W9-BAR-025

CROSS PURPOSES

CROSS PURPOSES

Pierce v. Society of Sisters and the Struggle over Compulsory Public Education

PAULA ABRAMS

The University of Michigan Press

Ann Arbor

Copyright © by the University of Michigan 2009
All rights reserved
Published in the United States of America by
The University of Michigan Press
Manufactured in the United States of America
⊚ Printed on acid-free paper

2012 2011 2010 2009   4 3 2 1

No part of this publication may be reproduced, stored in a retrieval system,
or transmitted in any form or by any means, electronic, mechanical,
or otherwise, without the written permission of the publisher.

A CIP catalog record for this book is available from the British Library.

Library of Congress Cataloging-in-Publication Data

Abrams, Paula, 1953–
    Cross purposes : Pierce v. Society of Sisters and the struggle over compulsory public
education / Paula Abrams.
        p.   cm.
    Case cited as: Pierce v. Society of Sisters of the Holy Names of Jesus and Mary, 268
U.S. 510 (1925)
    Includes bibliographical references and index.
    ISBN 978-0-472-11700-0 (cloth : alk. paper) —
    ISBN 978-0-472-02139-0 (e-book)
    1. Sisters of the Holy Names of Jesus and Mary—Trials, litigation, etc.
2. Oregon — Trials, litigation, etc.   3. Pierce, Walter Marcus, 1861–1954—Trials,
litigation, etc.   4. Educational law and legislation—United States—History—20th
century.   5. Due process of law—United States—History—20th century.   6. Church
schools—Law and legislation—United States—History—20th century.   7. Catholic
schools—Oregon—Portland—History—20th century.   8. Private schools—Law and
legislation—United States—History—20th century.   9. Religious minorities—Legal
status, laws, etc.—United States—History—20th century.   10. Catholics—Legal
status, laws, etc.—United States—History—20th century.   I. Title.

KF228.S57A38   2009
344.73'079—dc22   2009024929

For David, Madeline, and Justine

ACKNOWLEDGMENTS

This book began when my daughters entered St. Mary's Academy as high school freshmen. My curiosity was piqued when I realized that the 150-year-old school they attended had been the plaintiff in *Pierce v. Society of Sisters,* a case I taught every year in my constitutional law course.

The discovery and the recounting of the story of *Pierce* benefited from the generosity and expertise of many helpful people. I am grateful to the many librarians and archivists who extended assistance. I am particularly indebted to William J. Shepherd, Patrick Cullom, and Jane Stoeffler, at the American Catholic History Research Center and University Archives at the Catholic University of America. Their help in tracking down documents and citations saved me several cross-country trips. Robert Ellis from the National Archives in Washington, D.C., and Susan Hamson of the Columbia University Rare Book and Manuscript Library provided valuable information at key points in my research, as did Richard Tuske from the New York City Bar Library. Closer to home, John Fitzgerald of the National Archives, Pacific AK Region, and David Wendell of the Oregon State Archives helped resolve questions throughout my research. I greatly appreciate the hours of assistance from the librarians and archivists at the Oregon Historical Society. Finally Sarah Cantor, Director of Archival Collections at the Holy Names Heritage Center, provided helpful information and documents.

My special thanks go to Robert M. O'Neil, professor of law at the University of Virginia and director of the Thomas Jefferson Center for the Protection of Free Expression. He graciously contributed his time and expertise at several points in the development of the manuscript. His insightful comments proved invaluable to the completion of this project.

I am grateful to the administrators, staff, and teachers at St. Mary's Academy in Portland, including Christina Friedhoff, Patricia Barr, Alena Kelly, Sister Molly, Sister Sue, and Sara Salvi. They provided me with valuable information about the history of St. Mary's and access to important documents.

I appreciate the guidance and encouragement of Jim Reische and Melody

Herr, my editors at the University of Michigan Press, and the expertise of the staff at the Press who contributed to the production of this book.

My thanks to the many people at Lewis & Clark Law School who offered support and assistance throughout the research and writing of this book. Thanks to my colleagues who provided sound advice and encouragement. I appreciate the financial support of the law school through two summer research grants. I am grateful to Lynn Williams and the library staff for their help at so many points in my research. The book benefited from the research assistance of a number of talented students, especially Leslie Baze and Sarah Stauffer. I am particularly indebted to the word processing assistance of Lisa Frenz and Andy Marion, who patiently organized, revised, and kept track of my many edits and drafts

Finally, my deepest gratitude and love to my family, David, Madeline, and Justine, whose encouragement and support helped me take this project from dinner-table conversations to published work.

CONTENTS

Illustrations following page 86

INTRODUCTION   One Flag, One School

The message tacked to the St. Mary's Academy door just before midnight on November 7, 1922, confirmed the worst fears of the nuns and school-children asleep within. "The School Bill passed. Fiat!" Hours earlier, the people of Oregon became the first in the nation to approve a ballot initiative compelling public education for all children between the ages of 8 and 16. The law made criminals of parents or guardians who sent their children to private schools. The oldest Catholic school in the state, St. Mary's Academy had educated Portland children since 1859; now it faced certain closure. A late-night rain splattered the rows of darkened windows across the ivy-covered facade of the school at the corner of Fourth Street and Mill. The massive brick and stone building already looked deserted.

The passage of the School Bill ordained the ruin of both secular and religious private schools throughout the state. Of Oregon's 175,000 students, 12,000 attended private schools. More than three-quarters of these privately educated students attended schools operated by the Roman Catholic Church. Opponents of the School Bill, pointing to such statistics, charged that it was the product of anti-Catholic bigotry.

It was not that simple.

The Oregon School Bill emerged from the nativist furor sweeping the United States. Between 1901 and 1920, over 14 million immigrants came to America, the large majority of them from southern and eastern Europe, most of them Catholics and Jews. The Great War heightened hostility toward foreigners and to ideas perceived as anti-American. Victory did not alleviate this antipathy. As Americans struggled to "return to normalcy," many argued that immigrants who spoke different languages and practiced different religions were destabilizing the country and threatening the American way of life.

The country's preoccupation with nativism, patriotism, and ideological conformity reached its apex with the Red Scare of 1919–20. Headlines warned of Bolshevik "terrorists" who plotted to bring violence and revolution to America.[1] Attorney General A. Mitchell Palmer and his young assistant, J. Edgar Hoover, led a campaign to deport thousands of immigrant members of the Communist Party. The crusade to purge America of Bolshevist influence spread throughout all facets of society. One British journalist observed, "No one who was in the United States . . . in the autumn of 1919, will forget the feverish conditions of the public mind at that time. It was hag-ridden by the ghost of Bolshevism. . . . Property was in an agony of fear, and the horrid name 'Radical' covered the most innocent departure from conventional thought with a suspicion of desperate purpose."[2]

Radicalism also preoccupied the Supreme Court, which, like the nation, struggled to adapt to a world of vast and rapid change. The spate of wartime legislation restricting radical speech forced the Court to decide how far the government could go to suppress subversive influences. Like the rest of the country, the Court took a hard line on radicalism. Under the Espionage and Sedition Acts, it upheld convictions of immigrants, antiwar activists, and socialists for subversive speech. In case after case, the Supreme Court affirmed lengthy prison sentences for speech critical of the government and the war. Eugene Debs, the Socialist candidate for president through five elections, was among those whose antiwar speeches yielded ten-year prison terms.

The postwar Bolshevik hysteria fueled intolerance toward immigrants. The Bolshevist label was code for all things considered unAmerican. Patriotic societies argued that the "best antidote for Bolshevism is Americanism." For many Americans, the drive to assimilate immigrants became a patriotic mission to protect national security.

The call for compulsory public schooling grew out of this crusade to Americanize immigrants. Compulsory public schooling offered a potent means of acculturation, training impressionable children to become loyal Americans. In 1920, sociologist John Daniels proclaimed the virtues of public education: "[Children] go into the kindergarten as little Poles or Italians or Finns, babbling in the tongues of their parents, and at the end of half a dozen years or more . . . [they] emerge, looking, talking, thinking, and be-having generally like full-fledged Americans."[3] The public school, then, was to be the great American melting pot.

The Ku Klux Klan supported compulsory public education as part of its political agenda. Reconstituted in Atlanta in 1915 as the Invisible Empire and energized by the national success of the racist, pro-Klan film classic *The Birth of a Nation,* the Klan seized on the unrest in the country and embarked on a successful nationwide recruiting drive. It married racist, nativist, anti-Semitic, and anti-Catholic messages to fears of radicalism. The Klan de-nounced aliens, blacks, Jews, and Catholics as un-American "agents of Lenin." The KKK's postwar strategy of cloaking bigotry in the garb of pa-triotism was phenomenally successful. The Klan also benefited from a rising religious fundamentalist movement, whose members were drawn to Klan Protestantism. National membership surged in the early 1920s from less than 5,000 to more than 4,000,000. Shortly after his inauguration, Presi-dent Warren G. Harding became a member of the Klan in a secret cere-mony in the Green Room of the White House.[4] In the Klan's view, manda-tory public schooling would instill "100 percent Americanism" in every one of the nation's children.[5] It also would eliminate Catholic private education.

In the fall of 1922, Oregon adopted the model of Americanized, egali-tarian education envisioned by the champions of mandatory public school-ing. Populist and progressive politics, anti-Catholic and nativist sentiments, and fears of radicalism all made the state fertile ground for adoption of com-pelled public education, as did the Oregon initiative process, one of the country's most vigorous experiments in direct democracy. Each of these forces alone probably would not have yielded a majority vote, but together they moved Oregonians to embrace a dramatic social experiment.

The opponents of the School Bill were not ready to accept defeat. For St. Mary's Academy and other private schools in the state, the School Bill meant the dissolution of their work and calling. By the time the votes were tallied, the providers of private schooling in Oregon already were formulat-ing a strategy to challenge the new law. The Society of the Sisters of the Holy Names of Jesus and Mary, the dominant provider of Catholic educa-tion in the state and the founders of St. Mary's Academy, joined forces with Hill Military Academy, a nonsectarian private school. In the ensuing legal battle, the parties argued about parental rights, economic interests, Bolshe-vism, and state-controlled curriculum. When *Pierce v. Society of Sisters* was finally decided by the U.S. Supreme Court in 1925, it became a landmark case in constitutional law. The Court rejected the state's claim that it had the authority to impose compulsory public schooling. Parents, the Court decreed, have a constitutional right to decide how to educate their children, including the right to send them to private schools.

The *Pierce* decision has helped shape the course of modern American constitutional law. It continues to be extolled as the "Magna Charta" of American education by parents who seek to shape educational policy. The Court's recognition of parental rights also impacts the law over a wide spectrum of public policy matters, including health care, privacy, and religion. At the same time, *Pierce* stands as a pivotal decision in the judicial resolution of numerous controversies, including abortion, death with dignity, sexual preferences, and a host of family and personal liberties.

The story of *Pierce* vividly illustrates the stresses placed on American democracy during times of national crisis. Nativism endures as a persistent political force in American society. The pressure to conform to mainstream ideology and culture remains intense in times of national crisis, when immigrants become targets of hostility and fear. The passage of the Oregon School Bill and the litigation that followed reveal a country embroiled in nationalist fervor and willing to brand minority groups as unpatriotic. By striking down the initiative, the Supreme Court rejected the plebiscite's determination that immigrants, particularly Catholics, posed a threat to national security.

Pierce, despite its significance, is frequently misunderstood. In numerous opinions, the Court has treated *Pierce* like a constitutional chameleon, disputing whether the decision is primarily about privacy or the free exercise of religion or free speech rights. Outside the legal community, the common perception of *Pierce* is that it is a case rejecting anti-Catholic bigotry. That the perceptions of *Pierce* vary is not surprising; the decision speaks to all these values.

The chronicle of *Pierce,* from the Oregon initiative campaign to the chambers of the Supreme Court, reveals how deep-seated political and social conflicts lead to landmark decisions. The School Bill fight is an account of post–World War I America. The struggles that defined this era led to the passage of the Oregon law and shaped the legal challenges and Supreme Court decision that followed. The import of *Pierce,* and its modern progeny, emerge from this profound narrative.

PART I   Initiative

CHAPTER 1   One Hundred Percent Americanism

The Oregon School Bill fight was never simply a local issue. The inspiration for the Oregon School Bill came from a resolution adopted at Colorado Springs, Colorado, by the Supreme Council of the Scottish Rite Masons, Southern Jurisdiction, in May 1920. The resolution represented the will of Masons in 33 southern and western states.

> Resolved: That we recognize and proclaim our belief in the free and compulsory education of the children of our nation in public primary schools supported by public taxation, upon which all children shall attend and be instructed in the English language only, without regard to race or creed, as the only sure foundation for the perpetuation and preservation of our free institutions, guaranteed by the constitution of the United States, and we pledge the efforts of the membership of the order to promote by all lawful means the organization, extension, and development to the highest degree of such schools, and to oppose the efforts of any and all who seek to limit, curtail, hinder, or destroy the public school system of our land.[1]

The national leadership of the Masons and other supporters of compulsory public education wanted all children in America to attend public schools. Oregon became the center of an unfolding national debate on the merits of compelled public schooling. Many Oregonians called the

School Bill the most significant local political issue to agitate the state since slavery, but both the campaign and the ensuing litigation proceeded with a keen awareness of the national attention focused on Oregon.

The Oregon Masonic Grand Lodge adopted the Supreme Council's resolution in July 1920. The proposal garnered little political attention at the time. Nearly two years later, Republican state senator Charles Hall revived the languishing resolution and made compulsory public schooling the most contentious issue in the May 1922 Oregon gubernatorial primary, in which Oregon's incumbent Republican governor, Ben Olcott, faced primary challenges from five Republicans, including Hall and state senator Isaac Patterson.

In what the *New York Times* described as the "most bitter primary campaign in the history of Oregon,"[2] Senator Hall emerged as the primary challenger to Olcott. Hall brought compulsory public education to the governor's race by running on the platform "One Public School for All Eight Grades." He aggressively took his message around the state: "The public school is one of the fundamental factors in our system of government. I favor compulsory attendance in the primary grades. Teach pure Americanism to all pupils at an early age. Continue to strengthen and build up this typical American institution."[3]

While Hall traveled the state proclaiming the virtues of mandatory public schooling, white-hooded figures threatened the nuns and students of St. Mary's Academy when they walked down tree-lined Park Avenue. Some children were curious about the costumed figures, but most were frightened. At night, crosses burned on Portland's Mount Tabor and Mount Scott, on Skinner's Butte in Eugene, and on the hills surrounding smaller communities all over Oregon. These events were not unconnected. The fate of Oregon private schools became entwined with the rise of the most powerful political force in Oregon—the Knights of the Ku Klux Klan. Hall's support for compulsory public education secured him the endorsement of the Klan. Governor Olcott was a bitter enemy of the Klan and an opponent of compelled public schooling.

The Klan Moves into Oregon

The Knights of the Ku Klux Klan arrived in Oregon in 1921. They brought with them the "One Flag, One School" campaign, a centerpiece of the Klan's platform of 100 percent Americanism. The Klan oath included a vow to champion public education: "I believe that our Free Public School is the cornerstone of good government, and that those who are seeking to destroy it are enemies of our Republic and are unworthy of citizenship."[4] The Klan's aggressive support of compulsory public schooling would prove to be critical to the passage of the School Bill. The Klan brought to the campaign a formidable state political machine capable of delivering votes.

Some leading Oregonians, including Governor Olcott, initially underestimated the impact the Klan would have in their state. Kleagle Luther I. Powell, sent by the Klan's highest officer, the Imperial Wizard, proved to be an effective organizer and front man for the Klan; he rapidly recruited the mayor of Medford and so impressed the local paper, the *Clarion,* that it described the Klan as "the very antithesis of lawlessness." In September 1921, Governor Ben Olcott dismissed the influence of the Klan in Oregon, informing the *New York World* that "because of wholesome conditions in Oregon, with little discontent and a satisfied people, the Ku Klux Klan . . . has made little or no progress and I am informed it is now folding its tent like the Arab and as silently stealing away."[5]

Governor Olcott quickly came to rue his assessment that the Klan in Oregon made "practically no impression on our people."[6] The Oregon Klan recruited an estimated 20,000 new members statewide from a total population of nearly 750,000. In an address to the National Governor's Conference, Olcott expressed puzzlement that the Klan appealed to Oregonians: "We have not the so-called Catholic menace in Oregon; the Catholic population is comparatively small; we have no so-called Jewish menace in Oregon, because the Jewish population is also comparatively small. Some of the best citizens and the most far-seeing and forward-looking citizens of the state are Catholics and Jews. We have no negro population there, only a total of about 1800 negro votes in the whole state of Oregon."[7]

Olcott failed to appreciate that the meteoric rise of the Klan in Oregon was not simply about bigotry. The Klan's law-and-order platform resonated with diverse Oregon communities. In the lively port town of Astoria, the Klan successfully attracted citizens who abhorred the flagrant wantonness of the port culture, as well as those who felt threatened by the city's large Finnish population. Anti-Catholic sentiment swelled Klan membership in rural Tillamook, as did fears of labor unrest in a community heavily dependent on timber and dairy. In the urban communities of Portland, Eugene, and Salem, the Klan softened its nativist agenda with an antielitism message designed to appeal to conservative values of working-class and middle-class Protestants.

The Oregon Klan offered members Protestant solidarity and shared values. It required each applicant to certify that he was a "white male Gentile person of temperate habits, sound in mind, and a believer in the tenets of the Christian religion, the maintenance of white supremacy, the practice of an honorable klanishness and the principles of a pure Americanism."[8] The Klan's aggressive Protestantism resonated with the increasing numbers of religious fundamentalists in Oregon. The *Oregonian* in Portland reported on local Klan induction ceremonies in February and April of 1922, noting that the over 2,000 inductees came "from all the important walks of life in the city" and included "doctors, lawyers, business men of all kinds, railroad men, clerks, and citizens from other professions and employments." Journalist Waldo Roberts claimed, "Not the bad people of the State, but the good people—the *very* good people—are largely responsible for the transformation of the Oregon commonwealth into an invisible empire."[9] Benjamin E. Titus, a Portland journalist and briefly a member of the Klan, described the thrill of attending his first Klan meeting as "a feeling that I was now identifying myself with a body of citizens pledged by oaths and ideals as high and as holy as those that bound our forefathers when they founded these United States and consecrated them to liberty and preservation of human rights against all forms of unjust aggression."[10]

Portland Klan No. 1, the largest chapter in the state, with 9,000 members, became the center of Klan operations in Oregon. Fred Gifford, Exalted Cyclops, brought middle-class respectability to the face of the Klan. In his midforties, with steely gray hair, Gifford left a successful management career at Northwestern Electric Company for Klan leadership, increasing his monthly salary in the process from $250 to $600. Gifford's middle-class roots proved a valuable recruiting tool among Portland's urban middle-class population. Gifford made the School Bill a top priority, and his leverage among this socioeconomic group would yield votes.

Gifford's influence was due in part to his success in selling the Klan as a legitimate patriotic organization. In March 1922, the *Oregon Voter,* hostile to the Klan, interviewed Gifford and came away impressed. Gifford's description of the Oregon Klan invoked democracy and nationalism.

The objects we seek to attain are such that you, as an American citizen, will probably be in harmony with in the main. We are opposed to control of American public affairs by aliens, or by so called Americans whose primary allegiance is to some foreign power. We do not see how any genuine American could differ with us as to this. We are not anti-Catholic or anti-Jew or anti-anything, but pro-American.

Gifford responded with a smile to charges that the Klan threatened democratic values. He predicted, "After a few years, . . . you will not regard the Klan as a menace." The *Oregon Voter* article concluded by describing Gifford as "the reputed boss of Oregon politics, who within a few years is expected to control pretty much all of the legislative and public offices in the state."[11] In January 1922, Gifford inducted a number of state legislators into the Klan in a secret ceremony held in a Salem hotel.

Oregonians saw the ascendancy of the Klan confirmed on the front pages of their newspapers. A photo appearing in the August 2, 1921, *Portland Telegram* shows Gifford and King Kleagle Powell, in full Klan regalia, posing with Mayor Baker, Captain Moore of the Portland police, chief of police Leon Jenkins, district attorney Walter Evans, U.S. attorney Lester Humphrey, Sheriff Tom Hurlburt, and Philip S. Malcolm, inspector general in Oregon for the Supreme Council of the Scottish Rite Masons, Southern Jurisdiction. The two attorneys present later claimed that the Klan tricked the public officials into the photograph. According to the attorneys, the politicians attended a cryptically sponsored reception and agreed to pose for a photograph, only to have the hooded Klansmen pop out from behind the backdrop and into the picture at the last minute.[12]

Most of the Oregon press watched mutely as the Klan rose to political dominance during 1922. Governor Olcott complained that the Klan had "become so strong that the metropolitan papers of the state said not one word against them."[13] The Salem *Capital Journal* and the *Portland Telegram* waged the most aggressive editorial battles against the Klan. The editor of the *Capital Journal,* George Putnam, described the stakes in Oregon as a debate "over the efforts of unscrupulous grafters to commercialize religious and racial animosities for personal or political profit."[14] A number of other papers, including the *Medford Mail Tribune,* the *Corvallis Gazette-Times,* and the *East Oregonian* opposed the Klan, but the most prominent papers, the *Oregonian* and the *Oregon Journal,* stayed silent. The editor of the *Medford Mail Tribune,* Robert W. Ruhl, blasted his fellow editors for failing to take a stand on the power of the Klan in 1922: "During all this time in at least 80 percent of the newspapers of Oregon there was not the slightest editorial reference to this amazing development."[15]

The editorial silence stemmed both from the wide support for the Klan and from fear of retaliation. Papers that opposed the Klan felt its wrath. The Klan organized boycotts of opposition press. Advertisers reported visits by Klansmen, letters, and telephone calls, all threatening economic boycotts of their businesses unless they cancelled their advertisements in the targeted papers. Some editors suffered personal harassment, threats to their families, and smear campaigns. The *Portland Telegram* lost 5,000 subscribers and the lease on its new offices. Despite the meekness of the Oregon press, the Klan's activities in Oregon captured national media attention. In articles and editorials across the country, the national press excoriated Oregonians for their capitulation to the Klan. The failure of many in the local press to challenge the Klan would play a role in the success of the School Bill. Press criticism of the measure, for the most part, would be too little, too late.

The Klan as Political Machine

The meteoric ascent of the Klan in Oregon transformed the 1922 political campaigns, shaping the course of the governor's race and the fate of the School Bill. The Klan wielded such clout that the influential *Oregon Voter* timidly concluded in January 1922, "We would not regard membership . . . or activity in the Ku Klux Klan as disqualifying anyone from holding public office, even though we condemn the principles, purpose and activities of the Klan itself."[16] The *Catholic Sentinel,* a Portland weekly, warned Oregonians that Hall and other supporters of compulsory public education intended to destroy the Catholic schools in the state.

Klan activities undermined its claims to Protestant propriety. Near hangings and harassment and intimidation of minorities and of businesses that did not support the Klan spread throughout Oregon. Just six days before the primary, Governor Olcott tried to convince Oregonians of the threat posed by the Klan. On May 13, 1922, following a series of night ridings and near lynchings by the Klan in the southern Oregon town of Medford, Olcott issued an anti-Klan proclamation.

> Dangerous forces are insidiously gaining a foothold in Oregon. In the guise of a secret society, parading under the name of the Ku Klux Klan, these forces are endeavoring to usurp the reign of government, are stirring up fanaticism, race hatred, religious prejudice, and all of those evil influences which tend toward factional strife and civil terror. Assaults have been com-

mitted in various counties of the state by unknown, masked outlaws, the odium of which has reflected on the Ku Klux Klan. Whether or not these outlaws were connected with that organization is immaterial. Their vile acts demonstrate that the name of the organization may be used for evil purposes and that from the nature of its activities it has the moral effect of causing unthinking and misguided persons to enter into unlawful conspiracies and to perpetrate unlawful deeds.[17]

In his proclamation, Olcott ordered all law enforcement officers to make vigorous use of the state's antimask law to "insist that unlawfully disguised men be kept from the streets." But hooded figures continued to march through the streets of Oregon communities. At a Klan rally in Salem, an airplane strung with lights in the shape of a cross lit up the darkness, dipping its wings to frighten nearby citizens.

Klan sympathizers charged Olcott with political opportunism and allegiance to Catholics. A Klan spokesman accused Olcott of "an unwarranted attack bearing all the earmarks of Roman politics."[18] Olcott's proclamation consolidated Klan support for Senator Hall, and Hall came very close to taking the election. Olcott prevailed in the Republican primary, but by less than 600 votes out of the approximately 116,000 cast. The editor of the *Oregon Voter* observed that "bitter prejudice against the Catholics, based on their supposed domination in political affairs, was the actuating motive for the tens of thousands who supported Hall in May."[19] The Klan in Salem responded to Hall's loss by circulating a letter claiming, "Hall's opponents have stolen the nomination for a candidate whose every recent act has borne the indelible stamp of the Catholic Pope in Rome."[20]

Hall refused to accept defeat. He demanded a recount, charging fraud by Catholic Democrats illegally voting in the Republican primary, but he abandoned the challenge when the early tallies yielded additional votes for Olcott and evidence of fraud by Hall supporters.[21] With Klan backing, Hall decided to run as an independent in the governor's race, opposing Olcott and the Democratic candidate, state senator Walter Pierce. His candidacy assured that compulsory public schooling would remain a significant issue in the general election.

Despite Hall's defeat in the primary, the Klan claimed substantial political victory throughout the state. In Portland's Multnomah County, Klan-endorsed Republican candidates swept 12 out of 13 slots in the delegation to the Oregon House of Representatives. The *Oregon Voter* reported, "Religiously, the election was a torrid encounter." The paper concluded, "May 19 may pass into history as the Dawn of the Nightshirt Era in Oregon politics."[22] After the primary, Governor Olcott again blasted the Klan, this time in the national press, with a statement to the *New York Herald Tribune* warning, "No greater menace confronts the United States today than this monster of invisible government."[23] In a speech to the National Governor's Conference, Olcott admitted, "We woke up one morning and found that the Klan had about gained control of the state. Practically not a word has been raised against them."[24] With Klan assistance, the Masons' proposal for compulsory public education was about to become the political firestorm of an already combative campaign season.

CHAPTER 2   We the People

A small group of Oregon Masons, spurred by the statewide focus on compulsory public education during the primary, mobilized to place an initiative on the Oregon ballot in the November general election. Judge John B. Cleland, a Mason and Past Grand Master of the Grand Lodge of Oregon, drafted the initiative. The measure required public schooling for all children between the ages of 8 and 16, except for those physically or mentally "abnormal." Parents or guardians who violated the law were guilty of a misdemeanor and subject to a fine up to $100, 30 days in jail, or both. There were fourteen sponsors of the initiative, all prominent Masons. Robert E. Smith, president of the Lumberman's Trust Company in Portland, spearheaded the initiative campaign.

In a well-coordinated strategy, the Masons quietly circulated initiative petitions among its lodges and other Protestant patriotic organizations at 8:00 a.m. on Thursday, June 15. Signature collection ceased at 5:00 p.m. Smith claimed the collection of 50,000 signatures during that nine-hour period. The actual number of signatures collected appeared closer to 29,000, with 13,000 of those eventually rejected by the secretary of state, leaving 16,000 signatures, well beyond the 13,000 required by the state to place the initiative on the November 7 ballot. The Masons filed the initiative with the secretary of state on July 6. Smith boasted that the Oregon measure would be a model for the rest of the country.

The Forces behind the School Bill

On July 4, two days before the filing of the School Bill initiative, Father Edwin V. O'Hara, superintendent of Catholic schools in Oregon, staked out the Catholic position on the debate about to unfold. In an address to students at a summer session of the Marylhurst Normal School, Father O'Hara attacked compelled public education as an unjustified interference with parental rights. His speech, widely distributed in a pamphlet entitled *Freedom of Education,* argued that parents maintain the primary right and obligation of educating their children and that the state has the right to interfere only when parents fail to fulfill their duty. In the absence of parental neglect, he explained, the state must defer to parental choice: "these rights of parents are primitive and inalienable and may not be violated by the state without injustice; . . . the rights of parents to educate their children . . . is the most inamissible [*sic*] of human rights." O'Hara concluded that a state that fails to respect parental rights violates basic American principles: "the exercise by the state of its police power to drag children from the home of parents who are capable and willing to perform their full duty in the education of their children, would be an importation of tyrannous principles heretofore foreign to American tradition."[1]

The editor of the *Oregon Voter,* writing immediately after the secretary of state certified the School Bill for the ballot, concluded that anti-Catholic animus drove the proposal: "It is as an amendment to the Compulsory Education Law that this initiative bill comes before the public, although it is aimed at Catholic parochial schools."[2] School Bill sponsor Philip S. Malcolm released a public denial to the charge: "The attention of the Masonic Bodies of Oregon has been directed to statements that the compulsory public school bill is being initiated for religious purposes. Nothing is further from the real truth."[3]

The question of whether the Masons fronted the School Bill for the Klan bears inquiry. Of the fourteen sponsors, at least two were Klan officials. Malcolm, the Oregon inspector general of the Masons and the primary individual sponsor of the School Bill, openly aligned himself with the Klan. The Masonic endorsement of the proposal occurred at a special meeting of selected Masons called by Malcolm and Fred Gifford, also a Mason, in the spring of 1922.

The secrecy of Klan membership files leaves the extent to which the Oregon Klan infiltrated the Masons a matter of conjecture. The Klan's national platform included a proposal for compulsory public education and a pledge to protect America from the threat of "Bolshevist" and "Roman" influence in the private schools. The *Capital Journal* newspaper charged, in an editorial entitled "Masonry the Goat," that the Klan allied with the Masons to stimulate Klan membership. The *Journal* probably hit close to the mark. Klan strategy in other states included infiltration of Masonic lodges. The comments of one prominent Mason, William McDougal, represented at least a faction of Masonic sentiment: "I will say this much, that the Klan is composed of Americanborn, and if it comes to a show down I would rather be aligned with 100 percent American influences than with foreign influences."[4]

Oregon Catholics believed that Klan influence thrust the Masons to the leadership of the School Bill campaign. The Masons' push on compulsory public education initially surprised the Catholic community. The editor of the *Catholic Sentinel* commented during the signature drive, "It was not known generally that the Masons were actively pushing the measure, the general impression being that it was a Ku Klux Klan measure."[5] The *Sentinel* saw little threat from the initiative when it was first placed on the ballot.[6]

The relationship between the Klan, the Masons, and the School Bill exploded into controversy during the campaign, when a number of prominent Oregon Masons disavowed Mason support for the measure, charging Klan influence. When Inspector General Malcolm demanded that all Masons pledge their support for the School Bill, William Wheelwright, a leading Mason and chairman of the Oregon State Child Welfare Commission, publicly refused. He denied that the Masons favored the initiative. Noting that a number of Masons submitted statements against the measure for the *Voters' Pamphlet,* Wheelwright insisted, "Every Mason whom I have consulted (and I have seen many) had declared himself against the bill, with one exception."[7]

George G. Brown, state Masonic Grand Master, flatly denied official Mason sponsorship of the initiative, claiming that the School Bill "is not and never has been endorsed by the Oregon Grand Lodge of Masons" but had been "foisted upon the voters by the Ku Klux Klan." Brown insisted that endorsement of the School Bill by the Masons "was accomplished at a special meeting of hand-picked members of that order in Portland last spring, called by P. S. Malcolm and Fred L. Gifford, and attended only by delegates present at their invitation." The so-called endorsement, according to Brown, originated with a "radical faction of the Masonic order that fell in with the Ku Klux movement from the first."[8] Portland attorney and former

Grand Master W. C. Bristol denounced Malcolm and Gifford and other Masons campaigning for the School Bill for violating the basic principles of Masonry: "True Masonry does not countenance such intolerance, bigotry and infringement upon personal religious beliefs."[9] Although these leading Masons disputed Masonic sponsorship, a dominant faction of the Masons claimed public responsibility for the measure. Whatever the true strength of Mason support, the Mason-Klan connection proved advantageous. The alliance gave the Klan a respectable front organization, and it gave the Masons access to the Klan's political machine.

Direct Democracy and the Oregon Experiment

The initiative process set in motion by the Masons' signature drive made Oregon an attractive venue from which to launch a nationwide campaign for compulsory public education. Oregonians created the "Oregon System" of direct legislation, one of the most significant achievements of populism in American history, and they vigorously employed the initiative and referendum to effect social change. School Bill sponsors calculated that they had a greater likelihood of success if they brought the case for mandatory public schooling directly to the voters. Since 1902, the initiative process had been a powerful tool for transforming Oregon social policy.

The Oregon movement for direct legislation began in the late nineteenth century, when a poor economy and unsafe working conditions in mines and timber attracted many Oregonians to populism. They flocked to the People's Party and placed populist politicians in the statehouse. Populists achieved only limited legislative success however; the legislature also housed incompetence and corruption, the "briefless lawyers, farmless farmers, business failures, bar-room loafers, Fourth of July orators, [and] political thugs" who served as the "representatives of the monied and monopolistic classes."[10] Corporate officers, bankers, and railroad magnates, the "First Families" of Portland, controlled the legislature.

By the end of the nineteenth century, rampant corruption in the management of federal land grants and the political power of corporate special interests pushed Oregonians to a radical response. During the 1890s, an alliance of labor and farm interests joined to form the Joint Committee on Direct Legislation, a populist organization committed to bringing direct democracy to Oregon. Their literature promised that direct legislation, through the referendum and initiative process, would "make it impossible for corporations and boodlers to obtain unjust measures by which to profit at the expense of the people."[11] The joint committee and its successor, the Direct Legislation League, joined with the populist People's Party in an aggressive campaign to lobby support for a constitutional amendment authorizing lawmaking by initiative. The secretary of each of these groups, William S. U'Ren, populist, attorney, and political activist, became the primary architect of direct democracy in Oregon and a prominent figure in the national movement for direct legislation.

U'Ren and the populists faced an uphill battle in a Republican-dominated state. An editorial in the *Oregonian* called the proposal "one of the craziest of all the crazy fads of Populism," a "vagary nobody cares about."[12] Undeterred, U'Ren sought a larger political forum to build consensus for the proposed amendment. Elected to the state House of Representatives in 1897 on the populist ticket, U'Ren orchestrated the infamous Hold-up Legislature of 1897, exploiting infighting between factions of Republicans to prevent formation of a quorum in the House. After two months, the legislature went home without convening, but U'Ren came away with promises of support for the amendment from a number of powerful Republicans. U'Ren called in those Republican pledges to obtain legislative approval of the proposal during the 1899 and 1901 legislative sessions. By the time the amendment went to the voters in 1902, direct legislation enjoyed the support of all the political parties in Oregon except the Prohibitionists. The amendment passed in an 11–1 landslide, 62,024 to 5,668, amending the state constitution for the first time since statehood in 1859.

Direct democracy, dismissed only a few years earlier as a "socialist innovation," became the rallying cry of a citizenry fed up with public and corporate corruption.[13] Judge George Williams, president of the Direct Legislation League and a respected politician who had participated in the drafting of the Oregon Constitution, accurately captured the public's mood when he concluded, "In these days, when corporations and combinations of corporations have become so powerful, it seems to us that this amendment is necessary to protect the people from the aggressions of the money power of the country."[14] The "Oregon System," as the reforms became known around the country, provided the majority with a potent antidote to the special interests controlling the statehouse.

The vision of egalitarian, participatory democracy promised by direct legislation did not appeal to all Oregonians. Business interests and conservatives feared an empowered, radical majority, enamored of populist platforms and fomenting political chaos. Philosophical opposition came from those who considered direct legislation at odds with the representative form of government established in the U.S. Constitution. Some populists and progressives viewed direct democracy as simply another means for the wealthy and powerful to dupe the average citizen into passing laws against their best interests.

> How would you like to live in a state where the people can and do amend their constitution in the most radical fashion by a minority vote, where one-third of the voters decides the fate of laws affecting the other two-thirds, . . . where special interests hire citizens to circulate petitions asking for the recall of judges who have found them guilty; where men representing themselves as for the people, buy signatures with drinks, forge dead men's names, practice blackmail by buying and selling, for so much per name, signatures for petitions needed to refer certain measures to the people; a state where the demagogue thrives and the energetic crank with money, through the Initiative and the Referendum, can legislate to his heart's content . . . ?[15]

One prominent Oregonian, Ralph Duniway, son of suffragist Abigail Scott Duniway, went even further: "If the initiative and referendum is in force, I predict that men will be shot in the streets of Portland, that a state of anarchy will exist in Oregon, and that it will be necessary to call out the Federal troops."[16]

Despite these concerns, the state did not devolve into anarchy. The Oregon System also survived legal challenges at both the state and federal level. In *Kadderly v. City of Portland,* the Oregon Supreme Court rejected a claim that the amendment violated Article IV, Section 4, of the U.S. Constitution, which guarantees to each state "a Republican Form of Government." The Court found that in the direct legislation system, "the representative character of government still remains," that "the people have simply reserved to themselves a larger share of legislative power, but they have not overthrown the republican form of the government, or substituted another in its place."[17]

When the challenge to the Oregon System came before the U.S. Supreme Court, the Court, in *Pacific States Telephone & Telegraph Co. v. State of Oregon,* dismissed the case for lack of jurisdiction. The Court held that the constitutional authority to determine whether a state has a republican form of government resides with Congress, not the Court. The challenge presented a political question outside the jurisdiction of the Court.[18]

Direct Democracy and Oregon Politics

The strength of public support for the Oregon System and the vigor with which populists employed the initiative and referendum produced a veritable revolution in state government within a few short years. In 1904, Oregonians, by initiative, approved a direct primary law that included, well before the passage of the Seventeenth Amendment, a provision for the direct election of U.S. senators. In rapid succession, the citizens adopted an array of progressive legislation, including protective labor laws; recall power on public officials; a corrupt practices act; authorization for a state university; taxes on oil, railroad, utility, and communication companies; and extension of the initiative and referendum to local government.[19] By 1914, Oregonians added women's suffrage, abolition of the poll tax and the death penalty, proportional representation, and the requirement of indictment by grand jury to the list of reforms achieved through the initiative process. Nearly half of the states eventually adopted some form of the Oregon System, but during the first decade of the twentieth century, Oregon stood alone in aggressively employing it, putting twenty-three initiatives on the ballot.

The Oregon initiative, as used in the first two decades of the twentieth century, served the Progressive Era well. Direct legislation increased citizen involvement in the political process and reduced the influence of special interests. Many of the reforms expanded the rights and political participation of less powerful groups. U'Ren even achieved some success in assuaging conservative business interests that the system provided "ample insurance against revolutionary laws." During these heady, early years of direct legislation, state senator Jonathan Bourne described the Oregon System as "the best system of popular government in the world today" and "the safest and most conservative plan of government ever invented."[20]

The Oregon experiment in direct democracy turned national attention to the state. U.S. Supreme Court chief justice and former president William Taft reflected popular opinion when, visiting the Northwest, he described Oregon as a useful laboratory for dangerous political and social experiments. He maintained that Oregon was too remote from the centers of population in the Union for its innovations to pose a serious hazard to the rest of the country.[21]

Taft's assessment of Oregon as a venue for political experimentation proved accurate. Oregonians were proud of their reputation as innovators. Advocates of compulsory public schooling predicted that Oregonians would favor a measure that gave the people the power to enact a radical change in education policy, a change that could become a model for the rest of the country. Allen Eaton, scholar and Oregon legislator, observed in his 1912 book on the Oregon System, "From what has been said, it already must appear that the people of the state of Oregon enjoy a very wide political power—so wide that they may do anything in politics that they please to do."[22]

In 1922, Oregonians faced a decision on whether to use the power of the initiative to lessen, rather than expand, the rights of the Catholic and Lutheran minorities who maintained private schools. The initiative process allowed a powerful minority faction to put before the voters a proposal tainted by animus and untempered by legislative debate. It gave the homogenous, Protestant majority both the power and the opportunity to determine the fate of private education. The editor of the *Portland Telegram* described the attitudes of many favoring the School Bill: "We, the majority, have decided what is necessary. . . . The public schools please us. Why not make them please the other fellow? Why not march him up to the school of our choice and say to him in effect: 'There, take that, it's good for you.'"[23]

Oregon had garnered praise for its successful system of popular governance. But that was about to change. The School Bill would bring Oregon and the Oregon System scorn, not commendation. The use of the initiative to compel public education would be widely viewed as confirmation that direct legislation endangers unpopular minorities. The School Bill campaign would become notorious for its exploitation of voter confusion and prejudice.

CHAPTER 3   The Entering Wedge

Within days of the filing of the School Bill initiative with the secretary of state, Alexander Christie, archbishop of Oregon City, signaled his alarm about the proposal to Father John J. Burke, general secretary of the National Catholic Welfare Council (NCWC), clear across the country: "I am writing to you upon a matter of vital and urgent importance, and one to which I beg to ask your immediate and best attention." Christie's July 13 letter implored Father Burke for "immediate and substantial aid in the way of money" to mount the "most vigorous fight" against the School Bill. The archbishop's appeal to the NCWC placed the Oregon initiative at the center of a nation-wide battle for parochial education: "Oregon has been selected as the weakest link in the chain of States, and as the favorite battle-ground of radical and freak legislation.... If it carries in Oregon, it will gain tremendous momentum in other States in the West, and hence the desperate efforts its advocates are making to win the election, and the equal desperation with which we must oppose it." Christie predicted a "fair" chance of defeating the measure with "substantial" funds from the NCWC. He closed his letter with palpable urgency: "This is the situation. It is critical, imminent and unescapable."[1]

The success of the June signature campaign startled opponents of compulsory public education, most of whom assumed the controversy dead when its political champion, gubernatorial candidate Charles Hall, suffered defeat in the Republican primary. As the executive secretary of the

Lutheran Schools Committee described it, "Oregonians awoke one morning to read the news" that compulsory public schooling would be on the November ballot.[2] The filing mobilized opponents, particularly the Catholic and Lutheran leadership. Christie immediately claimed, "There is no time to be lost, for the work is large, complicated and difficult."[3]

Before Oregon: The Failed Michigan Campaign

Father Burke was no stranger to the issue of compulsory public education. The Oregon initiative was not the first attempt in the country to compel public schooling. In Michigan, the fledgling automobile industry drew large numbers of immigrants to Detroit. Nativist sentiment against Catholics and Germans fueled a 1920 Michigan initiative to amend the state constitution to mandate public education for all children between the ages of 5 and 16. The proposal sparked immediate controversy when the secretary of state refused to place the initiative on the ballot after the state attorney general, Alex J. Groesbeck, publicly issued an opinion concluding that the proposed amendment violated the Fourteenth Amendment of the federal constitution by destroying the economic interests of the school owners and teachers.[4]

The Michigan initiative sponsors sought a court order to compel the secretary of state to place the proposal on the November ballot. On October 1, the Michigan Supreme Court granted the order. The court held, five to three, in *Hamilton v. Vaughan,* that the secretary of state lacked authority to determine the constitutionality of a ballot measure. The dissent, siding with the attorney general, disagreed, arguing that the secretary of state need not certify a clearly unconstitutional ballot proposal. Concluding that the ballot measure impermissibly infringed on economic rights, the dissent also found that the proposal "takes from the parent the privilege of educating his children in parochial or private schools; indeed it takes from them the right to exercise any control over the education of their own offspring and gives such right to the state." The dissent complained that the proposal offered only divisiveness, "precipitating a bitter religious warfare in this commonwealth . . . where the net result can be but a nullity."[5]

The Michigan measure caught the attention of the Catholic national leadership. The administrative committee of the NCWC rightly perceived the proposal as a potential national threat. The committee requested that Father Burke arrange a meeting between the NCWC and the Michigan bishops. The Michigan bishops refused assistance from the NCWC, unhappy at the prospect of national interference in what they saw as a local matter. One Michigan bishop, Edward D. Kelly, complained to James Cardinal Gibbons, archbishop of Baltimore: "I was very much surprised that anyone had asked the NCWC to come into Michigan. . . . I do not think it at all necessary. Some of our priests and people are quite indignant that they should be considered incapable of handling the situation."[6] The Michigan bishops' refusal of NCWC assistance would have adverse repercussions in Oregon. Their rebuff squelched the development of an NCWC national strategy to oppose compelled public education, a consequence that would hinder the efforts of Oregon Catholics.

During the Michigan campaign, proponents charged that parochial schools function "only to perpetuate some foreign language, custom or creed." Accusations that Catholics sought to control the schools were interspersed with claims that parochial schools produced high percentages of criminals and unwed mothers. The leader of the initiative movement, James Hamilton, eventually became the King Kleagle of the Klan in Michigan. Between 1920 and 1924, the Michigan Klan's priority remained compulsory public schooling. Hamilton's campaign literature questioned, "Who Shall Educate Our Youth—Uncle Sam or the Pope?" and proclaimed that "any effort on the part of the German Lutheran people or Catholic people to prevent this meeting as is their custom will be absolute proof that parochial schools are not producing real American citizens."[7]

Michigan Catholics and Lutherans joined with leading educators and other religious denominations running parochial schools to oppose the measure. The Michigan Lutheran Church benefited from the expertise of the national Lutheran Church—Missouri Synod, an organization already seasoned from battles to protect its German-language schools against restrictive laws on foreign language instruction. Opponents met the attacks on their patriotism head-on, describing parochial schools' citizenship programs and the sacrifices made by Catholics and Lutherans to support the war effort, including the ultimate sacrifice from their young men fighting for America. One opposition ad proclaimed that "the spirit of Protestantism exhibits itself in love and tolerance" and "cannot agree to a dictatorship of religion or education." Another argued that Michigan's high literacy rate would plummet if private schools closed. The Lutherans' slogan during the campaign—"Whose Is the Child?"—emphasized the cultural and legal conflicts between parental authority and state power. Catholic bishop

Michael J. Gallagher, in an address before a large crowd, called the proposal "tyrannical," arguing that the government acted contrary to American principles when it essentially told parents, "we will not allow you to teach your children what you think—we will take them out of your arms and we will take them to schools where they must be taught as we think and not as you think."[8]

On election day in 1920, the Michigan initiative failed by a vote of 610,699 to 353,818. Michigan voters elected Attorney General Groesbeck as governor. Although defeated, the large number of votes for the initiative encouraged proponents to try again. Some Lutheran leaders, contemplating another costly campaign, favored "letting the enemy win by default at the polls" in order to mount a constitutional challenge to the initiative. But the Lutheran Campaign Committee, in a letter to Lutheran pastors and teachers, rejected that approach as too risky because the legal outcome was uncertain. Acknowledging that parental rights are "not clearly and specifically, but only impliedly, safeguarded" by the Constitution, the committee admitted that religious liberty challenges also could be problematic because "defending a school is not as easy as defending a church." The state could be expected to defend the measure by relying on its police power, that "dark continent of American jurisprudence" where limits on state power remained unclear. The committee advised Lutherans to pursue a vigorous campaign of education and opposition because they risked defeat by placing their trust wholly in the courts.[9]

In 1922, Michigan proponents of mandatory public schooling failed to collect sufficient signatures to place the measure on the ballot. While Michigan debated the fate of mandatory public schooling, numerous other states—including California, Texas, Oklahoma, Ohio, Wyoming, Arkansas, Nebraska, and Washington—considered similar measures. The Lutheran Schools Committee, a leader in the fight against compulsory public schooling, warned that the threat to private schools was a "national danger."[10]

Michigan proved to be a flawed choice as a test state for compelled public education. Substantial increases in ethnic diversity, typical in many states experiencing rapid industrialization, presented a double-edged sword for proponents of mandatory public schooling. Nativist sentiments ran high in the state. But the large immigrant population also meant more voters, increased organizing power, and, in some diverse communities, the enhanced tolerance born of shared experience. The financial burden of incorporating the many immigrant children attending private schools into public schools deterred many voters from supporting mandatory public education. The catalyst for the movement for compulsory public schooling lay more logically in a state like Oregon, a state that was only beginning to undergo the changes already well under way in regions that were more industrialized. Mason Robert E. Smith accurately captured the political climate.

> It is not that there is any immediate and particular danger here. But in the East the number of foreign-born and indifferent people is so overwhelming that such a bill as this one could never be put through. In accordance with the wishes of the supreme council of the Scottish Rite, therefore, we are beginning in Oregon, to set the example for the rest of the country.[11]

The First Oregon Appeal to the NCWC

Archbishop Christie and other Catholic leaders entered the School Bill fight acutely aware of the strategic dilemma it posed for the Catholic community. As the principal provider of religious education in the state, the Roman Catholic Church stood to suffer the greatest harm if compelled public schooling became law. The church also risked exacerbating Klan-inflamed anti-Catholicism if it mounted an aggressive public campaign. Already subject to accusations of Catholic conspiracies and Catholic political machinery, the Catholic leadership understood that a high-profile confrontation on the School Bill could backfire, reinforcing Protestant fears that parochial schools threatened public education. Charges of bigotry would be as likely to provoke hostility as sympathy. Christie, appointed archbishop in 1899 and widely respected for his eloquence, administrative skills, and financial expertise, stood to lose his life's work. He had devoted his office to the growth of Catholic education. Elementary and secondary parochial schools in Oregon expanded and thrived during his tenure. Seventy-five and in frail health, Christie took charge of the Catholic campaign with the passion of someone who knew his legacy depended on the outcome.

Archbishop Christie outlined his campaign plans in his urgent request to Father Burke for immediate financial assistance from the NCWC. He stressed the importance of reaching every voter and the secular press with literature attacking the initiative for "its fraudulent purpose, its destructive effects, its un-American spirit." He also planned to send public speakers to every community in the state. Not surprisingly, the campaign would require a large sum of money, Christie argued, because the small Catholic population in Oregon lacked financial resources and was spread throughout the large and sparsely settled state. Clearly concerned about the threat of passage, Christie warned Burke that the "fight must not be lost." Oregon, with its reputation for innovative legislation, would capture national attention if the School Bill passed. Just as Oregon's experiment with direct democracy inspired imitation throughout the country, so, too, could they expect compulsory public schooling to spread, with devastating consequences for Catholic education. Christie exhorted Burke to present his appeal at once to the NCWC and to impress on them the "absolute necessity and vital emergency of the situation."[12]

Father Burke well understood the import of Archbishop Christie's entreaty. Father James H. Ryan, associate director for legislation at the NCWC, had been following the progress of the School Bill and believed the situation to be serious. Thus, as early as June, he had advised the NCWC to lend its assistance. He characterized the Oregon initiative as the "entering wedge" in a nationwide battle forming over parochial education.[13] But Burke's reply to Christie on July 30 fell far short of the immediate and substantial assistance requested by the archbishop. Burke agreed that the Oregon campaign threatened Catholic education throughout the country. He saw the situation as critical and "onerous" and worried that passage in Oregon would ultimately lead to similar federal legislation, perhaps even a constitutional amendment. He also told Christie that the national Catholic assistance should be generous.[14] Unfortunately, that assistance was unlikely to come from the NCWC.

Created by Pope Benedict XV in 1919 to organize the protection of American Catholic interests, the NCWC fell victim to political infighting among the American Catholic hierarchy, and the dispute eventually reached the Holy See. On February 25, 1922, shortly after the election of a new pontiff, Pius XI, the Holy See ordered the dissolution of the NCWC through a decree issued by the Consistorial Congregation. Vigorous efforts by the administrative committee of the NCWC yielded a recall of the decree on July 4, but when Burke wrote to Christie, the pope's document of official support for the NCWC had not yet arrived, and the controversy had cost the NCWC considerable financial loss. After the dissolution decree, many of the bishops withheld the payments required by the NCWC. Cutbacks in staff to a "lamentably inadequate force" left Burke questioning whether the NCWC would even survive.

With this gloomy forecast, Burke promised Christie that the NCWC administrative committee recognized the seriousness of the Oregon situation and would consider Christie's request when it met in Chicago on August 11. On September 11, Burke, with deep regret, advised Christie that the administrative committee denied his request for financial assistance simply because the NCWC had no money to spare.[15]

The Oregon Opposition

Christie had not been idle while waiting to hear from the NCWC. He organized the Catholic Civic Rights Association; appointed prominent Catholics as members of its executive committee, including the archdiocese's attorney, Judge John P. Kavanaugh; and convinced Seattle attorney and Catholic convert Dudley G. Wooten to serve as its executive secretary. The Catholic Civic Rights Association went on to raise almost $50,000 for the campaign, but less than $200 came from outside Oregon. As Wooten described it, Oregon Catholics "fought this battle single-handed and unaided."[16]

Wooten brought political savvy and years of public service to the campaign. A native of Texas and a graduate of Princeton University and the University of Virginia School of Law, Wooten served Texas as a prosecutor, judge, and member of the state House of Representatives before being elected as a Democrat to the Fifty-seventh Congress in 1901. Unsuccessful in his bid for reelection, Wooten relocated in 1903 to Seattle, where he practiced law, served as a part-time judge, and won appointment to numerous prestigious public boards and commissions, including the State Board of Higher Curricula.

Wooten understood immediately the strategic impasse gripping the Catholic leadership in Oregon. From the earliest meetings of the Catholic Civic Rights Association's executive committee, Wooten detected two camps with conflicting approaches. Both distressed him. The more cautious faction "was for a passive and compliant campaign, . . . and pursuing a sort of let-alone, camouflaged attitude on the question." This group even advised that the use of the name *Catholic* be avoided. Other members advocated that the church go on the offensive: "there were those who favored an aggressive and militant assertion of Catholicism, a defense of Catholic dogmas, discipline and institutions, and putting the religious issue to the front as the paramount subject of discussion."[17]

Wooten perceived that both strategies suffered from extremism and that both spelled disaster: "Either course of action would have proved fatal, and it is doubtful which would have been the worse." Any attempt to mask Catholic opposition by "subterfuge or silence" was, he said, "foolish, cowardly and poor politics." At the same time, he argued that calling the Protestant public's attention to the church, Catholic doctrine, and religious bigotry "would serve only to further inflame public prejudice, would create side issues and irrelevant controversies, and cause the whole campaign to turn upon a religious quarrel, about which, in no age or country, have men ever been able to think clearly or to reason fairly."[18]

A more nuanced plan, which acknowledged the importance of the issue to Catholics without resorting to acrimony, offered a far greater likelihood of success to Wooten. Rather than emphasize or ignore religion, Wooten urged the executive committee of the Catholic Civic Rights Association to focus the campaign on the "natural and inalienable" right of parents to educate their children according to "their conscientious conception of parental and religious duty."[19] Parental rights had proved to be a successful campaign theme in Michigan, and Wooten was optimistic that it would resonate in Oregon.

Wooten's initial frustration with the executive committee's lack of political acumen reflected his broader disenchantment with the effectiveness of the Roman Catholic Church as a political force. The division within the Oregon Catholics struck Wooten as characteristic of "the lack of unity in counsel and solidarity in action that characterizes Catholics everywhere." Wooten, a convert, criticized hereditary Catholics for their inability to understand and communicate with non-Catholics. He chastised them for alienating non-Catholics and emboldening bigots because they are "too sensitive and self-conscious in the matter of their religious faith, . . . and they are more or less morbid on the subject, often imagining affronts and antagonisms that do not exist." As a result, Catholics often came across as "timid" and "cowardly" about their faith. Worse, hereditary Catholics failed even to recognize how unsympathetic they appeared, when it appeared obvious to converts. Wooten worried that their timidity made Catholics easy victims.[20]

Archbishop Christie, Wooten, and Bishop McGrath of Baker City devised a comprehensive canvassing strategy that employed the 130 Catholic parishes in Oregon in a door-to-door campaign to fight the School Bill. Local parish committees, pledging perseverance in opposing the initiative, identified voters by color codes, with white cards for Catholics, blue cards for non-Catholics who were undecided or open to persuasion, and yellow cards for "pronounced and incorrigible bigots." Parish members spoke to neighbors, organized speakers, and distributed over half a million copies of Wooten's pamphlet *24 Reasons,* which attacked, point by point, the misconceptions and misinformation distributed in support of the School Bill. Wooten argued that Catholics would defeat the initiative only if they mounted a vigorous defense of parental, religious, and educational liberties. Any other strategy amounted to appeasement and "pussy-footing" and was doomed to failure.[21] Wooten proved to be the most effective voice for his pamphlet, visiting every county in Oregon and speaking in all the principal cities.

The Missouri Synod Lutherans of Oregon met with far greater success in rallying national assistance to fight the School Bill. Dedicated to advancing religious education, Lutherans historically sought to build "a school with every church," and they operated a sizable network of parochial schools in Oregon. The Oregon Lutherans recognized the threat that the School Bill posed both in their own state and nationwide. Assailing the movement for compulsory public education as a "national danger," Rudolph Messerli, the executive secretary of the Lutheran Schools Committee advised a pastor in Nebraska to organize resistance early because "Failing in one state they will try in another or as soon as they find enough concerted interest in several states, they will attack more than one at the same time." Messerli concluded that the fate of the School Bill depended on whether the opposition could overcome two obstacles: the "general ignorance of the people of the fact that we already have compulsory education in our state, . . . and, the bitter antagonism which has been worked up against the Catholics by the K.K.K."[22] One of the largest Protestant sects in the state, the Lutherans could draw on considerable resources to fight the School Bill.

During the summer of 1922, the Lutheran Schools Committee, headquartered in Portland, sought the expertise of Rev. John C. Baur, who had managed the successful Lutheran opposition to the Michigan initiative in 1920. Baur, an Indiana pastor with a talent for organizing, counseled the committee on developing a statewide effort to track and influence public opinion. The Lutherans' campaign centered on distributing Baur's tract *The Truth about the So-Called Compulsory Education Bill* to all the voters in the state. Church youth groups throughout Oregon formed mailing clubs and circulated over 270,000 copies of the pamphlet. Baur also furnished literature from the Michigan drive, which the committee mailed to the editors of all the Oregon newspapers. Retaining the services of an advertising agency and a newspaper clipping bureau, the committee conducted a sophisticated operation that assigned pastors to respond to negative letters or editorials and that targeted advertising at uncommitted voters. It printed thousands of "Vote No" stickers.[23] The Lutheran opposition to the School Bill, signed by Rev. J. A. Rimbach, pastor of Portland's Trinity Lutheran Church, appeared as the first negative argument in the *Voters' Pamphlet* and drew strongly from the parental and religious liberty arguments in *The Truth*. The tagline of their campaign—"Who owns your child?"—came directly from the Michigan literature.

All this activity cost money, and the committee estimated it needed to raise $15,000 to cover its expenses, far too much to expect from Oregon alone. It secured $10,000 from the Missouri Synod headquarters in St. Louis, and in early August, Messerli sent letters to pastors throughout the state requesting their immediate assistance in raising the remaining $5,000 from the congregations. Circulars in both German and English, with envelopes attached, described the significance of the campaign to parishioners. A second letter followed, at the end of August, its tone more urgent, asking pastors for immediate action in forming local committees to conduct a door-to-door campaign to raise money and register voters, with special attention to registering women.[24] The local response to these instructions varied. In October, prominent attorney Stephen Arthur Lowell of eastern Oregon, a Congregationalist and a vocal opponent of the School Bill, complained to the committee about the ineffectiveness of its efforts in Pendleton, reporting that there "are many German Lutherans, and a considerable body of Finnish Lutherans here, and I am informed by people who have talked with some of them that apparently nothing has been done to advise them of the menace."[25]

The hierarchical organization of the campaign by the Lutheran Schools Committee also offended some Lutherans. David E. Lofgren, a leading Portland attorney, complained that the committee had violated the principle of all Evangelical Lutheran churches that "the laity control their own policies in regard to all public questions" and that "when they delegate any one to speak for them they particularly select the representatives themselves." Lofgren made no attempt to hide his displeasure: "Not since the days of reformation have the Lutheran laity allowed the clergy or any other class to think for them."[26]

Pierce Signs On to the School Bill

In September, the political dynamics of the campaign for compulsory public education shifted dramatically when the statewide standard-bearer of the proposal, Charles Hall, withdrew from the gubernatorial race because of a state statute prohibiting defeated primary candidates from running as independents. His withdrawal caused barely a ripple of concern among the Masons and Klan that had supported him; they had landed a far bigger fish. In early September, Democratic gubernatorial candidate Walter Pierce announced his support for compulsory public education and transformed the political alliances in Oregon. The Republican Party outnumbered Democrats nearly three to one, and most of the Oregon Klansmen and Masons voted Republican. But the anti-Klan stance of Republican governor Ben Olcott posed a strategic dilemma for the Klan. A Democratic candidate was far more attractive to the Klan than an independent.

Pierce knew he stood little chance of winning the statehouse unless he could draw votes from Olcott. But pandering to the Klan also posed significant political risks. The *Corvallis Gazette-Times* held little regard for Pierce's integrity and quite accurately predicted before the May primary, "If Mr. Olcott is nominated, Mr. Pierce will be strongly for the Ku Klux Klan. If Mr. Hall is nominated, Mr. Pierce will be the most raving individual in Oregon against invisible government." After Pierce announced his support for the School Bill, the *Oregonian* reported that "old-line democrats washed their hands of his campaign."[27]

The press disdain expressed for Pierce failed to acknowledge his considerable political clout. Short and stocky, but with a commanding presence, Pierce ranked as one of the state's most influential populists. Indeed, before his run for governor, the *Oregon Voter* assessed his political strengths differently: "As a campaign orator he is without a peer in the state, especially in addressing working people or rural gatherings. His personality is affable, he avoids cherishing personal grudges, he enjoys championing the cause of the unfortunate and he is well-liked wherever he is known. His sense of humor is keen and his heart is big."[28] A two-term state senator, Pierce exemplified the political sentiments of many Oregonians. A rancher, former teacher, and lawyer, Pierce embodied the contradictions that defined postwar America. He championed progressive economic and labor measures, while inviting charges of racism for his votes on social issues. In 1919, he introduced a full employment amendment to the state constitution to protect the interests of war veterans, proclaiming, "For long years it has been my belief that it is the duty of our government to afford full opportunity for those who desire to work."[29] That duty apparently extended only to certain segments of society: Pierce supported an anti-Chinese bill prohibiting white women from working in Chinese restaurants. He also voted against a measure to eliminate discrimination against blacks in places of public accommodation.[30] In 1918, Pierce made his first run for governor but lost to incumbent Republican governor James Withycombe by over 15,000 of the 81,000 votes cast. In the 1922 campaign, as in 1918, Pierce ran primarily as a populist against big business and in favor of tax reform. He initially rejected Klan overtures to support compulsory public education, predicting that the proposal had no chance of success.

By the summer of 1922, however, Pierce was prepared to cut a deal with the Klan for Klan support. Pierce's populist campaign aligned well with the Klan's nativist message. Exactly how far Pierce went to obtain Klan support remains shrouded in the secrecy of Klan membership roles. Shortly after the election, the La Grande Provisional Klan in eastern Oregon issued a personal invitation to Pierce to attend their next meeting on November 21, 1922. In one of the "best" meetings "ever held in the state of Oregon," the minutes from November 21 name "Klansman Walter M. Pierce, governor-elect," as an honorary member in attendance. Pierce thanked the Klan members for the support of "100% Americans." The Klan secretary urged members, "Let us bid Klansman Pierce God's speed in his new undertakings." A former Klan member claimed that "it was understood among Klansmen that Pierce had become a member of the Klan in Pendleton, although I cannot verify this fully."[31]

Pierce certainly was not above anti-Catholic sentiment. Shortly after the election, Pierce advised a constituent, "Our Catholic friends in this country are very quiet now. I am inclined to think that their days of great activity will cease for a time but we must remember that 'Rome never sleeps.'"[32] If Pierce was a Klan member, it is likely that he was inducted by Gifford during the summer of 1922. Gifford offered Pierce Klan backing. In turn, Pierce endorsed compulsory public education. Gifford claimed he also received a promise from Pierce of control of 50 percent of state patronage offices if Pierce won the election, a promise denied publicly by Pierce.

On September 3, 1922, Pierce gave Gifford a letter pledging his support for the School Bill. He issued a public statement the same day. In the statement, Pierce led with what he hoped would be the centerpiece of his campaign: tax relief. But most of the statement addressed the School Bill. Pierce emphasized his nativist, Protestant roots: "I am a Protestant, the ninth generation in America. Every one of my ancestors has been a Protestant for over 300 years. My wife and all her relatives are Protestants." He then insisted that religious prejudice played no part in his support for the School Bill: "I did not bring religion into this campaign. I refuse to meet it. It is not the issue. We are living in America, the land of the free, the 20th century, where every one can worship God as he pleases." Pierce pitched the School Bill as a populist initiative: "Every one of our six children was educated in the public schools. I believe in the free public school. . . . I believe we would have a better generation of Americans, free from snobbery and bigotry, if all children . . . were educated in the free public schools of America."[33]

CHAPTER 4   Good Enough for All

In a heavily Republican state, Pierce's endorsement of compulsory public schooling expanded the potential pool of voter support for the School Bill. Pierce's influence among populists was likely to yield votes for the measure. What that yield might be was difficult to discern among a citizenry with a reputation for political independence. By August, the campaign to capture the populist and progressive heart of Oregon had begun. School Bill sponsors dealt the first card in a hand calculated to meld themes of patriotism, egalitarianism, and nativism into a winning combination.

Voter Confusion Boosts the School Bill

The secretary of state approved the ballot title requested by the Masons. The Masons called their initiative the "Compulsory Education Bill," a title liable to confuse voters on the purpose of the measure. Oregon already had compulsory education; mandatory attendance laws were enacted in 1889, requiring children between the ages of 9 and 15 to attend school. The ballot title's omission of the word *public* obscured the actual objective of the initiative and led some voters to think they were voting to assure the continuation of mandatory attendance requirements.

Complaints that the sponsors intended to mislead voters with the ballot title dated from the signature-gathering phase. The weekly *Portland Spectator* reported that sponsors secured signatures by assuring citizens that the purpose of the initiative was "to give every child an education."[1] Wooten's pamphlet *24 Reasons,* prepared for the Catholic Civic Rights Association and providing reasons to oppose the bill, lists as reason 1 that the bill "secured a place on the official ballot by fraud, misrepresentation, and misunderstanding of many of those who signed the petitions." Interviews with petition signers suggested that perhaps thousands signed under the belief that the measure was merely a proposal for compulsory school attendance.

Proponents exploited misconceptions about the purpose of the School Bill throughout the campaign. They urged citizens to vote "yes" for "Compulsory Education." This misnomer gave School Bill advocates the strategic advantage of charging their opponents with harming Oregon's children by being "anti-compulsory education." In addition to reaping the benefits of any confusion generated by the ballot title, School Bill supporters successfully used the ballot title as a campaign slogan. The ballot title made it easy for supporters to distill the campaign to a simple proposition, "Are you for the public schools or against them?" Other ads fostered confusion on the purpose of the measure by claiming that a "yes" vote would save "Free Public Schools."[2]

The opponents tried to alert voters to the real purpose of the initiative, calling it the "so-called Compulsory Education Bill." In a pamphlet entitled *Remember Oregon* printed after the election, Wooten wrote, "A potent influence in the election, as it was cunningly contrived it should be, was the false and misleading title given to the bill. . . . The effect of this deceptive name misled thousands of voters, and created such confusion in the minds of thousands of others that they refrained from voting at all." Wooten acknowledged the advantage that the ballot title may have given its sponsors: "It served to put the opponents of the measure in a false light before the general public, by making it appear that they were warring against compulsory education in the free public schools."[3]

The Selling of the School Bill

Mason P. S. Malcolm ran the sponsors' campaign from his office in Portland. Malcolm worked closely with the Federation of Patriotic Societies (FOPS), which early on endorsed the initiative. Although the FOPS membership roles remained secret, the federation drew members from influential Protestant organizations, such as the Orange Lodges, Knights of Pythias, and Oddfellows. A local outgrowth of the anti-Catholic and nativist American Protective Association, it maintained ties to many prominent Oregonians. The FOPS achieved recognition primarily for publishing a "yellow ticket" of endorsed candidates prior to state and local elections.

The FOPS split with Klan leader Gifford over his favoritism toward public utilities. Gifford's close ties to public utilities spawned charges that the Klan used the School Bill as a smoke screen to distract populists and progressives from controversial economic proposals advanced by big business. The *Portland Telegram* reported, "The Klan in Oregon represents the capitalization of religious prejudice and racial animosity by public service corporations as the means of sidetracking the public mind from economic issues. With the people foolishly fighting over religion and fanning the fires of fanaticism, they have forgotten all about the agitation against 8 cent street car fares, high telephone and other service rates and reduced wage scales, that before the advent of the Klan threatened the profits of big business."[4]

Whatever their differences, Gifford and the FOPS saw eye to eye on the School Bill. The Masons, the Klan, and the FOPS orchestrated the election strategy, but the real power came from Gifford and the Klan. Gifford's Portland office served as headquarters for the Committee on Americanization of Public Schools. Malcolm wrote most of the campaign literature and offered voters a simple and compelling message: vote for the School Bill if you favor public education.

"Do you believe in our public schools?" queried the first line of the *Voters' Pamphlet* argument in favor of the School Bill. The pamphlet included only one argument in favor of the School Bill, submitted by the fourteen Masons who sponsored the bill. Proponents sought to keep voters firmly focused on the merits of public education. With 93 percent of schoolchildren already in public schools, the numbers favored a strategy that reinforced the wisdom of supporting public education and that raised suspicion about the relatively unfamiliar world of private schooling. The *Voters' Pamphlet* argument was designed to appeal to Oregonians of diverse political persuasions. "Americanism" justified the School Bill, and patriotism cast a big net in postwar Oregon. Advertisements in favor of the measure proclaimed, "Our nation supports the public school for the sole purpose of self-preservation."[5]

The Masons' pamphlet entitled *Reasons Why*—in response to the Catholic Civic Rights Association's pamphlet *24 Reasons*—urged voters to

"HONOR THE PUBLIC SCHOOL," through an education "IN CITIZENSHIP" and "DEMOCRACY." One ad, entitled in large letters "Public School Bill," quoted extensively from a statement by Theodore Roosevelt endorsing public education and reminding voters that public schools "are the creators of true citizens by a common education." Another described the School Bill vote as "the test of good citizenship." Campaign materials exploited the exalted view of public education held by progressives. One ad, entitled "Free Public Schools, America's Noblest Monument," pictured a colossal school, towering over the Washington Monument, the Capitol, and even Oregon's Mount Hood. Enlarged text described the public school as the "ONE thing that is important in this nation." A lengthy argument repeated, in all capitals, key words like *democratic* and *citizenship*, in conjunction with *public school*. Pictures of beautiful Oregon public schools dotted another advertisement captioned "Portals of the Nation's Future, Free Public Schools." This ad extolled the public schools: "Through them the coming generation of workers, thinkers, doers and achievers come and go, learning the principles of democracy—the basic things upon which depend the life and permanency of a nation of free people."[6]

School Bill advocates promised that compulsory public schooling would bring assimilation: "Mix the children of the foreign born with the native born, and the rich with the poor. Mix those with prejudices in the public school melting pot for a few years while their minds are plastic, and finally bring out the finished product—a true American." They argued, "Our children must not under any pretext, be it based upon money, creed or social status, be divided into antagonistic groups, there to absorb the narrow views of life as they are taught. If they are so divided, we will find our citizenship composed and made up of cliques, cults, and factions each striving, not for the good of the whole, but for the supremacy of themselves. A divided school can no more succeed than a divided nation."[7] One of the most frequently distributed ads on behalf of the School Bill simply proclaimed, "Free Public Schools, Open to All, Good Enough for All, and Attended by All." Gifford's advocacy for the Klan similarly stressed patriotism and an antielitist message aimed at middle-class progressives: "We also are for compulsory education in the public schools in a real sense. By that, I mean that no child should be permitted to be educated in the primary grades at any private school. Some private schools are denominational, and some are intended merely snobbish. We do not believe in snobbery, and are just as much opposed to private schools of the so-called 'select' kind as we are to denominational private schools. All American children should be educated on the same basis, in our American public schools."[8]

Other pro–School Bill campaign literature aggressively proclaimed the class-leveling function of public education. A widely distributed ad showed joyous children playing in a schoolyard dominated by an oversized American flag. Entitled "Free Public Schools for Red-blooded Children," the ad questioned, "Do we want a nation of red-blooded men, women and children, or do we want a nation of blue-bloods?" It described "happy, smiling children—red blood coursing in their veins" because "in their class rooms and playgrounds they learn . . . that common fellowship is at the very root of all American achievements." The ad claimed that public school children "learn to know that station alone—class in society—does not count" and that only public school children gain the "viewpoint of the vast multitude—of those who form the backbone of the country." Other ads argued that "wealth does not count, poverty does not hinder," for the only hierarchy is the "aristocracy" of learning. The Masons' pamphlet *Reasons Why* reminded voters that the "public school is the United States in miniature," where "the little citizens that are to be the future voters sit side by side, all EQUAL," and where they "realize—most precious knowledge—in early youth that it is what YOU ARE, not what your father HAS or what your grandfather WAS, that makes the difference in this world."[9]

The strength of the populist and progressive movements in Oregon played directly into the hands of School Bill proponents. Edward Alsworth Ross, a prominent progressive sociologist of the era, spoke in terms very similar to that of School Bill advocates when he described the role of public school teachers: "to collect little plastic lumps of human dough from private households and shape them on the social kneadingboard."[10] The progressives' attachment to public education brought middle-class Oregonians, particularly in Portland, a long way toward supporting the School Bill. The endorsement of the School Bill by a number of prominent Oregonians attested to the significant strategic advantage of a campaign designed to draw populists and progressives. One of the most well-known supporters of the initiative, William F. Woodward, a businessman popular with labor, Republican leader, and chair of the Oregon State Council of Defense, claimed that the "enduring success" of democracy could only be assured through an informed electorate, educated in citizenship produced by public schools. An articulate public speaker, Woodward garnered applause every time he proclaimed that "no private school, whatever its genesis, no matter how conducted, can equal for the purposes under which our nation exists the public school, which draws unto itself every child without regard to birth, creed, race or affiliation."[11]

Few other groups campaigned for the School Bill. The *Oregon Teacher's Monthly* came out in favor of the measure, commending the School Bill for securing to all Americans the "nationalizing influence" of public education. The editor praised compulsory public education, claiming it would serve as "an antidote for the inevitable class consciousness and possibly lopsided or snobbish private school attitude."[12] The president of Oregon State University and a number of public teachers also spoke in favor of the School Bill but did little to actively support it. For the most part, public school teachers and administrators remained silent. Protective of public education, they tended to equate criticism of the initiative with criticism of public schools.

None of the major papers in Oregon supported the School Bill. Aside from the weekly Klan mouthpiece, the *Western American,* editorials in support of the School Bill came from small, rural presses. The *Cottage Grove Sentinel,* typical of papers endorsing the measure, praised the School Bill in an editorial as a bold progressive step justified by "national necessity." The *Sentinel* criticized private schools for creating class distinctions detrimental to Americanization: "If private schools divide us into classes of rich and poor, Catholic and Lutherans, and so on, and lead one class to believe they are better citizens than some other class, they are out of harmony with our theory of democracy." The *Sentinel*'s editors insisted that "foreigners cannot be Americanized if Germans are permitted to attend their school, the Swedes to attend their school . . . and so on down the line." They refused to give credence to what they described as "the religious issue," because they observed cordial relations between Catholics and Masons. The paper did acknowledge that the School Bill raised complex policy concerns, but it concluded with a flourish, "Brilliant minds have sincerely opposed every great progressive move of the world's history and it is possible that this is history repeating itself."[13]

Despite a campaign designed to attract a broad voter base, School Bill proponents faced significant obstacles. Support for the measure suffered from the public rift between Masons. Endorsement by the Klan generated hostility in the many Oregonians who abhorred the Invisible Empire.

But the School Bill debate inflamed Oregonians, and the campaign benefited from voter anxiety and discontent. Many Oregonians viewed the measure as a symbolic referendum on postwar Oregon and America. To some voters, the initiative made evident the need to reform education in order to advance patriotism and assimilation. To others, the School Bill stoked fears of unwelcome change brought by growing numbers of non-Protestant immigrants. Still others viewed the School Bill as the vanguard of a classless society. Some voters simply wanted to send a message to Catholics. By the end of the summer, the School Bill cast a long shadow in Oregon, darkening the state with antagonisms that fostered alliances between egalitarians and bigots. As proponents of educational and social reform joined hands with the Klan, the superpatriots, and the nativists to champion the School Bill, opponents understood they would need considerable skill to fight the powerful currents underlying the measure's appeal.

CHAPTER 5   Who Owns Your Child?

Archbishop Christie, Wooten, and the leadership of the Lutheran Schools Committee argued that Oregonians would oppose the School Bill if they could be persuaded to see compelled public education as a draconian government intrusion that threatened personal liberty. Their efforts benefited significantly from the work of the Non-Sectarian and Protestant Schools Committee, a cooperative affiliation of secular school principals, Episcopalians, Lutherans, Adventists, and other prominent Protestants. This group mounted a high-profile attack on the School Bill that employed some of Oregon's most prestigious citizens. Members of its executive committee included a former Portland city commissioner, a former president of the Oregon Bar Association, and leading private school educators. The committee coordinated a large speakers' bureau, consisting of over fifty opponents of the School Bill, and funded an extensive advertising campaign.

The Opposition Rallies around Parental Rights

School Bill opponents united in their conviction that compelled public education violated fundamental liberties. Their strategy centered on reminding voters that protection of individual liberty and religious freedom formed the essential core of American democracy.

Dudley Wooten remained insistent that the Catholic campaign focus on parental rights. His conviction caused considerable debate among the Oregon Catholic leadership, some of whom pushed for a strategy stressing religious liberty. Wooten strongly disagreed; he argued that appeals to religious liberty risked alienating Protestant majorities. By contrast, every voter could identify with the protection of parental prerogatives. Wooten prevailed. The Catholic campaign narrative challenged the Masons' call to nationalism; it countered the image of an all-powerful state with that of parents proudly standing for the right to educate their children in the school of their choice.

The Lutheran leadership, with guidance from veterans of the Michigan campaign, had every incentive to re-create the successful Michigan strategy, and they, too, made parental rights the centerpiece of their campaign. Their submission in the *Voters' Pamphlet* pitted state power against parental prerogative, with a series of questions beginning with, "Who owns your child? The state? Who feeds and clothes your child? The State?" It charged that the School Bill, if enacted, "will deal a terrible blow to your constitutional rights, confiscate your parental authority and undermine your personal liberty."[1] Each of the remaining six negative arguments in the *Voters' Pamphlet,* filed by diverse religious and nonsectarian groups, championed the significance of parental rights in a democratic society.

Campaign literature stressed the link between parental rights and American fundamentals. One ad, captioned "In Justice to American Principles," asserted that the right of parents to choose a school for their child is one of the "inalienable rights" protected by the Declaration of Independence. Another, entitled "A Mother's Guiding Hand" and depicting a mother reading to her children, proclaimed, "Yours is the child. Yours is the right and duty to have a direct hand in guiding and educating," and warned that the School Bill would destroy maternal dominion. Ads from the Catholic Civic Rights Association invoked a higher authority in the struggle between parents and state, insisting that "God gave parents their children" and that "governments cannot rightfully take them away."[2]

Pamphlets, popular campaign tools, offered detailed analysis of how the School Bill threatened parental authority. Wooten's pamphlet *24 Reasons* argued that the initiative represented another step in the "weakening and final destruction of the duties and obligations of parenthood." It described the encroaching presence of the state in family matters as an alarming development, given that experts deemed the "decay" of parental authority as one of the "greatest evils extant in this country," contributing to juvenile delinquency and crime.[3]

The opponents' vigorous assertion of parental rights obscured the absence of legal precedent for their claim. The Constitution contains no references to parental authority, and there was no Supreme Court decision holding that the Constitution protected the rights of parents to control the education of their children. The tenets of a number of religions, including Catholics, Lutherans, and Adventists, recognized the right and duty of parents to care for and educate their children. The establishment of parochial schools occurred, in large part, to assure the fulfillment of these obligations in a manner consistent with church doctrine. The protection of parental rights in secular law fell far short, however, of the status of an "inalienable" fundamental right as claimed by School Bill opponents. Advocates who argued that the Fourteenth Amendment protected parental rights as a "privilege or immunity" or as a "liberty" did so in an effort to make precedent rather than invoke it. Shortly before the election, a group of prominent attorneys from around the state pronounced the School Bill unconstitutional on several grounds, including a violation of the privileges and immunities clause of the Fourteenth Amendment. Arguing that parents retained the "privilege" to supervise and direct the education of their children, they offered little legal support for their conclusion, citing only the argument of the dissent in *Hamilton v. Vaughan,* the Michigan case rejecting the authority of the secretary of state to refuse to place the initiative for compulsory public education on the ballot.

Catholics and Lutherans were not alone in their fight against the School Bill. The Seventh-Day Adventists, who relied heavily on a system of religious schools to educate their children and prepare them for missionary work, also devoted significant efforts to defeating the measure. Jews, despite their strong support for public education, vigorously opposed the initiative, appalled by the bigotry that tainted the debate. The Jewish League for Preservation of American Ideals took out full-page advertisements against the measure. Charging that the School Bill threatened the religious liberty of every creed in the United States, the league warned that "from Oregon, the move will spread to all states, and as it travels North, South and East, bitter bigotry and intolerance will take the place of friendship and brotherhood." African Americans, too, spoke out against the School Bill, attacking the "diseased mental state" produced by prejudice.[4] Secular private schools mobilized distinguished graduates to champion the virtues of educational diversity. Protestant pastors without ties to parochial education campaigned against the measure, even though the Portland Ministerial Association, the state's largest clergy organization, "declined" to take a position on the School Bill, largely because many Protestants supported it.

The Cold Facts

The anti–School Bill forces directly confronted attacks that private schooling suffered from incompetent tutelage and questionable patriotism. Characterizing the School Bill as a "war against a phantom,"[5] opponents called the measure an overreaction to a nonexistent problem. They argued that with less than 6 percent of schoolchildren attending private schools, private education posed no threat to public schools, nor were the Oregon private schools inferior to public schools. The Non-Sectarian and Protestant Schools Committee charged that the state had not found one private school in Oregon deficient in teaching Americanism or failing to adhere to instructional and curriculum requirements set by the state. Dudley Wooten contended that private schools "Americanized" immigrants as well as the public schools: "Actual statistics will show that there are as many nationalities represented in the private schools as in the public schools; that the discipline and intercourse of the pupils are just as democratic . . . ; that racial and class distinctions are as little permitted . . . ; and that there is absolutely no difference in the tone and teaching . . . in matters affecting American ideas and ideals."[6] Ads reminded voters that the founders and great patriots of the early days of the American Republic all attended private schools or received private tutoring. Public education provided no guarantee of patriotism, because many "anarchists" and criminals graduated from public schools.

School Bill critics countered charges of private school elitism by emphasizing how private schools, far from being elitist, served special needs not satisfied by public education. Private schools provided not just religious training but the extraordinary discipline of military schools, meticulous care and attention to those with learning difficulties, the single-gender environment desirable for some, and home and schooling for orphans. The *Oregon Voter* calculated that pupils in private and parochial schools received two to five times the teaching attention as those in public schools. The denial of elitism, however, often relied on arguments that reinforced elitist stereotypes, as when School Bill opponents bemoaned the potential fate of Yale and Harvard. State monopoly of education, they argued, would destroy great institutions, innovation, and competition.

The anti–School Bill forces publicized criticisms voiced by leading educators throughout the country such as Yale University president Arthur Hadley; author and former Columbia University professor Dr. Edward T. Devine; and a former U.S. commissioner of education, Philander Claxton. Columbia University president Dr. Nicholas Murray Butler claimed that the measure should be called "a Bill to render the American system of education impossible in Oregon."[7] Many of Portland's elite, educated in private schools and with children in private schools, led the opposition to the School Bill. Their ardent support for educational diversity did not diminish their quite obvious personal stakes.

The finances of compulsory public education favored the anti–School Bill forces. The economic downturn after World War I made money tight in Oregon. If the School Bill passed, thousands of students attending private and parochial schools would be forced into public schools. Taxpayers would be responsible for capital expenses for buildings and grounds enhancement and for increased per annum operating expenses. While calculations of the actual financial impact varied somewhat, most objective assessments predicted a substantial impact on public education resources. By adding between 9,000 and 12,000 new students to the public schools, both the *Oregonian* and the *Oregon Voter* estimated a minimum of three million dollars statewide to expand classrooms and facilities, with over half that amount incurred in Portland. Estimates of the additional annual statewide revenue necessary to cover the per pupil costs for the new students ranged from $650,000 to over one million dollars per annum. Opponents argued that passage of the School Bill guaranteed, at minimum, a million dollars in new taxes. Portland, in the midst of what would be a failed effort to bring a world's fair to the city in 1925, would, presumably, find additional taxes most unwelcome. Some commentators warned that these estimates did not account for the likelihood that the state could incur significant financial liabilities from successful lawsuits brought by private schools and former private school teachers seeking redress for lost income.

Opponents made the financial risks of School Bill support personal, particularly for those Klan members who mistakenly assumed that the secrecy of Klan membership rolls shielded them from public accountability. At a massive members-only Klan rally in Portland's Civic Auditorium, a group of young Catholic men and at least one priest slipped into the parking lot and copied the license numbers on the cars. When confronted by the police, the group deflected police suspicions by, quite accurately, explaining that "some Catholics got into that meeting." The subsequent match of license numbers with public records revealed the Klan connections of many leading businessmen, a disclosure that found its way into the Portland newspapers. The publication of Klan members' names gave Catholics an opportunity to respond in kind to the Klan's "100 Per Cent Directory" of approved businesses.[8]

St. Mary's Academy transacted considerable business in the Portland community. Mother Mary Flavia, the superior of St. Mary's, described by Father O'Hara as "the foremost religious educator of her time in the Northwest," decided to hold her business associates accountable for their positions on compulsory public education. She telephoned a number of the unmasked businessmen, advising them that St. Mary's could not continue to do business with those who sought to eliminate private education. To others, Mother Flavia sent a letter on October 21 that admonished them to think carefully about their position on compulsory public schooling.

> Gentlemen:
>
> We appeal with confidence to you in the attack to destroy the private, parochial and denominational schools and colleges by placing on the ballot at the November election a measure entitled a Compulsory School Bill.
>
> We need not remind you of the hundreds of thousands of dollars brought to our state and Portland in particular by the large attendance at the colleges, academies and private schools, add to this the maintenance, the money spent by the pupils, and you have an additional large sum of money brought to our city and state.
>
> Our business relations for many years have been most pleasant and beneficial, and in the hour of our trial, may we not appeal to you, yours, your people and friends to vote down this bill, thus preserve children to be wards of the parents, religious freedom be preserved and education remain unmonopolized.
>
> You know we have consecrated our lives to education and we appeal to you not only from a business standpoint, but in the interest of the children brought under our care and we can point with pride to the splendid achievements of our institutions in giving Oregon a refined, educated womanhood.[9]

The publication of the identities of numerous Portland Klan members signified the intensity with which the School Bill controversy played out on the pages of those newspapers willing to take a stand against the measure. The *Capital Journal*'s aggressive crusade against the School Bill culminated in a series of editorials that criticized the economic, political, and social implications of the measure. Analyzing the financial burden on the state posed by the closure of all private schools, the *Capital Journal* argued that the cost in dollars and cents to the taxpayers "is the least part of the cost to the state"and that the School Bill would stamp Oregon as a "freak" state, a "fool," execrated as the "most intolerant commonwealth," for its interference with parental and religious liberties. Predicting that passage of the initiative would deter educated Americans from moving to Oregon and drive current residents from the state, the *Capital Journal* foresaw future economic development shackled by the perception of Oregon as "an unsafe place either to invest or to live, a state where there is constant meddling by cranks and fanatics, not only with government and property, but also with individual liberty and freedom of conscience."[10]

In October, as election activity escalated, opponents faced evidence that the School Bill enjoyed considerable popular support. William Wheelwright, a leader of the Non-Sectarian and Protestant Schools Committee, debated the School Bill with prominent proponent William Woodward. They played to a packed house in Portland, and their debate was reprinted in its entirety in the *Oregon Voter*. Woodward emerged as the clear crowd favorite from this debate, an outcome that did not surprise Wheelwright or the committee. This politically savvy group understood the appeal of the School Bill. The committiee cautioned its speakers, "Remember that many are just beginning to grasp the dangers involved in this bill. You will go into audiences often strongly against you at the start."

Wheelwright encountered the most intractable problem confronting School Bill opponents: religious bigotry. Early in the debate, Wheelwright attacked the dishonesty in the School Bill sponsors' denial of religious bigotry. He charged that it was common knowledge that the measure was aimed primarily at Catholic schools: "There are some cases that are too plain for argument, and this is one; the hardest thing in the world is to prove the obvious."[11] Wheelwright concluded his address with a plea for religious tolerance, an appeal that, little more than one month before the election, fell flat. The audience sat in stony silence, in marked contrast to the applause they lavished on his adversary's adulation of the public schools.

CHAPTER 6   Romanism

The official campaign on behalf of the School Bill remained, for the most part, focused on patriotism and assimilation. Anti-Catholic bigotry was kept to subtext. But outside the *Voters' Pamphlet* and the ads displayed prominently in major newspapers, some School Bill supporters waged a far more nefarious campaign, conceived in religious bigotry. The movement for compulsory public schooling tapped into deep suspicions about Catholics. The Klan fomented this antipathy to draw support for the School Bill.

Anti-Catholicism in Oregon History

Anti-Catholic sentiment was not new to Oregon. The large migration of Protestant settlers brought with them hostility toward Catholics, learned in communities of the East and Midwest. Prior to statehood, French Catholic and Protestant missionaries clashed throughout the region. Many Oregon Protestants held Catholics responsible for inciting the Whitman Massacre, when members of the Cayuse tribe attacked the Whitman Mission in 1847, killing several of the Presbyterian missionaries and taking fifty hostages. After the attack, Henry Spalding, a Protestant missionary among the Nez Perces in the area, mounted a campaign charging Catholic provocation of the Cayuse. The perception of Catholic responsibility persisted during the highly publicized trial of Cayuse perpetrators two years later. This bias found its way into the publications of local historians and remained part of the history taught to Oregonians.

Anti-Catholic attitudes rose sharply during World War I, when Catholic immigrants migrated to Oregon to work in factories and shipyards. A number of Protestant ministers in Portland preached sermons fanning fears of Roman influence. Newspaper editor, J. E. Hosmer, caused a scandal when he planted a spy in a Benedictine convent in an effort to disgrace the Roman Catholic Church with evidence of immorality. When the spy, Mary Lasenan, found nothing amiss, Hosmer published a defamatory pamphlet entitled *The Escaped Nun from Mount Angel Convent, or The Last Stand of Desperate Despotism,* in which he falsely claimed Lasenan had been kidnapped by the nuns and subjected to sexual abuse by priests. Convicted of criminal libel, Hosmer spent 100 days in jail for contempt, refusing to pay a $200 fine.[1] On his deathbed, Hosmer recanted and apologized.

Hostility toward Catholics became an increasing part of Oregon public policy. Anti-Catholic measures were introduced throughout the 1921 legislature. A bill to prohibit certification of Catholic-run schools for teacher training just missed passage, as did a proposal to replace Catholic and Protestant chaplains at the state penitentiary with the Salvation Army. The legislature held hearings on a bill that would prohibit any teacher in public school from wearing the garb of a religious order, and legislators blasted the presence of nuns in public schools. One Oregon Catholic reflected the foreboding felt by many: "Noon today witnessed the closing of a legislative session which has given us great uneasiness, casting a cloud no bigger than the hand of a man."[2]

Discriminatory legislation presented only one of the threats to Catholics. Near hangings, night riding, and other acts intended to terrorize or pressure minorities and enemies of Klan members occurred throughout the state. Sister Mary Etherlind, who walked children from St. Mary's Academy to Sunday Mass, was one of the many nuns regularly confronting hooded figures on horseback who rode onto the sidewalk to frighten the children. Public school children taunted their Catholic contemporaries with calls of "Cat-likker! Cat-likker!"

Charges arose that Catholics sought to destroy public education. The Portland School Board elections of 1921 generated a field of candidates who promised that "no Catholic's place will be safe." Running on an anti-Catholic platform, the winning candidates credited their success as "a victory of the great majority of the people in this city who believe in maintaining our free public school system on a strictly nonsectarian basis as against a certain minority who by their thorough organization eternally persist in meddling with our education institutions."[3] Portland's mayor at that time, George L. Baker, became an early advocate of compulsory public education to force Catholic children into the public system.

Suspicions of a Catholic conspiracy against public education led to discrimination against Catholic teachers in the public schools. Application forms for public school employment required disclosure of religious affiliation. Fearful Catholic employees listed "Christian." They dressed in disguise to attend church, often to no avail. Catholic teachers and employees received terse termination notices: "Your services are no longer needed in this school system." No explanation and certainly no recommendation accompanied these notices. Similar incidents occurred throughout Oregon. Teachers in the southern Oregon town of Medford traveled as far as Eugene, in the central Willamette Valley, to attend Mass without detection. As one Oregonian described the efforts to purge public schools of Catholic teachers, it was "not a question of Catholic's [sic] having the right to follow the teaching of their Dago Pope, but the right of Protestants to educate their children by the best public school system in the world."[4]

Anti-Catholicism Fuels the School Bill

The Masons' aggressive support of compulsory public education contained mixed messages, combining an appeal to patriotism and antielitism with blatant bigotry. From the early 1920s, the national Mason publication, *New Age,* conducted a vigorous campaign on behalf of compelled public schooling. Some of their appeals played directly on nativist fears and prejudices: "Once concede that an alien church can interfere with the education of the citizen, and you must concede that an alien political committee or dictator can do the same." The Oregon Masons published a number of ads rife with anti-Catholic messages. One drafted by Malcolm charged that opponents of the School Bill include "those who believe the rights of church should take precedence over the rights of the state."[5]

Gifford's public statements on behalf of the School Bill generally abjured the blatant, inflammatory attacks on Catholics that risked alienating moderate voters. But Gifford occasionally failed to disguise his contempt for Catholics: "We do feel that as the allegiance of Catholics is to a foreign power, the pope, that their clannish attempts to extend the temporal power of the pope over the offices of this country is opposed to the best interests of America."[6] To Klan audiences, Gifford spoke even more bluntly, throwing them the "raw meat" of bigotry he claimed they craved: "Somehow these mongrel hordes must be Americanized; failing that, deportation is the only remedy." Gifford relished his power, chanting at Klan rallies, "Who made the Klan? Who is going to put over the School Bill for the Klan?" while the audience roared back, "Gifford!"[7] While Gifford generally avoided public pronouncements of bigotry, he proved less successful at muzzling other Klan leaders, such as Rev. Reuben Sawyer, Klan leader and pastor of Portland's East Side Christian Church, whose garbled message sounded a veritable potpourri of religious bigotry, nativism, and patriotism: "The Ku Klux Klan swears allegiance to the flag and not to the church. . . . One of our purposes is to try to get the Bible back into the schools, such as it was in the old days. The little red schoolhouse on the hill is the cornerstone and foundation for our government. Within the next few years we hope to see only native born Americans rule the government instead of foreigners."[8]

While the anti-Catholic strategy preyed on Protestant fears that Catholics answered only to Rome, it also fostered antipathy toward Catholic schools. Proponents urged voters to protect the public schools from the "Roman monopoly" and the "catechized monstrosities [who] would destroy all of our public schools." Masonic supporters of the initiative, proclaiming the "truth" as to the official position of Masonry on the public schools, boasted that all Masons pledge to protect the public schools from the "assaults of those who would destroy and create in its stead a system of parochial schools, supported by public taxation, dominated and controlled by and under the absolute influence and power of an autocratic hierarchy, upon ideas foreign in conception and directly contrary to the theory of . . . American democracy."[9]

Allegations of substandard education in private schools intermingled with insinuations about the appropriateness of the curriculum, particularly in parochial schools. The disseminators of these innuendos never offered evidence to support their claims. On the surface, these criticisms purported to be directed at the adequacy of citizenship instruction in religious schools. But they also played on Protestants' lack of familiarity with Catholic schools. Sometimes implied, sometimes explicit, these charges all made the same point: Catholics could not be trusted to teach American patriotism, because they were committed to instructing loyalty to Rome over loyalty to country.

The anti-Catholic campaign exploited Protestant Oregonians' ignorance of Catholic religion by portraying the Roman Catholic Church as a secretive cult, beholden to suspicious and immoral practices. Dr. James R. Johnson, Portland Klan leader, traveled Oregon making inflammatory speeches accusing Catholic priests of misusing the confessional to obtain sexually stimulating disclosures. Johnson and other Klan members paraded a series of disgruntled ex-nuns and ex-priests before audiences eager to hear scandalous tales of sexual and physical abuse within the Catholic cloister. Ex-nun Elizabeth Schoffen, the most infamous mouthpiece for the Oregon Klan, denounced the church before packed auditoriums. Schoffen served for many years as a floor supervisor at St. Vincent Hospital in Portland, but she left her order and turned on the church when she was transferred to a less-prestigious assignment. Speaking as "Sister Lucretia" and drawing on her purported 31 years of experience as a nun, she spread sordid accusations about depraved behavior at St. Vincent. On October 8, 1922, at one of her more seamy appearances, restricted to "men only," a man representing over 50 physicians attempted to distribute flyers protesting her attacks against St. Vincent. He was beaten until unconscious and dumped outside town. The Sisters of St. Vincent responded with a public refutation of Sister Lucretia's charges. They also requested that Mayor Baker of Portland launch a public inquiry to prevent further damage to the hospital's reputation, an invitation that Baker refused.[10] In response, a group of 58 non-Catholic physicians paid for a full-page advertisement protesting the vilification of the sisters through crude and malicious falsehoods.

These attacks on Catholics took on new relevance to many Oregonians upset about the explosive political issue of public school teachers wearing religious garb. Approximately 20 nuns worked in public schools throughout Oregon, both as teachers and principals. These nuns wore the habits of their religious orders during the school day. Gifford lost no time in circulating campaign ads built around pictures of public school classes posing with their teacher in religious garb. The ads simply instructed voters, "Find the Teachers—then THINK!" Other ads identified the nuns teaching in public schools and their salaries, then quoted part of a statement by Theodore Roosevelt, who opposed "any appropriation of public money for sectarian purposes." The juxtaposition of these pictures with the charge that Catholics sought to control the public schools provided powerful propaganda for School Bill proponents. One of the first acts taken by the Klan-dominated

1923 legislature would be the enactment of a law banning teachers from wearing religious garb in the classroom.

The Oregon Klan's pamphlet on the School Bill, *The Old Cedar School,* exemplified Klan strategy toward working-class Oregonians. Part populism, part religious bigotry, *The Old Cedar School* managed both to deny religious animus and to excoriate multiple minority religions for their elitist efforts to destroy public education. The pamphlet offered a dialogue between an unsophisticated farmer and his troublesome children, who married Catholics, Episcopalians, Methodists, and Seventh-Day Adventists and who intended to reject the Old Cedar School in favor of private religious schools. In the foreword, King Kleagle Luther Powell wove populist and progressive themes, claiming that the School Bill campaign represented a "battle of the mass of humanity against sects, classes, combinations and rings; against entrenched privilege and secret machinations of the favored few to control the less favored many," and that those who opposed the initiative "wished to work their children and collect their earnings." According to Powell, the Klan supported the School Bill because the former had a duty to protect public schools from the onslaught of private religious education, not because it desired the "destruction or injury of any religious sect."[11]

The Old Cedar School ridiculed its opponents, mocking a fictional intellectual windbag named Hon. Ab. Squealright and Catholic education at the "Academy of St. Gregory's Holy Toe Nail," where children learned "Histomorphology, the Petrine Supremacy, Transubstantion . . . together with the Beatification of Saint Caviar."[12] It did not equivocate on charging minority religions with a conspiracy to destroy the public schools. A full-page cartoon at the end of the pamphlet depicts the Old Cedar School, with its loyal, old teacher in the doorway, welcoming children of all backgrounds and religions, while the American flag waves atop the bell tower. But holding the children back are Catholic, Episcopalian, Methodist, and Seventh-Day Adventist mothers. As a Catholic priest approaches the school with a burning torch, an Episcopalian bishop, a Seventh-Day Adventist minister, and a Methodist superintendent hack at the foundation of the school with large mallets. The pamphlet's last image, also covering a full page, shows the school in flames, toppled from its foundation, with the old schoolteacher dead in the doorway, his hand futilely grasping the cord of the burning school bell, as the American flag, severed from the tower, ignites. The Catholic priest walks away, his torch extinguished, a smile on his face.

In the pamphlet, as elsewhere in the Klan campaign, the Klan threw the opposition's accusations of religious persecution back in the faces of their opponents, charging them with manufacturing claims about religious bigotry merely to protect their elitist institutions. Kleagle Powell derided a multitude of religions, not only in Oregon, but throughout history, including "Mohammedans," polygamists, and "head-hunters," which "howled" religious persecution whenever the enlightened majority intervened to halt their brutal practices. Powell concluded his litany of purported falsities with the example of "church organizations which have burned countless thousands as heretics who differed from them in religious beliefs, [who] cry religious persecution when it is proposed that children shall learn common school studies." The true religious bigotry, claimed Powell, came "not from its supporters, but from those who would aid the gradual and insidious absorption of the public school for their own selfish purposes."[13]

The Catholic Response

Powell's assailment highlighted the political risks that School Bill opponents faced if they denounced the religious bigotry in the School Bill campaign. Religious freedom arguments required a carefully nuanced strategy. Moderate voters perhaps could be persuaded that the School Bill threatened religious liberty. These arguments could easily backfire if voters perceived them as charges of religious prejudice. School Bill opponents often found themselves on the defensive when they attempted to debate the impact of the measure on religious liberty. Catholics, acutely sensitive to the potential backlash, devised a strategy that championed the importance of religious liberty and tolerance to all Americans and that downplayed religiously divisive attacks.

In their *Voters' Pamphlet* argument, the Catholic Civic Rights Association asked voters to celebrate harmony, not discord, and unity rather than division. They described how the Puritans, the Huguenots, the Cavaliers, the Quakers, and the Catholics, among others, sought refuge in America because they "craved" civil and religious liberty. Their argument alluded to anti-Catholicism only in general terms, claiming that Oregon, with its highly educated and patriotic citizens, "has been free from racial and religious strife for a long time" and should not fall prey to "agitation that will estrange old friends and neighbors and that will devide [*sic*] our people into classes and factions."[14]

Catholic speakers often quoted President Thomas Jefferson. In response to a worried inquiry from Ursuline nuns in New Orleans fearing the closure of their school at the time of the transfer of the Louisiana Territory to the United States, Jefferson assured the sisters that "the principles of the Government and Constitution of the United States are a sure guarantee to you that it will be preserved to you sacred and inviolate, and that your institution will be permitted to govern itself according to its own voluntary rules, without interference from the civil authority." He concluded his letter with a tribute to educational diversity, widely repeated by School Bill opponents: "Whatever diversity of shade may appear in the religious opinions of our fellow-citizens, the charitable objects of your institution can not be indifferent to any; and its furtherance of the wholesome purposes of society by training up its young members in the way they should go, cannot fail to insure it the patronage of the Government it is under. Be assured it will meet with all the protection my office can give it."[15]

To selective audiences, the Catholic critique resounded with far more passion and anger. In his July 4 speech before a predominantly Catholic audience, Father O'Hara blasted the School Bill for its blatant bigotry: "Let there be no misunderstanding concerning the purpose of the proposed school legislation. No labels or protestations can conceal the end in view; let no man deceive you with vain words—the measure is conceived in a hatred of religion and in the hope of crippling its free exercise."[16] The Non-Sectarian and Protestant Schools Committee urged its speakers to address the "real animus of this bill," by asking their audiences whether they viewed their Catholic neighbor as "such a bad person."[17]

Religious Liberty and the Federal Constitution

School Bill opponents proclaimed a national, federally protected right to be free from state interference with religion, a right that had not been recognized by the Supreme Court. The First Amendment limits only the authority of the federal government, not the states. The Supreme Court had rejected claims that the First Amendment applied to the states through the due process clause of the Fourteenth Amendment. Most of the campaign literature ignored that fact, using language that specifically connected the voter to the federal constitution or that made vague references to religious liberty. It was common for ads and pamphlets to assert that the School Bill violated religious "liberty" protected by the federal constitution or to argue that the measure interfered with the "free exercise" of religion. An ad by the Non-Sectarian and Protestant Schools Committee entitled "In Justice to American Principles" quoted the Declaration of Independence and the First Amendment as support for their contention that freedom of speech and religion are rights secured for all Americans.

The absence of federal constitutional precedent for the religious liberty proclaimed by School Bill adversaries did not mean that these claims were manufactured for the fight against compulsory public education. To the contrary, the idea that religious liberty constituted a fundamental American principle deserving of federal constitutional protection enjoyed widespread support across the country. By the mid-nineteenth century, the rallying cry of religious liberty carried particular relevance to disputes involving education and religion.

Many Americans associated religious liberty with separation of religion from state. Minority religious groups who understood religious oppression, including Jews, Baptists, and atheists, strongly supported separation, as did many secularists who believed religious influence should be excluded from government.[18] But nativists and anti-Catholic groups, such as the Klan, argued for an "American" constitutional principle of religious separation to protect Protestant dominance. They supported separation to preclude states from lending public assistance to Catholic schools. The platform of the American Federation of Patriotic Voters, a nativist organization, supported "absolute separation of church and state, as guaranteed by the constitution," and the safeguarding of public schools from "ecclesiastical influence or control."[19] Religious liberty, as separation, became a justification for a variety of measures intended to reduce Catholic influence and opportunity.

Catholics and others who disliked the religious bias underlying many separationist arguments challenged this narrow and often hostile definition of religious liberty. Adopting the language of the separationists, they proclaimed that religious tolerance represented the true "Americanism." The opponents of compelled public education specifically asserted that religious liberty included the rights of parents to educate their children at parochial schools. Dudley Wooten described the religious principle at stake.

The State has no more right to force parents who believe in religious instruction as an indispensable part of true education, to send their children to the public schools where religious instruction is impossible, than it has to force those who do not believe in religious education to send their children to sectarian schools. Americanism means what the men who made it declared it to mean, which is the freedom and equality of all men in the enjoyment of their natural rights."[20]

The *Voters' Pamphlet* submission by the Lutherans agreed: "Under the constitution of the United States . . . you enjoy religious liberty; that is the liberty to worship God according to the dictates of your conscience and to rear your child according to your religion."[21] Seventh-Day Adventists described religious liberty in even more specific terms: "Some believe it is their inalienable and constitutional right to educate their children for missionary service. To many parents this has become a religious duty and it is an 'exercise' of their religion, and a matter of conscience."[22] By invoking religious liberty as an "American" constitutional principle, School Bill opponents sought to draw on deep convictions held by many Americans. That the Supreme Court had yet to legitimize these convictions mattered little to most citizens, who either misunderstood the law or assumed the Court would validate their views.

Some School Bill opponents tried to turn religious hatred to their advantage, claiming that the vitriolic campaign actually advanced Catholicism in Oregon. At a mass rally in Portland, A. F. Flegel, a well-known Mason, Methodist, and attorney, insisted that the initiative "is doing more to promote the advance of Catholicism than anything that has taken place in this country in a century." Arguing that the "blood of the martyr is the seed of the church," Flegel spoke of packed Catholic churches and an assessment by a priest in eastern Oregon that, after years of declining church attendance, "our people have rallied to the church with an intensity and unanimity that I have never known." Flegel also found evidence of a backlash against the initiative by many Protestants who, "by the thousands," express "intense sympathy for Catholics, simply because they feel they are not getting a square deal." Describing School Bill supporters as the "greatest missionaries" for Catholicism, Flegel concluded that "had the sponsors of this bill lain awake nights trying to devise ways and means for promoting the very thing they seek to check, they could not have served Catholicism more effectively."[23]

As summer pushed into fall and the campaign heated up, the anti-Catholic assault became more public and personal. The Klan attempted to undermine opponents by accusing Protestant adversaries of being Catholic or part of the Catholic "machine." The most prominent victim of the misinformation campaign, Governor Olcott, faced rumors spread throughout the state that he and his wife were Catholic and sent their children to Catholic school and that his deceased sister, a Methodist Sunday school teacher before her death, was alive and living as a nun in San Francisco. False statistics of the number of Catholics appointed by Olcott to government positions circulated as evidence of Olcott's obeisance to the Catholic machine.

Newspaper editors opposed to the Klan or the School Bill also fell prey to deceitful charges. Gifford regularly assailed adverse editorials as the work of Catholics. In an editorial entitled "Liars and Us," the *Bend Bulletin* alleged, "Ever since we began our argument against the Ku Klux Klan, reports have been coming to us of a story going about to the effect that the editor . . . was a Catholic." Remarking on reports that the paper was "controlled by the Catholics," the *Bulletin* lamented that "people have been asked to boycott us on that account."[24] Hugh Hume, the editor of the weekly *Spectator,* faced similar false accusations. The public status of the recipients of these attacks put them in the awkward position of denying the allegations while at the same time trying to assure voters that they would be proud to be Catholic and were only protesting the "unconscionable" lying of their attackers. As in the Michigan campaign, misinformation spread about the propensity of parochial school graduates to engage in criminal behavior. Distortions of Catholic scripture also surfaced. Anti-Catholic speakers ranted that "the law of the Church says drink all you can," a dramatic misinterpretation of Christ's counsel to his disciples at the Last Supper to "drink ye all of this."[25]

The Klan-sanctioned diatribes against minority religions illuminated a fundamental inconsistency in the Klan's position on the School Bill. Klan leaders failed to be troubled by the hypocrisy of an agenda that both touted public education as "open to all" and reviled religious minorities. While the Klan obviously anticipated that native-born Protestantism would dominate the public schools, its contempt for minorities undermined its idyllic portrayal of public education.

Smaller hypocrisies emerged. Gifford had sent his two daughters, Mary and Marcella, to St. Mary's Academy between 1914 and 1916, and his son attended Hill Military Academy even during the campaign. Other prominent supporters of the School Bill were alleged to have children in private schools, Catholic spouses, or spouses who attended private schools. A number of School Bill proponents were themselves products of private school education.

The anti-Catholic sentiment fueling support for the School Bill was not simply a matter of religious bigotry. The School Bill campaign exploited hostility toward Catholics primarily by suggesting that Catholics posed a risk to American democracy. School Bill proponents played on fears that immigrants, including Catholics, brought to America a radical political agenda and then nurtured that agenda in private schools. Opponents underestimated how strongly this message resonated with Oregonians. The religious prejudice exploited during the campaign was symptomatic of a more profound unease among Oregon voters, the apprehension that dramatic social change and the forces of radicalism threatened their world and American democracy.

CHAPTER 7   Seeing Red

Supporters and opponents of the School Bill put forth very different visions of democracy. Proponents championed the prerogatives of the majority. They envisioned a society where immigrants and minorities assimilated to majority values and where the interests of the community dominated those of the individual. Opponents claimed individual liberties were the cornerstone of democracy. To them, an enlightened government protected minority rights as vigorously as it legislated majority values. While a political and philosophical chasm divided these positions, both sides of the School Bill agreed on one significant premise: the fate of compulsory public education would influence the course of American democracy.

In 1922, the greatest perceived threat to democracy came from Bolshevism. Most Americans abhorred the authoritarian, highly centralized government imposed in Russia after the 1917 Russian Revolution. To the adversaries in the School Bill fight, mandatory public schooling evoked a shared trepidation, the infiltration of Bolshevik ideas into American society. Both sides stirred fears of radicalism to gain voter support. The School Bill campaign became, in part, a debate over the best way to combat radical influences in society. Supporters believed mandatory public schooling essential to instill patriotism and eliminate the risk that private schools would teach un-American values. Opponents equated compelled public schooling with the state monopoly of education found only under communist governments. Only two days before the election, voters reading the Sunday *Oregon-*

ian encountered a full-page ad warning that "the public school is the SCHOOL OF AMERICA, and the ONLY school," and that he who "hesitates in his loyalty to THAT school . . . is a traitor." Several pages later, another full-page ad responded, "Remember that Russia now has state monopoly of schools."[1]

Red Scares in Oregon

Debates over radicalism were not new in Oregon; they dated back to statehood and the rise of populism. A vigorous labor movement made socialism an issue prior to World War I. Disgruntled workers in newly industrialized businesses flocked to the Socialist Party and to militant labor unions like the West Coast Shingle Weavers' Union and the International Union of Shingle Weavers, Sawmill Workers, and Woodsmen. The Oregon ranks of the Industrial Workers of the World (IWW, or "Wobblies") grew with thousands of dissatisfied loggers and mill workers.

During the war, newspapers excoriated not only the "Huns" but also pacifists and socialists. In 1917, the front-runner in the Portland mayoral race, Will Daly, lost the election after, two days before election day, the conservative *Oregonian* published an editorial exposing Daly, a registered Republican, as a member of the Socialist Party. The paper speculated, "If the people elect Daly, we shall have a socialist for Mayor. . . . There will be encouragement for strikes and countenance of industrial agitation for the sake of agitation."[2]

Vigilante squads roamed the state, poking haystacks in search of Germans and radicals. To Portland mayor George Baker, the "Reds" posed a far greater threat, however, than German immigrants. The thousands of workers who descended on Portland to work in the wartime shipyards brought a rowdy, often lawless environment to parts of Portland, but the police often seemed indifferent to these mundane forms of disorder, focusing their attention on tracking down radicals and uncovering "plots" against the government. Floyd Ramp, a respected farmer and Socialist, spent eighteen months in prison for violation of the Espionage Act in telling a group of soldiers that they were "fighting to protect John D.'s [Rockefeller] money."[3]

The rapid collapse of the burgeoning Portland shipbuilding industry after World War I led to unrest, and Oregonians succumbed readily to fears of a "Red" conspiracy, even blaming the radicals for a virulent flu epidemic. The IWW wooed returning servicemen by providing basic food, clothing, and shelter. "Well, come along with us," the group encouraged, promising, "Our organization will be very glad to give you a meal or two until you get back on your feet and we will give you a suit of clothes."[4]

Such fears prompted Oregon governor James Withycombe, in his January address to the 1919 legislature, to ask for enactment of a law to punish radicals for treason, urging the legislature to act quickly: "Now while poisonous influences of sedition and sabotage are fresh in our minds it might be well to set down in the statutes Oregon's appraisal of I.W.W.ism and other forms of disloyalty."[5] That same month, when a council of workmen, soldiers, and sailors formed in Oregon, Mayor Baker warned the legislature, "IWW agitators and organizers are finding a fertile field in which to spread their dangerous propaganda. . . . We must put down this Bolshevik movement and do it now or they will put us down."[6]

Instability in Seattle, a hotbed of both IWW agitation and vigilante response, created dread of a regional descent into anarchy. The Wilson administration selected Charles L. Reames, the U.S. attorney for Oregon and widely considered the top prosecutor in the West, as special assistant in charge of radicalism cases in Seattle. But Reames's aggressive plan for wholesale deportation of alien IWW members met resistance within the Wilson administration and fed public fears that the government could not control the spread of radicalism.[7]

The Seattle General Strike of February 6, 1919, which threw Seattle into a panic and frightened the rest of the country with the prospect of revolution, triggered alarm in neighboring Oregon. After the strike, Seattle mayor Ole Hanson kept the focus of national media attention on the Pacific Northwest, as he toured the United States describing the attempted "Bolshevik revolution" in his part of the country. Hanson charged that the Wobblies "want to take possession of our American Government and try to duplicate the anarchy of Russia." Seattle papers warned, "STOP BEFORE IT'S TOO LATE . . . This is America—not Russia." National headlines were no less inflammatory, claiming, "REDS DIRECTING SEATTLE STRIKE— TO TEST CHANCE FOR REVOLUTION," and notifying readers that "the [Bolshevik] beast comes into the open." The Seattle General Strike, the May Day bombings, and a series of additional strikes throughout 1919 spawned a Bolshevism hysteria throughout the country, including Oregon. Mayor Baker of Portland captured the political mood in 1919 when he implored citizens to "forget selfish purposes and interests and harness our activity to purge the country of the evils of Bolshevism."[8]

The IWW's demands for a restructuring of the relationship between industry and government and their willingness to use violence made them an easy political target. In 1918, the Oregon Bar Association unanimously supported the drafting of legislation that would "stamp out . . . IWWism and all other isms, . . . Bolshevists, anarchists [and] . . . others of their ilk."[9] The criminal syndicalism bill, proposed to the 1919 Oregon legislature, made it illegal for a person to advocate violent political or industrial change or belong to an organization that advocated violence. The sponsor of the bill, Senator Walter A. Dimick, implored his colleagues to recognize the urgency of the political situation: "The Bolshevists have written the darkest pages in history today, and the movement is carrying westward and is showing its hand in the form of the I.W.W. which defies all law and all mankind." Senator B. L. Eddy agreed, calling the Bolsheviks "a deadly ferret clutching at the throat of the American eagle."[10]

The *Oregon Journal* gushed that the bill would "preserve Americanism," for "Evil in the human heart was the motive power of Bolshevism."[11] Mayor Baker of Portland, in his statement of support for the bill, informed the legislature that 135 of the newly returned servicemen had already become Bolshevists.[12] But some Oregonians found the bill troubling. The conservative *Oregon Voter* wrote that the bill raised one of the most momentous issues of the day, whether "those who agitate violence as a remedy for industrial wrongs may be denied the privilege of free speech, free press and a free assemblage for their advocacy of crime or sabotage."[13] The legislature should be reluctant to pass the measure, the editorial suggested, because any infringement of fundamental rights should be carefully considered.

Walter Pierce, a state senator at the time, was the only senator to oppose the measure. Embracing populist themes, Pierce argued to his unresponsive colleagues that economic hardship, not "evil in the heart," caused social unrest.[14] He insisted that Bolshevism would disappear if workers could be assured of a decent living: "There is a cause of this Bolshevism, this turmoil which is spreading over the world and perhaps society must reorganize itself." Worrying that the bill might incite unrest, Pierce urged the senators to "remove the cause and not wave a red flag in the face of those who are protesting evil conditions."[15] After the bill became law in January 1919, Pierce commented that the "people of Oregon, like all people in world affairs, yielded to the hysteria going through the country."[16]

On November 11, 1919, during an Armistice Day parade, American Legionnaires in Centralia, Washington, stormed the IWW headquarters. Four veterans died in the ensuing melee. Angry citizens captured IWW leader Wesley Everest, already driven from Coos Bay, Oregon, for IWW activities, and turned him over to authorities. That night, a mob pulled Everest from the jail and lynched him from a railroad bridge, riddling his body with bullets. Some witnesses reported that the mob castrated Everest before lynching him. Officials failed to arrest anyone for Everest's murder, even though eleven members of the IWW stood trial for the deaths of the veterans. The media fueled popular misconceptions that the Wobblies fired into a peaceful parade. Government officials, fearing a national IWW uprising, arrested or detained Wobblies throughout the country.

Nationwide raids targeting radicals and conducted by Attorney General A. Mitchell Palmer on January 2, 1920, yielded 28 arrests in Portland, the greatest number of such arrests on the West Coast. An additional 29 members of the IWW waited trial on charges of criminal syndicalism. The *Oregon Journal* devoted most of its front pages on January 3 and 4 to the results of the "Red Raid," with headlines that proclaimed a nationwide communist conspiracy to overthrow the government and with coverage of the IWW trials in Portland and Centralia, Washington. The January 4 *Oregonian* carried national and local stories of the raids. Printing a picture of a group of those arrested in Portland, the *Oregonian* boasted that its photographer experienced little difficulty in getting the group to pose, since "all it takes is a package of cigarettes to get 'Reds.'"[17] Portland radicals made headlines when they predicted that the "nation would be shaken to its foundations within the next few months" and that radicals would seize control of Portland's government in the next election.[18]

The *Oregonian* editors called for the arrest of every radical in the country, demanding that the convicted be placed in concentration camps. Politicians complained that the courts failed to mete out sufficiently harsh punishments to radicals, letting them off with minor fines or parole. In February 1921, the legislature gave Oregon one of the most stringent antiradicalism statutes in the country, by unanimously passing a more comprehensive version of the 1919 criminal syndicalism law.

The Portland police created a secret communist detail, known as the "Red Squad," to investigate radical activity. The head of the Red Squad, police officer Walter B. Odale, a former intelligence officer during World War I, first gained notoriety for his zealous efforts to destroy the IWW in Portland. With his appointment to the Red Squad, Odale pursued alleged communists and communist sympathizers with a single-mindedness bordering on obsession. Odale peppered his conversations with references to the power of the communist "united front" and blamed communism for every conceivable social problem, from the disintegration of family life to labor unrest to the growing crime rate. Working out of an unmarked office paid for through private donations, Odale and his associates made use of a network of spies and informants to collect information. They compiled long lists of suspects from around the state and papered their office with charts correlating "subversive" individuals, associations, and activities.[19]

Oregon Nativists Cry Wolf

Many of the suspected radicals in Oregon, as throughout the country, were immigrants, Catholics, or Jews. In truth, Oregon had scant reason to fear disruption by immigrants. In 1920, only 13 percent of Oregonians were foreign born, approximately 8 percent were Catholic, and less than 0.4 percent were black. But racial and religious prejudices survived as a legacy of the Anglo-Saxon pioneer migration into Oregon. The original Oregon constitution ratified in 1857 contained an exclusion clause, prohibiting blacks and mulattoes from entering the state and denying legal rights to those already in the state. In 1859, Oregon became the first state admitted to the Union with an exclusion clause written into its constitution. The clause was still on the books when the School Bill passed. The state constitution also prohibited Chinese who were not already residents from owning property. Anti-immigrant sentiment, already present in Oregon, rekindled easily.

The 1918 statewide primary election sowed the nativist seeds of the School Bill battle. Patriotism dominated all other issues in the campaign. The American Patriotic Association described Father Edwin O'Hara, superintendent of Catholic schools, as a radical, ignoring that he was on active duty in Europe as an army chaplain. Nativist legislation in Oregon rose after the war. In 1919, the legislature passed a language bill prohibiting "the teaching of any subject other than foreign languages in public or private schools, except in the English language."[20] A special session of the legislature called in January 1920 unanimously adopted a joint resolution urging Congress to restrict landownership by aliens. The 1920 legislature enacted additional restrictions on speech, making it unlawful to publish or sell any newspaper or periodical in a foreign language unless the publication also contained a literal translation in English.

Newspaper coverage of IWW activities and the Palmer raids repeatedly highlighted the alien status of radicals. Although less than half of those arrested in the local Palmer raids were "alien 'Reds,'" the front-page *Oregonian* story on January 3, 1920, read, "20 Communists Held as Plotters—Deportation Is Object." The *Oregon Journal* followed suit, with front-page headlines promising, "Local Bolsheviki Will Be Deported."[21] Descriptions of the "foreign element" matched the national news reporting of "alien anarchists." The Sunday, January 4 *Oregonian* devoted pages of coverage to radicalism, juxtaposing a story on the New York immigrants scheduled for deportation, "Swarm of Radicals Fills Ellis Island," with a local article titled "Reds to Be Deported," which described the nationality of each radical arrested in Portland. One supporter of the School Bill typified the views of many when he opined that although the majority of immigrants are "good," there has also been "a vast deal of dangerous immigration, that wishes to perpetuate here all the old world hates and evils." He argued that compelled public schooling promised a "universal melting pot where America can take the children from even the . . . hordes of foreign born who are themselves beyond help in visualizing the aims and the destiny of America, and starting them on a safe, sane, righteous way of thought and life."[22]

Nativism across America

The political climate in Oregon exemplified an intolerant national history. The association of immigrants and Catholics with radicalism began long before World War I. From the earliest days of the Republic, political and cultural forces attributed radical politics to foreign influence. Anti-Catholicism contributed to the Protestant migration from Europe to colonial America. Catholics in some of the colonies suffered disenfranchisement and preclusion from any office of trust and honor. Fear of foreign agitators dated back to the founding of the country, when Congress, apprehensive that the victors in the French Revolution sought to export political insurrection, passed the Alien and Sedition Acts of 1798, which, among other things, authorized the president to deport aliens dangerous to the peace and safety of the United States.

The political tension generated by nativism pervaded politics during the last decades of the nineteenth century. In 1884, Rev. Samuel Burchard, a Republican, attacked the Democrats as the party of "Rum, Romanism and Rebellion." The epithet became an issue in the 1884 presidential election, when the popular Republican candidate, James G. Blaine, failed to repudiate the slur, lost the Irish American vote, and was defeated by Democrat Grover Cleveland. Blaine maintained he would have won the election "but for the intolerant and utterly improper remark of Dr. Burchard." The Haymarket Square bombing in Chicago in 1886, during a protest by anarchists, generated virulent hostility toward immigrants across the country. Although the bomber was never found, the trial, conviction, and hanging of a number of German anarchists cemented the public perception of immigrants as lawless and violent. Nativists, insisting that immigrants personified radicalism, argued that "there is no such thing as an American anarchist," because "the American character has in it no element which can under any circumstances be won to uses so mistaken and pernicious."[23]

The 1901 murder of President McKinley by the anarchist son of Polish immigrants spurred Congress to pass the Immigration Act of 1903, the first immigration law to exclude immigrants because of their political beliefs or deny them citizenship. The law precluded entry and naturalization by anarchists and those who advocated or believed in the forcible and violent overthrow of government. In the years leading up to World War I, the public identification of the IWW with radical aliens led to increasingly restrictive immigration laws. President Wilson twice vetoed literacy test requirements, only to have Congress override the veto in 1917 and enact legislation also providing for the deportation of any alien advocating violent political action.

World War I roused nativism into national hysteria. Immigrants, Germans and Russians in particular, represented the enemy, and the country presumed their loyalties remained elsewhere. Theodore Roosevelt proclaimed "America for Americans" and charged immigrants still attached to the country of their birth with "moral treason."[24] He linked immigrants to radicals by describing "Russian exiles of the Bolshevist type" and "Germanized Socialists," and he spawned violent hostility to Germans by recommending the shooting or hanging of any German who showed disloyalty.[25] Congress passed the Espionage Act in 1917, which made it a crime to interfere with the operation of the armed forces. One year later, Congress toughened the Espionage Act with the Sedition Act, which prohibited disloyal or abusive language about the government or armed forces during war. Both laws were used aggressively against radicals and immigrants.

Although the war fanned prejudices against immigrants, the collective focus of the country remained on achieving victory. Armistice Day endowed

America with a renewed pride in democracy. But peace also brought domestic disruption and shattered the sense of collective purpose. The industrialization of war had created a vigorous economy stimulated by the partnership between the federal government and private industry, and the postwar collapse of this economic linchpin caused spiraling inflation and hardship. The tenuous wartime truce between labor and management disintegrated into industrial unrest. During 1919, over four million workers participated in more than 3,600 strikes.[26] The public widely perceived the labor instigators to be immigrants "soaked" in the doctrines of Bolshevism. With the war behind them, America turned to destroying the enemy within.

In 1919, most of the country watched with trepidation the Bolshevik-inspired upheavals in Germany, Italy, Poland, and Hungary. As labor unrest erupted throughout America, the public branded workers and labor leaders as "foreign leeches." In real numbers, American Bolsheviks consisted of probably less than 70,000 members of the fledgling American Communist Party and the American Communist Labor Party, but the Bolshevik label attached to far greater numbers.[27] The term *Bolshevist* quickly became an epithet not only for radicalism but also for difference, whether political, religious, or cultural. Bolshevism symbolized the antithesis of democracy, the antimatter to democracy's matter. Governor Nestos of North Dakota made national news when he was forced to the public defense of North Dakota farmers charged as radicals and Bolshevists. The United Mine Workers published a series of articles alleging the existence of a Moscow-controlled communist plot to overthrow the government, funded by "liberal American intellectuals."[28] In a time of economic and political instability, Bolshevism became both the cause and the description of the "evil" threatening society.

The Supreme Court Weighs In

The Supreme Court validated national fears of a Bolshevik menace. A series of unanimous opinions penned by Justice Oliver Wendell Holmes, Jr., in 1919 upheld convictions, under the Espionage and Sedition Acts, of immigrants, antiwar activists, and socialists for subversive speech during the war. Dismissing arguments that the First Amendment protected their speech, the Court found that anti-American, antiwar speech posed a "clear and present danger" to the war effort. In the first major case, *Schenck v. United States,* the Court upheld the conviction of Charles T. Schenck, general secretary of the Socialist Party in Philadelphia, under the Espionage Act of 1917, for distributing, during wartime, leaflets challenging the war and the draft. The leaflet, which reprinted the text of the Thirteenth Amendment's prohibition on slavery, described military conscription as despotism and urged recipients to "Assert Your Rights." It advised, "Do Not Submit to Intimidation." The Court found that the distribution of some of these leaflets to draftees constituted a "clear and present danger" of harm to the country and justified Schenck's conviction for obstructing the recruitment of soldiers and causing insubordination in the armed forces.[29]

Similarly, in *Frohwerk v. United States,* and *Debs v. United States,* also wartime cases, the Court upheld convictions for antiwar speech that carried 10-year sentences. Jacob Frohwerk's conviction resulted from a series of articles critical of the war, published in a newspaper, the *Missouri Staats Zeitung,* during 1917. The Court warned that "it is impossible to say that it might not have been found that the circulation of the paper was in quarters where a little breath would be enough to kindle a flame."[30] The Court also affirmed the conviction, under the Espionage Act, of Eugene Debs, former presidential candidate and a leader of the Socialist movement, for giving a 1918 speech that criticized the war and advocated the Socialist platform.[31] Debs served just over two and one-half years of his sentence before his 1921 release by President Harding in a general Christmas amnesty. While incarcerated, Debs ran for president as the Socialist Party candidate, receiving 919,799 votes, or 3.4 percent of the total votes cast.

In the last of the 1919 cases, *Abrams v. United States,* the Court upheld conspiracy convictions, under the Sedition Act of 1918, of five Russian immigrant defendants who wrote, printed, and distributed two leaflets—one in English and one in Yiddish—attacking American intervention in Soviet Russia. The English pamphlet urged, "Awake! Awake, You Workers of the World! REVOLUTIONISTS." The Yiddish pamphlet, entitled "Workers—Wake Up," also called for a general strike. The Court, describing the defendants as "alien anarchists," found that the "plain purpose of their propaganda was to excite, at the supreme crisis of the war, disaffection, sedition, riots, and, as they hoped, revolution in this country."[32] This time, Justice Holmes dissented, however, joined by Justice Brandeis, arguing passionately that the pamphlets failed to present the "present danger of immediate evil or an intent to bring it about" that justifies interference with First Amendment liberties. Holmes agreed that the power to punish subversive speech is greater during war, but he belittled the pamphlet as a "silly leaflet" unlikely to have any effect on the war effort.[33] While Holmes's dissent laid the foundation for a more tolerant approach toward radical speech, one that the Court would eventually adopt, a majority of the Supreme Court in 1919, like most of the country, showed little tolerance for radicalism.

Purging Radicalism and Protecting Patriotism in the Schools

The national fixation on patriotism and nativism widened into an obsession with ideological conformity that culminated in the Red Scare of 1919–20, with the arrests of over 7,000 people alleged to be radicals. Warren G. Harding, in his 1920 campaign for president, offered a return to "normalcy," but the country, while desperate to recapture a sense of prewar innocence, had been transformed. Arrests on one day, January 2, 1920, numbered over 3,000 in 33 cities. While the collective hysteria dissipated by the end of 1920, the fear of Bolshevism remained rooted in the national consciousness. Antiradicalism led to the passage of the Emergency Quota Acts and Immigration Acts of 1921–24, which set country-by-country immigration quotas.

The vigilant crusaders against radicalism argued that patriotism through public education was necessary to national security. By 1923, 80 percent of the states mandated citizenship classes, up from just 2 percent in 1913. Over three-fourths of the states also enacted laws requiring compulsory flag displays and exercises and English-only instruction.

The demands placed on public education to guarantee patriotic indoctrination led to increased scrutiny of teachers and curriculum. The conservatives who led the patriotism movement saw academic freedom as a threat to the teaching of 100 percent Americanism. In 1921, the American Bar Association admonished the country that radical teachers were corrupting children by indoctrinating "questions into the unformed minds of the coming generation." An ABA committee report urged "every true American" to "stem the tide of radical, and often treasonable, attacks upon our Constitution, our laws, our courts, our law-making executives, and our flag." The report advised schools against " graduating a student who lacks faith in our government."[34]

Many teachers who merely taught about Bolshevism lost their jobs in witch hunts for "Red" schoolteachers throughout the country. The New York City school superintendent undertook a quest to find out "Who's Red and Who's True Blue," probing the personal beliefs of schoolteachers—

justifiably, he insisted, because loyalty does not allow for "9 to 3 patrio-tism."[35] Teacher loyalty oaths, required in only five states before the Red Scare, rapidly became law in over half the states. Textbook purges made headlines, with states demanding removal of any "unpatriotic" statements and insisting on "purification" of government and history books. Private schools came under attack, particularly elite colleges, which were de-nounced as "radical institutions." The patriotic societies singled out profes-sors, labeling them radicals and leaders of "parlor red" seminaries, including such liberals as Felix Frankfurter of Harvard, who later won appointment to the Supreme Court.

The specific threat to education posed by Bolshevist indoctrination made headlines, which claimed, "Reds Are Ruining Children of Russia." Sto-ries like "Russia's Third Front," describing Russian schools as "nurseries" of Bolshevism, aggravated fears that impressionable children could easily be influenced by radical ideology. Proponents of compulsory public education pointed to these news accounts as evidence of the risk to democracy posed by private schools. But the Bolshevik experience played to both sides of the debate over compelled public education. The Soviet Union made news around the country when it banned all private schools, primarily to elimi-nate religious education.[36]

The School Bill and Bolshevism

These stories resonated with Oregonians, who showed little tolerance for radical influences in the schools. The *Oregonian* charged that children were "the prey of theoretical propagandists in our institutions of education."[37] Oregon banned any textbook "that speaks slightingly of the founders of the republic, or of the men who preserved the union, or which belittles or un-dervalues their work."

Sponsors of the School Bill capitalized on the public mood, fomenting the public's dread of radical immigrants. They called for immediate and ur-gent action against radical elements: "We must now halt those coming to our country from forming groups, establishing schools and thereby bringing up their children in an environment often antagonistic to the principles of our government."[38] The Mason pamphlet, *Reasons Why,* described "vicious, un-American elements that hate the public school . . . , like that English Governor of Virginia." One ad proclaiming, "Our republic is in danger," charged that "foreign born boys and girls . . . are corrupting the morals and blighting the free truth-loving spirit of our public school boys and girls."[39] School Bill proponents did not hesitate to tell voters that a politician who failed to support the public school as the "ONLY school" should be considered "a traitor to the spirit of the United States" and that "your vote should tell him so."[40]

The anti-School Bill forces also played the radicalism card, and they generally wielded it more frequently and directly than the advocates for the measure. They gambled that the public would reject compelled public schooling when it recognized the parallels between the Oregon proposal and the state-controlled education policy of the Bolsheviks. Governor Ben Olcott described the stakes in stark terms as a choice between "Americanism" and radicalism. He attacked candidate Pierce for assisting the "Reds," reminding voters that state senator Pierce had cast the only vote against the Oregon criminal syndicalism law. Even Portland Socialist Party leader C. W. Barzee, after first promising Pierce his support, later attacked the School Bill as tyrannical for giving the state the power to use state monopoly of education as a vehicle for pro-government propaganda.[41]

Opposition literature labeled the initiative the "School Monopoly Bill." The Lutheran campaign captured the essence of the opposition strategy by asking, "Who owns your child? The state?"[42] Leading Protestant businessmen published a statement to remind voters that "this measure imitates the method of public education which brought Prussia to her deserved destruction—giving the state dictatorial powers over the training of children and destroying independence of character and freedom of thought." They cautioned that the real danger came from a more recent political model: "In the present-day Russia the Bolshevist government treats the child as the ward of the state. This measure proposes to adopt this method and to substitute state control for the authority and guidance of the parents."[43] The argument signed by principals of leading nonreligious private schools concluded its rather pragmatic analysis of the benefits of private schooling by attacking the School Bill as "Prussian in spirit and method and . . . a piece of majority tyranny" that "represents an anti-American effort to standardize the individual."[44] The Seventh-Day Adventists described the measure as "un-American," warning that "the government that turns its citizens into subjects and makes them mere cogs in a wheel, without any rights of their own, is a government that is transforming itself into a tyranny."[45] A group of Presbyterian ministers called the proposal "inimical" to human welfare because it "is based on the philosophy of autocracy that the child belongs primarily to the state."[46]

Mindful that the public's loathing of Bolshevism arose primarily from hostility toward the concept of an all-powerful state, opposition pamphlets, advertisements, and speaker talking points peppered their criticisms with persistent references to the link between state monopoly and tyranny. The Lutheran Schools Committee pamphlet questioned whether the "flower of our youth" fought and died in World War I only "to make democracy safe for a state control of the national mind?"[47] School Bill opponents cautioned voters that government efforts to eliminate religious schools aided Bolshevist plots because religion stood as a bulwark against godless Bolshevism. The most broadly distributed literature, the campaign ads, placed the question of tyranny squarely in front of the voter. Full-page ads entitled "In Justice to American Principles" warned, "Remember that Prussia tried the system of state monopoly of schools. Remember that Russia now has state monopoly of schools."[48] Other advertisements questioned why Oregon would seek to establish a system of education that is based on the autocratic philosophy that the child belongs to the state and is "unknown in the wide world except under Lenine [sic] in Russia."[49]

Catholic campaigners in particular found the "Bolshevik menace" an attractive alternative to attacking religious intolerance. Dudley Wooten's pamphlet *24 Reasons* embedded "despotism," "tyranny," "state monopoly," and "Sovietism" in over one-third of the arguments against the measure. Reason 11 states flatly, "The Oregon bill was inspired by the principles and practices of Russian Sovietism."[50] Wooten lectured extensively throughout Oregon, delivering an address entitled "The School Monopoly Bill or the Government Ownership of Children." Father O'Hara, a war veteran, campaigned actively against the measure, passionately describing his postwar pride in the triumph of American principles over autocracy, only to find those principles threatened by the Prussianism of education embodied in the School Bill.

Press editorials on the School Bill generally avoided the inflammatory labels spewing from both campaigns. The *Capital Journal* admonished voters that passage would make Oregon the "freak" state of the union, the only one that "substitutes for the American system of individualism the German kaiser's system of collective education and the Soviet idea that the child is the property of the state."[51] The press outside of Oregon passed a much harsher judgment on the measure. The weekly *San Francisco Argonaut*, in an editorial entitled "Prussianism in Education," typified the national coverage by excoriating the School Bill as a proposal that "out-Prussias Prussia" by imposing an anti-American absolute monopoly that casts children in a common mold.[52] But the majority of Oregon editors preferred a less combative tone, describing the School Bill as "incompatible" with American principles of liberty.

Editorial cartoonists delighted, however, in exploiting the hysteria over radicalism. One typical cartoon depicted the "Compulsory Education Bill" as an enormous stockpot. Six chefs poured ingredients into the pot. Each chef bore a distinct name—"Bolshevism," "Prussianism," "Class Hatred," "Persecution," "Hate," and "Spite." A black-coated man in a tall hat, tagged "Religious Revenge," stirred the pot, as its bitter fumes filled the night sky. The caption read, "Mixing the Devil's Broth." Another cartoon, which appeared in the Portland papers, took aim both at the Klan and gubernatorial candidate Pierce for their autocratic views. Titled "Three Souls with the Same Thought," it portrayed Pierce, "the wandering boy," and Vladimir "Lenine" flanking a white-robed Klansman. "Lenine" and Pierce beamed as the Klansman held high a placard, signed by "Lenine—Head Bolshevik," proclaiming, "State Monopoly of Schools Is an Absolute Success in Russia."[53]

CHAPTER 8   The Majority Will

In the dwindling days of the Oregon School Bill fight, labor unrest in Portland brought home the threat of radicalism exploited in campaign rhetoric. On October 13, a walkout by 1,000 members of the International Longshoremen's union and the Marine Transport Industrial union, a branch of the IWW, shut down the Portland waterfront. Portland mayor George Baker fomented public anxiety, condemning the strike as a Wobbly-led insurrection and insisting repeatedly that the city was in the throes of a revolution. Baker called for all patriots to come to the defense of Portland and law and order.[1] The city council passed an emergency ordinance authorizing Baker to hire 74 special officers, who, along with the police department, were ordered to take whatever steps were necessary to prevent the IWW from methods of "terrorism and disruption." Klan Grand Dragon Fred Gifford offered Baker, unconditionally, the full strength of the Oregon Klan to assist in combating the Red menace.[2] The police swept the waterfront, arresting over 500 strikers and other IWW members throughout the city. Federal officials stirred further alarm when they claimed they were unable to prosecute the IWW or other antigovernment radicals under existing federal laws governing peacetime activities. If an IWW meeting "had occurred three or four years ago," they let the public know, "we'd have the county jail filled to capacity this morning." They explained, "We'd simply have placed a cordon of soldiers about the place and taken those we wanted."[3]

Then, on October 19, Mayor Baker spread the word that IWW leaders, rallying workers across the country with the slogan "On to Portland," expected 25,000 members to descend on Portland. The jails and courts filled with vagrants; anyone coming into town was suspected of subversive activities. The newspapers were quick to point out the number of aliens among those arrested. The *Oregonian* informed its readers that a study of the names and nationalities of those arrested revealed that over one-fourth were foreign born and that the majority who claimed American citizenship possessed, nonetheless, names with a "decided foreign tinge." As the paper described them, "unpronounceable Polish, guttural Teutonic and weird Russian combinations of consonants predominate on the police docket." The appearance of those arrested only compounded their subversive air, for they were "unkempt, unshaven, . . . and strangers to soap and water." Labor sympathizers staged a protest at the city jail, and a red flag hung briefly from a jail window, which the papers described as the "blood-red banner of anarchy."[4]

Those arrested who could not prove at least six months of Portland residency were offered the choice between jail time and permanent exile from Portland. Most left town. Drifters and the unemployed who were swept into the police dragnet faced vagrancy charges. Deportation proceedings began immediately against all noncitizens arrested. Defense attorney B. A. Green, challenging the arrests, shouted in open court, "If you don't stop this persecution, God Almighty himself can't keep these wobblies out of Portland."[5]

On October 25, the strike ended, and Mayor Baker abruptly halted the raids, just as defense attorneys prepared to file suit against the city. There had been no IWW violence. But people were upset with the unrest that seemed to hang over the city.[6] The press miscalculated the seriousness of the public mood, an error that plagued press coverage throughout the School Bill campaign.

As with the rise of the Klan, many of the major newspapers said little about the School Bill until late in the campaign. Those papers that supported the Klan or feared their wrath either came out in favor of the initiative or kept quiet. While none of the major papers supported the School Bill, most took their time in opposing it.

With less than three weeks until the election, the *Portland Telegram,* the most prominent newspaper that came out early against the School Bill, pointedly accused the other Portland dailies of shirking their responsibilities by failing to take a position on the measure. The *Telegram* also berated the "stupidity" of those Democrats who sought to divert voters' attention from the School Bill and from Democrat Walter Pierce's support of the measure by pretending that taxes, from which Pierce promised relief, remained the dominant issue for voters. George Putnam, editor of the *Capital Journal* and an early and vehement critic of both the Klan and the School Bill, blasted the "pussyfooting" of the Portland daily press. Taking to task both the *Oregonian* and the *Oregon Journal*, Putnam wondered, "Is it possible that the Journal, like the Oregonian, once fearless and forceful, has likewise become fearsome and decadent, caring more for pocketbook than for principle, and too timorous and pusillanimous to voice its conviction, barters its honor for a mess of klan pottage, lest it lose a subscriber or an advertiser?"[7] Despite this scathing characterization of much of the Portland press, the Klan's *Western American* still referred to the papers as "Portland's pope-bossed, Jew-kept, scandal mongering dailies."[8]

In late October, as autumn colored the forests and cooled the air, editorials against the School Bill cropped up in small towns all over the state. From Klan strongholds in southern Oregon, the *Klamath Falls Herald* and the *Roseburg Review* criticized the measure's interference with parental and religious liberties and expressed disgust at the exploitation of religious prejudices. The *Bend Bulletin* in central Oregon and the *Astoria Budget* along the Oregon coast published similar commentaries. In the Willamette Valley, the *Corvallis Gazette-Times*, in an editorial entitled "Take It to Yourselves," advised voters to stand in the shoes of religious minorities whose patriotism had been unfairly questioned.[9]

The *Telegram* reprinted the editorials and cited them as evidence that public sentiment had begun to shift against the initiative. It also reminded voters that the eyes of the country watched the Oregon debate. The paper reprinted an article from the social science magazine *The Survey* that attributed the existence of the School Bill to a national failure in inculcating tolerance and described Oregon as "acutely revealing a general national disease."[10] On November 6, the day before the election, the *Telegram* published a front-page story entitled "K.K.K. Plot to Control the State." Written by political editor Henry M. Hanzen, it warned that Pierce and Klan legislative candidates stood poised to seize control of the state and enact compulsory public schooling even if the initiative failed at the polls. While Hanzen predicted defeat for both the School Bill and Pierce, he urged voters to recognize that they faced a choice between tolerance and state-sponsored bigotry.

In Portland, while the School Bill debate filled the front pages of the two remaining Portland dailies, the *Oregonian* and the *Oregon Journal*, their editorial pages stayed silent. The *Oregonian* buried its editorial position in a series of long articles entitled "Education and the State," which examined the legal, financial, and political arguments for and against the School Bill. Unconvinced that the measure threatened religious liberty, the *Oregonian* ultimately decided to oppose the initiative, for violating parental rights. The final article in the series, published on the day before the election, offered only tepid resistance to the proposal, insisting that the editors did not "underestimate" the benefits of compulsory public education. Claiming that the paper was "the last to say that the proponents of the measure are not actuated by a sincere motive for the public welfare," the *Oregonian* dispassionately concluded that the state should pursue vigorous regulation of education rather than abolition of private schools, because of the "weighty" concerns of minority rights and increased taxation.[11]

The *Oregon Journal* refused to take a position on the School Bill before the election. Instead, it expressed dismay that the measure distracted voter attention from the "all-important question" of tax policy posed by the platforms of the gubernatorial candidates, Governor Olcott and Walter Pierce. While the paper admitted "there cannot be too many sources of school training," it dismissed religious liberty claims as propaganda and blamed the Catholics for their predicament because nuns teaching in religious garb in public schools had "inflamed prejudice."[12] *Capital Journal* editor Putnam, in a blistering attack, accused the *Oregon Journal* of being a mouthpiece and apologist for the Klan and blamed the paper's "shameful" silence for the flourishing of the Portland Klan.[13]

Democratic gubernatorial candidate Walter Pierce, the purported standard-bearer for compulsory public education, proved to be a less-than-vigorous advocate. Pierce preferred tax reform to school reform, and as the campaign progressed, School Bill proponents became increasingly upset with his tepid support. With most Democrats aligned against the School Bill, Pierce attempted to appease both sides. Republican Charles Hall publicly accused Pierce of playing "Dr. Jekyll and Mr. Hyde." Hall expressed disgust at Pierce, whom Hall claimed shamelessly ignored the School Bill before hostile audiences then gushed with enthusiasm for compulsory public education in more favorable venues.[14] Pierce's votes as a state senator in 1905 in favor of legislation authorizing private schools and religious corporations came back to haunt him in the campaign with accusations of hypocrisy and rank opportunism. The *Capital Journal* described the situation: "Walter Pierce heads the yellow ticket, having paid the price. But is he so ashamed of his bargain that he dare not champion the compulsory school bill in his campaign and substitutes instead a tearful plea for reduction of taxation. . . . Walter Pierce is evidently for anything or opposed to anything that will get him a vote."[15]

As election day drew near, Pierce privately predicted that the School Bill would fail, and he moved to distance himself further from it. Pierce's brother, Charles, toured eastern Oregon, quietly informing Protestant clergymen opposed to the initiative that his brother no longer supported the measure. Pendleton judge Stephen Arthur Lowell attacked Pierce's expedience in a public statement, blasting Pierce as a "man whose opinions change with every political exigency."[16] In communities that expected to defeat the School Bill, Pierce let it be known through a variety of spokesmen that he had shifted his position.[17]

Fraudulent ads fomenting anti-Catholicism circulated in the last days of the campaign. Purporting to be from the "Catholic Welfare League," the ads blasted the "unholy heretic" Protestant orders and cautioned Catholics to "Beware" of political tickets circulated as propaganda pieces by these "villainous" groups. Framed by large crosses, the ads exploited distrust of Catholic loyalty by reminding Catholics of their duty: "Nationalities must be subordinated to religion and we must learn that we are Catholics first and citizens next." The ads concluded by urging Catholics to vote "only for Catholics." These propaganda pieces were published as part of larger ads bearing the caption "Good Americans! Attention!" and warning members of the Protestant patriotic societies that Catholics, not Protestants, injected religion into the political campaign. This spate of false advertisements generated counteradvertising identifying the misleading information and thoroughly confusing many voters.[18]

As the campaign drew to a close, the *Portland Telegram* sensed a shift in the public mood on the School Bill. The paper perceived a "significant change in the attitude of a large group of people,"[19] a repositioning of former supporters who had taken a closer look at the measure and concluded that parental choices should be respected. By election eve, most of the newspapers in the state agreed with the *Telegram,* predicting defeat for the measure. A protest song, "School Bills, School Bills," penned to be sung to the tune of "School Days, School Days," captured the disgust with intolerance observed by the papers.

In killing a cat, 'tis a popular way
To coat with sweet sugar the pill,

So the kitty all purring and eager and gay
Will gulp it and get very ill;
In killing a school, it is sometimes the rule
To use not the brutal sand-bag,
But to make exhortation about education
And flap the American Flag. . . .

The camouflage art we learned in the war
Will help in political play,
And a camouflaged bill is a splendid thing for
The stowing of rivals away.
All faiths and all creeds we may tolerate
Without any quibble or fuss—
We may tolerate—but we beg here to state
They must think precisely with us.

CHORUS—

School bills, school bills,
Dear old freak and fool bills.
Bring out the standard they used to raise
Back in the witch-burning bygone days.
"Freedom shall flourish,—but we'll flay
Whoever thinks some other way
Than we, when they vote." (Signed K.K.K.)
Though it may be hard on the kids.[20]

By November 6, the last day of the campaign, most of the papers predicted defeat for both the School Bill and Democrat Walter Pierce. The *Capital Journal*'s election eve editorial attacked the School Bill as a strategy by the Klan to "build a political machine to control the affairs of state, and seize the spoils," and it warned that a Klan victory on election day would shatter the state for years, if not decades.[21] The *Oregonian* dismissed the measure as "on its last legs and likely to be defeated." As for the gubernatorial campaign, the paper pegged it a "horse race," acknowledging that many voters in this overwhelmingly Republican state could bolt party lines because of the School Bill. Nonetheless, the paper also portrayed Pierce as "on downgrade," concluding that he lacked the political strength to spur the wholesale desertions by Republicans necessary for his success.[22]

Pierce had alienated both Democrats and Republicans. In the last week of the campaign, Pierce's principal financial supporter deserted him, publishing large advertisements in newspapers throughout the state exhorting Pierce to oppose the School Bill because it is hostile to "true Americanism."[23] The Democratic Party expected Pierce to lose 30 percent of the Democrats because of the School Bill. The *Oregonian* described the distrust aroused by Pierce: he obtained "support by pledging himself to the school bill, but his failure to stress the measure in his speeches has recently caused his sincerity to be viewed with suspicion." The paper questioned Pierce's credibility, concluding, "The campaign utterances of Pierce have been a series of misstatements and exaggerations and as fast as one of his misstatements has been nailed and exposed he has followed it with another equally without foundation." Anticipating 70 percent voter turnout, the *Oregonian* called the School Bill the "determining factor" in the election, and while it recognized strong support for the measure in rural Oregon, the paper predicted its overwhelming defeat in Portland's populous Multnomah County.[24]

Election day dawned on November 7. The *Oregonian* greeted voters with a headline on IWW unrest: "Another Near Riot at Docks Quelled." The rain forecasted for the morning held off until the polls closed. Sunny skies and unseasonably mild temperatures brought large crowds of voters to the polls. Voting was orderly, despite the bitter campaign and the "deep rooted feeling which prompted an immense army to march to the ballot boxes."[25] At St. Mary's Academy, as at the many private schools throughout the state, the air crackled with apprehension. Nuns maintained a telephone vigil, collecting results as the voting progressed. The votes in favor of the School Bill led throughout the day. Opponents had outspent supporters by four to one, to no avail. By midnight, the outcome was clear. The School Bill passed by a margin of 115,506 to 103,685, garnering 52.7 percent of the vote. Voter turnout for the election was high, with 241,267 of the 333,055 registered voters casting ballots, approximately a 72 percent voter turnout. But of the 241,267 voters who went to the polls, over 22,000 did not cast any vote on the School Bill.[26] Those who abstained from voting on the School Bill amounted to almost double the margin of victory. Dudley Wooten charged that thousands of voters abstained because of confusion about the measure.[27]

The strength of the victory came from the communities in the

Willamette Valley, not from the rural Klan strongholds. In Portland's Mult-nomah County, voter turnout hit 72 percent. The *Oregonian* claimed that Portland "brought out the largest registration in the history of the community." Women, in particular, flocked to the polls, leading the *Oregonian* to comment, "Not since women were given the ballot in Oregon have so many attended the polls in Multnomah County." The School Bill passed by a margin of two to one in Portland, where the vote divided the city as clearly as the Willamette River. Precincts east of the river, working-class and middle-class neighborhoods with strong Klan support, carried the measure by a ratio of four to one. Eight percent of these voters bypassed the gubernatorial race, coming out solely to vote on the School Bill. The more upscale neighborhoods west of the river handily defeated the initiative by a margin of more than two to one, with 75 precincts opposing the measure and just 31 in favor.[28]

Governor Olcott's opposition to the School Bill and the Klan cost him the election. The vote that carried the School Bill also swept Walter Pierce into office by 31,000 votes. Candidates sponsored by Fred Gifford and the Klan fared very well, placing Gifford at the apex of his power as a political boss and setting the stage for a Klan-dominated legislature when it convened in 1923. Multnomah County voters sent a slate of Klan-controlled politicians to represent them in the state legislature. Klan candidates even prevailed on the bench, with Multnomah County retaining all Klan-endorsed circuit judges; only the Catholic incumbent lost his judgeship. One Klan-sponsored Democratic candidate even captured Oregon's third congressional district and headed to Washington.[29]

Oregonians awoke on November 8 to what the *New York Times* called a "Democratic landslide" and found the eyes of the nation focused on their sparsely populated state. The *Times,* which had initially reported, inaccurately, that the School Bill "went down to defeat after a hard fight," rebounded with a major front-page story, titled "What the Klan Did in Oregon Elections," and opined that Oregonians should use the three years until the effective date of the measure to "think it over."[30] Across the country, editorials questioned not only the constitutionality of the law but also its wisdom. They fretted that if not struck down, the law could, as the *Baltimore Sun* argued, "jeopardize the peace of the whole country."[31]

Oregon editors suddenly discovered their voices, assailing the measure as a disgrace to the state. The *Oregonian,* which had predicted defeat of the measure by odds of 10 to 7, blamed its passage on anti-Catholicism and the invisible government created by the Klan. In its postmortem following the election, the paper called the School Bill "the most upsetting factor in the history of Oregon since the agitation over slavery."[32]

Archbishop Christie, who had devoted twenty-three years to establishing Catholic education in Oregon, was not about to let the destruction of private education go unchallenged. Immediately after the election, Christie, declaring that the "battle was not ended," announced his intentions: "Only one course of action remains to be pursued; the bill must be carried to the courts." The archbishop knew that the Klan and the Masons envisioned the Oregon law as the entering wedge in a nationwide campaign. Christie fully appreciated the seriousness of the challenge: "No rest will be taken until the highest court in the land has rendered a decision and for this reason perhaps the passing of the bill is a blessing in disguise. We are now in a position to settle the question of the rights of religious schools once and for all time."[33]

Vote 314 X YES

and Have

Free Public Schools

OPEN to All
GOOD enough for All
ATTENDED by All

All for the Public School and
the Public School for All

One Flag! One School! One Language!

P. S. MALCOLM, 32°,
Inspector-General in Oregon,
Ancient and Accepted Scottish Rite

(Paid Advertisement)

A common and misleading ad on behalf of the School Bill—published in the *Eugene Daily Guard* on November 4, 1922—urges a "yes" vote to protect free public education. (Courtesy Oregon Historical Society, #004197.)

Three Souls With the Same Thought

STATE MONOPOLY OF SCHOOLS IS AN ABSOLUTE SUCCESS IN RUSSIA

N. LENINE—HEAD BOLSHEVIK GOVERNMENT RUSSIA—

An editorial cartoon published in the *Portland Telegram* on October 26, 1922, attacks the School Bill as a Bolshevik-inspired proposal and links supporters, including the Klan and Klan-backed gubernatorial candidate Walter Pierce, to Leninist policies. (Courtesy Oregon Historical Society, #004198.)

An illustration from *The Old Cedar School,* the Oregon Klan's pamphlet on the School Bill, depicts the private school threat to public schools. An Episcopalian bishop, a Seventh-Day Adventist minister, and a Methodist superintendent hack at the foundation of the public school while mothers from the same faiths block their children from attending. A Catholic priest approaches with a burning torch. (Courtesy Oregon Historical Society, #004199.)

The final illustration from *The Old Cedar School* shows the public school in flames, its teacher dead in the doorway, and the American flag toppling, while the Catholic priest walks away with a smile on his face. (Courtesy Oregon Historical Society, #004194.)

Alexander Christie, archbishop of Oregon City, 1924. Christie devoted his life to Catholic education, and led the Catholic campaign against the School Bill. (Photograph by Steffens-Colmer, courtesy Holy Names Heritage Center.)

A panel of three federal judges, Ninth Circuit judge William B. Gilbert and district judges Charles E. Wolverton and Robert S. Bean, found the School Bill unconstitutional. (Courtesy Oregon Historical Society, #08840.)

John P. Kavanaugh, a former county judge and Portland city attorney, argued on behalf of the Society of the Sisters of the Holy Names of Jesus and Mary in the federal district court case challenging the School Bill. (Courtesy Oregon Historical Society, #011692.)

William D. Guthrie, a prominent New York attorney, served as lead counsel for the Society of the Sisters of the Holy Names of Jesus and Mary. Guthrie directed the Oregon litigation and argued the case before the U.S. Supreme Court. (Photograph reproduced with permission of the University Archives, Columbia University in the City of New York.)

St. Mary's Academy, Portland, ca. 1925. One of the largest schools owned by the Society of the Sisters of the Holy Names of Jesus and Mary, it is the oldest Catholic high school in Oregon. It opened its doors in 1859, the same year Oregon became a state. (Photograph by A. L. Ransford, courtesy Holy Names Heritage Center.)

PART II   Judgment

CHAPTER 9   A Great Cross

Within two days of the election, School Bill opponents announced plans to challenge the measure. They knew the Klan-controlled legislature was unlikely to repeal the law. The measure would not go into effect until September 1926, but the repercussions were likely to begin almost immediately. Among those who stood to lose their positions were the staffs of 39 private schools throughout the state, including 440 Catholic teachers in elementary education. These educators bore responsibility for over 9,000 students, with over 6,000 children in Portland. Joseph A. Hill, principal of Hill Military Academy and executive secretary of the Non-Sectarian and Protestant Schools Committee, told the *Oregonian* that a lawsuit would be filed as soon as the interested parties resolved numerous strategic decisions.[1] The Lutheran Schools Committee advised the national Missouri Synod's secretary of schools of the formation of a multidenominational committee to decide the most expedient course for bringing a case to the courts.[2]

Archbishop Christie, despite poor health, moved quickly to mount a multifaceted assault on the School Bill. Christie requested that the Knights of Columbus appoint a committee to monitor the activities of the new Klan-dominated legislature, set to convene in January 1923. Immediately after the election, Christie and a number of local priests formed the Catholic Truth Society, headquartered in downtown Portland and under the direction of Father Charles M. Smith. By November 30, the group had convinced the *Oregonian* to publish a weekly "Catholic Question Box" to inform Protestant Oregon about Catholic education and doctrine. Speakers hired by the Truth Society traversed the state, playing to capacity crowds and garnering the wrath of the Klan. While the Truth Society could help shift public opinion more favorably toward Catholics, Christie knew that the courts presented the best opportunity for ridding Oregon of the School Bill.

The Catholic Leadership Responds

On November 22, Christie and the bishops of the local ecclesiastical province met in Seattle and unanimously approved a three-part resolution to pursue legal action against the School Bill. The group agreed that the constitutionality of the measure should be challenged as soon as possible and pursued to the Supreme Court of the United States. Their second and third resolutions requested that the National Catholic Welfare Council, which had just been renamed the National Catholic Welfare Conference, assume the responsibility of bringing the case to the Supreme Court and fund the litigation. Christie, who had unsuccessfully sought the assistance of the NCWC during the campaign, hoped the conference would be deeply concerned now that the School Bill had become law. Catholic leaders from around the country, such as Archbishop Michael J. Curley of Baltimore, expressed alarm at the results of the Oregon election. Curley warned that the victors in Oregon "planned to carry the work to other parts of the Union with the object of creating such an atmosphere as made the prohibition amendment possible," and he denounced the legislation as "state socialism, setting up an omnipotent state that will claim ownership of individuals, body and soul."[3] Christie, in a letter to Father Edward J. Hanna, chairman of the administrative committee of the NCWC, thus asked once again for the assistance of the NCWC, because "this matter concerns the entire body of Catholics" and because the campaign had exhausted his resources. In his brief letter, he expressed confidence that "surely the Bishops of this country will not stand by inactive while the faith is being strangled in our innocent children," adding, "Our case to-day will be theirs to-morrow."[4]

January brought torrential rains and extensive flooding to Oregon. At St. Mary's Academy, the nuns kept up morale for the sake of their students while privately wondering whether the future would bring them any students to teach. Mother Mary Flavia, superior of St. Mary's Academy, advised the nuns and staff of her school, "Be prudent and hopeful in your words to the girls . . . and to everyone. This law is a great cross. But, and I have this on judicious advice, the bill will probably be declared unconstitutional. Let us trust in Almighty God. Let us trust in our constitution."[5] Meanwhile, the Klan-permeated legislature moved quickly to pass a statute preventing public school teachers from wearing religious garb in the classroom, a predictable outcome given the furor generated during the campaign over pictures of nuns in full habit teaching in public schools. Klan Kleagle Luther I. Powell moved north out of Oregon and began organizing a campaign in Washington State to place an initiative for compulsory public education on the Washington ballot.

On January 11, the administrative committee of the NCWC convened a special meeting at Loyola University, Chicago, to consider Christie's request. While Christie's petition brought the committee together, the NCWC had been following the situation in Oregon closely. Father Burke, general secretary of the NCWC, had been quietly collecting information and opinions since the election. Just two days after the election, Dr. Michael Slattery, executive director of the National Council of Catholic Men, a lay department of the NCWC, wrote Burke that after "very thoughtful consideration," he was "convinced that the successful carrying of the amendment in Oregon will open up the same question in many other states." Slattery advised Burke that litigation was the only way to resolve the matter and insisted that the case was far too important to be left in the hands of the Oregon Catholics. To Slattery, the School Bill case offered the NCWC a great opportunity to demonstrate to the nation that the Catholics would not stand for any infringement of their rights. Hinting at disgruntlement among the Oregon Catholic hierarchy, Slattery disclosed he had "evidence" that School Bill campaign chief Dudley G. Wooten lacked the competence and influence to inspire confidence in those who worked with him. While Slattery conceded it might be too much to say that the campaign was lost because of poor leadership, the Oregon experience convinced him that the NCWC should take charge of the litigation and retain the best constitutional attorneys in the country. Slattery closed his memo with a plea to bring the matter before the administrative committee with all due haste.[6]

Father Burke had also received an analysis of the election from the director of the NCWC, Justin McGrath, who, like Slattery, blamed the Oregon outcome, in part, on local Catholic errors, but errors of a very different type. McGrath did not see the Oregon election as evidence of a nationwide rise in anti-Catholic sentiment. Discussing elections in New York, Missouri, and California, where Catholic candidates prevailed in the face of vicious anti-Catholic campaigning by their opponents and the Klan, McGrath concluded that the Oregon vote could not be explained as part of a national surge in the power of the Klan. Instead, he perceived Oregon as somewhat of an anomaly, the one state in which a "platform of intolerance appears to have been wholly successful" and the only state in which the "bigots appear to have been the decisive factor."[7] McGrath found the largely native population of Oregon to be similar to that of numerous other states, particularly California, where Klan efforts failed despite a strong nativist political climate. McGrath looked for something other than Klan-provoked bigotry to explain the results in Oregon.

He found it in an innocuous postelection dispatch from John O'Hara, editor of the *Catholic Sentinel* in Portland, who opined that the widely circulated pictures of nuns wearing religious garb while teaching in public schools made effective propaganda for School Bill proponents. McGrath hypothesized that these pictures caused non-Catholics to fear a Catholic conspiracy to control public education and that they voted accordingly. While he admitted that he was not fully informed on the reasons the Oregon Catholic leaders authorized nuns to teach in public schools, McGrath plainly viewed the choice as a major mistake, one certain to create apprehension in non-Catholics. He criticized the poor political judgment of the Oregon hierarchy, which had failed to see the potential backlash because it was so pleased to get nuns into public schools. McGrath blamed the Oregon Catholics in part for the disaster and concluded that "it is not the part of wisdom to do everything that we are invited to do." McGrath assumed that the nuns had been invited to teach in public schools where rural communities had difficulties finding teachers. But in an addendum to his original memo, McGrath expressed his outrage on learning from the *Christian Science Monitor* that in some school districts, Catholic majorities on the school boards had hired the nuns, despite protests by the Protestant minorities: "If this statement represents the truth . . . the result in Oregon is not surprising." To McGrath, the Catholics in Oregon "sowed the wind, and reaped the whirlwind."[8]

Father Burke had these opinions in mind when the administrative committee met on January 11. Archbishop Christie attended the Chicago meeting at the request of the committee and brought along the Portland archdiocese's attorney, Judge John P. Kavanaugh. Christie and Kavanaugh had been busy in Chicago, and they arrived at the meeting with a commitment by the national Knights of Columbus to donate $10,000 toward litigation challenging the School Bill. The archbishop and his attorney, along with Oregon Knights of Columbus state deputy P. J. Hanley and Portland Knight and attorney Frank Lonergan, had presented their appeal to the Knights' Supreme Board of Directors on January 6 and obtained the financial backing to pursue a "test fight" to protect parochial education.[9] At the NCWC meeting on January 11, Kavanaugh, speaking at Christie's behest, explained that even though the School Bill would not go into effect until September 1, 1926, Oregon Catholic schools had already suffered loss of morale and 50 percent devaluation of their properties. He argued this adverse impact on the schools' economic interests provided grounds for challenging the law before it went into effect. Kavanaugh expressed confidence that the Supreme Court would find the law unconstitutional.

Archbishop Hanna brought before the committee other attorneys to assess the merits of a court challenge to the law. Patrick J. M. Hally, a former Michigan circuit judge and veteran of the Michigan battle over compulsory public schooling, advised the committee that the Supreme Court could be expected to respond favorably to claims of family and parental rights. Judge Thomas D. O'Brien, former Minnesota Supreme Court justice, agreed and argued that a legal challenge should focus on religious liberty and fundamental rights of parents, not property rights. Judge Kavanaugh anticipated that several suits would be filed, testing both personal and property rights. Judge O'Brien expressed some concern that the Court would be unwilling to hear the case because the law had not yet gone into effect.

Father Burke had been collecting his own legal opinions. In December, Bishop Carroll, a member of the administrative committee, forwarded to Father Burke a legal opinion he received from attorney J. A. Walsh, replete with vague assertions of constitutional violations, and requested Burke to obtain opinions from respected attorneys prior to the Chicago meeting.[10] Burke sought out William D. Guthrie, prominent Catholic attorney, Columbia University law professor, and frequent advocate before the Supreme Court. Guthrie responded on December 20. Claiming ill health, Guthrie replied that he was unable to undertake a thorough study of the matter, but he agreed to provide a general opinion in time for the January 11 meeting. Guthrie described the case as "an extremely delicate and difficult one" that required the "most competent" and, as Guthrie penned in by hand, the most "experienced" professional direction. He concluded by dismissing Walsh's legal analysis as one that did not directly address the real issues.[11]

Despite his illness, Guthrie responded to Father Burke well in advance of the January 11 meeting. Recuperating in Atlantic City and unable to re-search fully the law, Guthrie nonetheless outlined for Father Burke his first assessment of the case and the appropriate litigation strategy. While Guthrie believed the Oregon law violated personal liberty guaranteed by the Fourteenth Amendment, he stressed to Burke that the courts had not yet considered the validity of compulsory public education. Guthrie thought the issue a "close" and "very delicate" question of constitutional law, but one worth a careful investigation.[12]

Guthrie's conclusion accurately assessed the legal challenges confronting the plaintiffs. Given that the courts had upheld the broad authority of the state to compel school attendance and to set curriculum, it was not clear whether the Supreme Court would find the state lacked the power to com-pel public school attendance.

Common Schools and Mandatory Attendance Laws

The philosophical justification for mandatory school attendance in America rested directly on the connection between education and successful gover-nance. The founding fathers recognized the need for an educated citizenry in a representative democracy. Thomas Jefferson wrote, "Preach, my dear Sir, a crusade against ignorance; establish and improve the laws for educating the common people." Washington, in his farewell address as president, ad-vised, "In proportion as the structure of government gives force to public opinion, it is essential that public opinion should be enlightened." John Adams wrote passionately about the importance of education to democracy, describing it as "indispensable" to free government. Similar sentiments found their way into several state constitutions and the Northwest Ordi-nance of 1787, which provides, "Religion, morality and knowledge being nec-essary to good government . . . schools and the means of education shall for-ever be encouraged."[13] In 1789, Massachusetts enacted the first statewide school law, requiring larger communities to provide schooling.

Federal policy during the nineteenth century recognized the importance of education to governance and pushed for establishment of public schools. A House committee report on education land policy published in 1826 con-cluded, "The foundation of our political institutions . . . rests in the will of the People. . . . How then is this will to be corrected, chastened, subdued? By education—that education, the first rudiments which can be acquired only in common schools."[14] Federal land grants provided new states property for the establishment of public schools.

After the Civil War, as a condition for admission to the Union, Congress required new states to establish nonsectarian public schools open to all. Reconstruction spurred the movement for common schools in the South. By 1889, almost half of the states contained preambles in their constitutions extolling the importance of education and the duty of the state to provide public schools.

By the late nineteenth century, the influx of immigrants into America presented new issues for the fledgling system of common schools. Between 1870 and 1920, the population of the United States rose nearly 60 percent, from 63 million to over 100 million. Most of the population increase resulted from immigration, with over 28 million immigrants arriving during this period. As the country became more heterogeneous, fears surfaced, among many in power, that the new residents did not understand or appreciate American values. One educator of the times reflected a common sentiment that "people have come here who are not entitled to freedom in the same sense as those who established this government."[15] Public schools provided a vehicle for assimilating new immigrants. By 1900, more than 30 states and the District of Columbia mandated school attendance.

The proponents of compulsory public education envisioned the Oregon School Bill as the next step in a nationwide transformation of education, because they believed that the hard issues concerning state authority over education had already been resolved. The enactment of mandatory attendance laws had generated bitter controversy in many states. Parents fought the laws, arguing that mandatory school attendance deprived them of their inalienable rights to raise their children without interference from the state. Opponents charged that universal, compulsory schooling was "monarchical" and "antidemocratic." But the progressives who led the movement for common schools had convinced the politicians and the courts that all children should attend school.

Cases challenging mandatory attendance laws failed. The courts typically recognized common-law parental rights of care and control over their children but inevitably concluded that the state's educational interests prevailed. In numerous decisions, the courts even went so far as to hold that the common-law duty of parents to educate their children extended both to the children and to the state. In a 1901 Indiana case, the Indiana Supreme Court described the parental obligation in unequivocal terms: "One of the most important natural duties of the parent is his obligation to educate his child, and this duty he owes not to the child only, but to the commonwealth."[16] Most of the courts took mandatory education very seriously, rejecting efforts by parents to avoid attendance laws by refusing to vaccinate their children or by deciding to homeschool their children without state approval.[17]

Education and the Progressive Era

During the first two decades of the twentieth century, laws for mandatory school attendance had been the central, but not the only, item on the progressive agenda for educational reform. Mandatory attendance also enhanced the enforcement and effectiveness of hard-won child labor laws.[18] The progressives' vision of a comprehensive public education system included both extensive state regulation and a greater role for the federal government in educational policy. States would maintain the primary authority to regulate education, but as the federal courts increasingly upheld the exercise of federal legislative power over traditional state concerns, progressives remained optimistic that a national education program could be justified. The Morrill Acts of 1862 and 1890, providing federal land grants to establish state universities, evidenced a willingness by Congress to exercise some involvement in educational policy. In 1914, Congress enacted the Smith-Lever Act, which provided federal land grants and financial assistance to agriculture, home economics, and mechanic arts in land-grant schools. The Smith-Hughes Act of 1917 took federal involvement one step further, with Congress offering the states funding for programs in vocational education. Some progressives viewed these congressional overtures as the first steps in establishing minimum national requirements for education.[19]

In education, as in other social and economic reforms, the progressives proposed a fundamentally different relationship between the individual and the state. The progressive view of expanding state regulation over education created a tension between state authority over the child and parental control. Many educational reformers welcomed this tension, with one prominent progressive, Stanford professor Ellwood Cubberly, exulting that "each year the child is coming to belong more to the state and less to the parent."[20]

The intense nationalism of the postwar years intensified the interest in regulating education. Some reformers doubted whether local control over education could ever again be adequate to serve the needs of a rapidly transforming country that stood poised to emerge as a world power. They argued that the United States could establish a world-class education system only if the federal government enacted a national education policy. Many described American education as "ill." One reformist colorfully wrote, "It is not merely indisposed, it is sick. It has measles, whooping cough, diphtheria, scarlet fever, small-pox, scrofula, erysipelas . . ."[21] The Towner-Sterling Bill and similar federal bills introduced after the war proposed a cabinet-level federal department of education to oversee education policy and offer grants to the states to help eliminate illiteracy and "Americanize" the foreign-born. The federal financial incentives provided to the states in these bills opened the door to the possibility of federal control of educational content, at least to the extent necessary to inculcate good citizenship.

The progressives' push to federalize education met with resistance from prominent private educators who viewed the proposals with alarm. They argued that Congress lacked the constitutional authority to regulate education, a power reserved to the states under the Tenth Amendment. While these educators claimed that any extensive regulation of education jeopardized academic freedom, they found the prospect of a federalized educational policy particularly threatening. Columbia University president Nicholas Murray Butler spoke for many private educators when he criticized the bills to create a federal department of education as an exercise in "doing ill that which should not be done at all."[22] Challenging the federal government to keep its "hand off the schools," Butler dismissed the progressives' "illusion" of a federalized system, insisting that "standardization, Government-made uniformity, and bureaucratic regulation are not the allies of education but its mortal enemies."[23]

Religious schools joined in the opposition to federalized education, fearing government interference with their curriculum. The NCWC made opposition to the federal proposals one of its top priorities. Father James H. Ryan, director of education for the NCWC, depicted the federal bills as "dangerous, vicious and a wolf in sheep's clothing." Sounding a theme common to the opponents of education regulation, Ryan bluntly rejected the progressive ideal of a benevolent state, describing as "utter bunk" the philosophy that the "child does not belong to the parents, but to the state."[24]

While the country debated the appropriate role for the federal government in education, greater consensus existed on the need to improve education at the local level. Most educators supported state regulation of education to improve quality and achieve consistency. Many also agreed that states should be regulating education more aggressively to promote assimilation. For some advocates of assimilation, compulsory public education represented a reasonable step forward from mandatory attendance laws, a step that would advance important national priorities. It was precisely this argument of incrementalism that worried Guthrie and the NCWC. Guthrie advised Burke to consider a court challenge with caution; a decision by the Court upholding compelled public education as a reasonable extension of state authority would be the death knell of Catholic education.

Father Burke read Guthrie's letter to the assembled administrative committee of the NCWC on January 11. Despite a Supreme Court that generally was very receptive to economic liberty claims, Guthrie recommended that the constitutional challenge to the School Bill rest primarily on parental and religious liberties, not economic rights. Guthrie wrote that an attack on the law alleging only interference with property interests might not adequately protect the Roman Catholic Church in the future. Guthrie also expressed concern over the very practical difficulty of filing suit when the law was not due to go into effect until 1926. Admittedly, Guthrie had not thoroughly researched the question, but he advised Father Burke that it could be difficult to convince the courts that the matter was ripe for litigation prior to the effective date of the measure. The courts could conclude the suit was premature because there would be no justiciable grievance until the law went into effect.[25]

To the Catholic leadership, the School Bill case presented the most dramatic, but by no means the only, threat to Catholic education. The NCWC faced challenges to private religious schooling at both the state and national levels. The agenda for that day included review and approval of numerous pamphlets prepared by the Education Department of the NCWC to combat national campaigns by the Scottish Rite Masons and National Education Association, advocating strict regulation of private schools. The NCWC also actively opposed the creation of a federal department of education, which it believed would "mean the creation of a super-State, an autocracy to the nth degree," and an education model that would lead to "nationalized children."[26] The gathered committee members recognized that the fate of the School Bill was likely to drive the future of American education. After excusing the visiting attorneys, the committee voted unanimously to grant Archbishop Christie's request for assistance and assume responsibility for litigation challenging the School Bill.

CHAPTER 10 Turf

With NCWC approval granted, Bishop Muldoon of the NCWC's administrative committee cautioned about the potential for a turf battle between local and national leadership. The $10,000 gift from the Knights of Columbus resulted from the personal appeals of Archbishop Christie and Judge Kavanaugh, and Kavanaugh expected to continue working on the case. Bishop Muldoon urged the committee to reach a clear understanding with Archbishop Christie that the NCWC, while committed to consultation with Christie, retained the "deciding voice" in selecting the attorneys and directing the litigation.[1] Father Hanna appointed Bishop Edmund F. Gibbons, chairman of the NCWC Legislative Department, and Archbishop Dowling, chairman of the Education Department, as a subcommittee to meet with Father Burke, prepare a formal agreement between the NCWC and Archbishop Christie, and draft a letter to be sent to the Catholic hierarchy throughout the country requesting financial support for the litigation.

The subcommittee returned to the meeting that same afternoon, drafts in hand, and by the end of the day, the administrative committee approved both the terms of the agreement with Archbishop Christie and the form of the letter to be sent to the dioceses. The proposal to Christie offered $100,000 for litigation of the case, with $40,000 to cover debts already incurred, on the understanding that "there be full co-operation and agreement in regard to the choice and employment of counsel, the general account of the case, and the expenditure of funds."[2]

Most important, the agreement put the case under the direct control of the NCWC, requiring that "before any important step be taken by the Archbishop of Oregon, in the conduct of the case, or by the lawyers engaged, previous consultation and agreement must first be had with the Administrative Committee of the NCWC."[3] Archbishop Christie quickly agreed to these terms. Father Hanna requested that Archbishop Dowling and Bishop Gibbons continue as a subcommittee to oversee the litigation and assigned Dowling the task of notifying Kavanaugh that the NCWC would be taking charge of the case. The NCWC's acceptance of the case put Kavanaugh's status in question and also created tensions with the Knights of Columbus, who had just donated $10,000 to challenge the School Bill. The NCWC did not want the Knights involved and expected Christie to return the funds. Hanna drafted a letter to the Knights for Archbishop Christie's signature, thanking them for their generosity but refusing their assistance.

The administrative committee expected the bishops around the country to raise the $100,000. The letter sent to the dioceses, written by Father John B. Fenlon, explained that "the movement to imitate the Oregon school law has already spread to several other states, and threatens to spread still further," making it "necessary to act quickly and to endeavor to prevent great damage to our schools." Describing how Archbishop Christie "begged" for assistance, the letter concluded that "the Oregon need is immediate and urgent," and it requested the bishops to send aid without delay. The committee left the manner of fund-raising to the judgment of each diocese, but Archbishop Dowling, as treasurer of the NCWC, bore responsibility for collecting the funds.[4] The letter suggested the litigation strategy already proposed by Guthrie, advising the bishops that a Supreme Court decision affirming the parental right of education would protect Catholic schools nationwide. Bishops around the country responded promptly to the NCWC request, and by April 7, the litigation fund contained nearly $52,000.

The NCWC advanced its litigation strategy with an aggressive public relations campaign intended to inform the public about religious education and the dangers of compelled public schooling. It churned out press releases of speeches given across the country by educators, politicians, and civic leaders condemning compulsory public education. It distributed over 35,000 pamphlets prepared by the Education Department of the NCWC to public officials, clergy, legislators, and teachers. In March, the NCWC formed the Catholic School Defense League and launched a national recruitment effort at five dollars per membership. The publicity program constituted the most ambitious and comprehensive public relations undertaking by the Roman Catholic Church in the United States and became a model for future litigation on behalf of interest groups.[5]

The Catholic hierarchy well understood the threat to religious education presented by the School Bill. The movement for compelled public schooling was hardly the first effort to destroy Catholic education. The NCWC recognized that the fight for compulsory public education represented, in part, the latest round in a pitched battle by Protestant groups to subject all schoolchildren to Protestant based moral and religious training in the public schools.

The marked rise of Protestant fundamentalism during and immediately following World War I generated strong support for compulsory public schooling. The term *fundamentalist* originated during this period, when, in 1920, conservative Baptist leader Curtis Lee Law used the term to describe those Christians ready "to do battle royal for the Fundamentals."[6] Fundamentalists rejected the "modernism" movement in Protestant theology because it attributed scripture to human, rather than divine, origin and drew from social science and scientific methods of analysis to interpret scripture. Anti-Catholicism ran high among fundamentalists, who accepted only "original," pre-Roman Christianity.

Fundamentalists perceived the social and political upheavals in the country as a threat to conservative values. Conservative Christians saw public education as symbolic of the conflict between fundamentalism and modernism and sought to influence school curricula in Bible reading and the sciences. The teaching of evolution in public schools galvanized fundamentalists into a nationwide antievolution campaign that would culminate in the Scopes "Monkey Trial" in 1925. Fundamentalists demanded a public education system responsive to majoritarian values. They found compulsory public education attractive because it eliminated private schools that might teach modernism. William Jennings Bryan, antievolution crusader and defender of the antievolution law in the Scopes trial, explained the fundamentalist perspective: "If it is contended that an instructor has a right to teach anything he likes, I reply that the parents who pay the salary have a right to decide what shall be taught."[7] Bryan's assessment reflected the attitude of Protestant prerogative that defined public education from its earliest days.

Religion and the Molding of American Education

The initial movement for common schools included many Protestant ministers and clergy who assumed that public schools and churches served the same moral educational purposes. The curriculum in early common schools included Bible reading, prayers, and hymns, all taught from Protestant texts.

Horace Mann, a Massachusetts Unitarian and recognized leader of the movement for common schools, touted the ideal of free, universal, and secular education. The reality of the common school was anything but secular. Mann, the Massachusetts secretary of education, argued in 1837, in the first annual report of the Massachusetts Board of Education, for the "entire exclusion of religious teaching" from public schools. What Mann really meant was the exclusion of any one particular Protestant dogma. While Mann prohibited religious teachings "peculiar to specific denominations but not common to all," he also championed moral education based on Protestant religious texts. Under Mann's vision, Protestant Bible reading became the cornerstone of moral education: "our system earnestly inculcates all Christian morals; it founds its morals on the basis of religion; it welcomes the religion of the Bible; and in receiving the Bible, it allows it to do what it is allowed to do in no other system—to speak for itself." Mann's state curriculum required daily reading from the King James Version of the Bible.[8]

Early tensions existed between different Protestant sects—particularly between liberal Protestants, such as Unitarians, and evangelical Protestants—as to what form of Protestantism should be taught in the public schools. Mann's strategy, which found support as the common schools spread throughout the states, offered a generic Protestantism, grounded in Protestant Bible reading without specific doctrinal instruction or interpretation. The active assistance of Protestant clergy and civic leaders to the growth of common schools depended on this compromise, which assured religion, but not sectarianism, a place in public education. By the early 1900s, approximately three-fourths of the common schools in the country required Bible reading, by either legal or curricular mandate.

The push to increase Protestant influence in the public schools coincided with the nativist movement of the mid-nineteenth century, led by the American Know-Nothing Party. The Know-Nothings' political platform favored curbs on immigration (particularly from Catholic countries) and strongly Protestant public schools. In the 1850s, the Know-Nothings successfully captured both public attention and political office. The nation's first mandatory attendance law, passed by the Massachusetts legislature in 1852, originated with the Know-Nothings, in part, as a way to force Catholic children into common schools. An editorial published in the *Common School Journal* after the law's passage reflected the prevailing sentiment.

> The English Bible, in some way or other, has, ever since the settlement of Cambridge, been read in its public schools, by children of every denomination; but in the year 1851, the ignorant immigrants, who have found food and shelter in this land of freedom and plenty, made free and plentiful through the influence of these very Scriptures, presume to dictate to us, and refuse to let their children read as ours do, and always have done, the Word of Life. The arrogance, not to say impudence, of this conduct, must startle every native citizen, and we can not but hope that they will immediately take measures to teach these deluded aliens, that their poverty and ignorance in their own country arose mainly from their ignorance of the Bible.[9]

Catholic immigration during the nineteenth century helped solidify the Protestant compromise. By 1900, there were 12 million Catholics in America, many of them immigrants. Most were poor; with the exception of the Irish, many were from southern and eastern Europe and did not speak English. When their children entered the public schools, they encountered both cultural and religious hostility. Textbooks often contained blatantly anti-Catholic references, denigrating both Catholic religion and loyalty. Compulsory reading of the King James Bible outraged Catholic parents, because the Roman Catholic Church considered it a sin to read this text. Catholics read from the Douay Bible, which the church authorized as the approved English translation and annotation of the scriptures. The Protestant compromise of Bible reading without commentary also alienated Catholics. Catholics rejected Bible reading without comment, or "private interpretation," because it denied the authority Christ gave the church for teaching and interpreting.

Catholic resistance to the reading of the King James Bible sparked retribution and violence. In Boston in 1834, the anti-Catholic diatribes of Rev. Lyman Beecher spurred a frenzied mob to burn down the Ursuline Convent in retaliation for Catholic criticism of Bible reading in public schools. In Philadelphia, between 10 and 20 people died in the Bible Riots of 1844. Catholic children suffered violence for their resistance, preyed on by other children and even school administrators. In 1859, a Massachusetts court held that a school acted within its authority when it beat a Catholic student who refused to read the Protestant version of the Ten Commandments.[10] Leaders in the Roman Catholic Church were accused of conspiring to destroy public education when they called for a compromise on Bible reading, either by excusing Catholic children from Bible reading or by allowing them to read the Douay Version.

Early legal challenges to mandatory Protestant Bible reading failed. Between 1854 and 1924, in 25 cases throughout 19 states challenging Bible reading, the courts upheld the right of schools over student protests by a ratio of 5 to 1. Three-fifths of the complaints involved Catholics. The cases concerned a variety of issues, from use of the Bible for instruction to daily religious exercises and prayers from the Bible. Courts typically agreed with the schools that Bible offerings functioned as nonsectarian lessons in personal and civic virtue, rejecting constitutional arguments that protected minority religions from majoritarian will.[11]

In a significiant case, *Donahoe v. Richards,* Bridget Donahoe, a fifteen-year-old Catholic girl in Maine, suffered expulsion in 1854 for refusing to read the King James Bible. Her priest told her it was a sin to use the Protestant Bible. The court upheld the expulsion, rejecting the argument that the reading of the Protestant Bible constituted religious education. While recognizing that the public schools should not engage in religious instruction, the court found,

> But the instruction here given is not in fact, and is not alleged to have been, in articles of faith. No theological doctrines were taught. The creed of no sect was affirmed or denied. . . . The Bible was used merely as a book in which instruction in reading was given. But reading the Bible is no more an interference with religious belief, than would reading the mythology of Greece or Rome be regarded as an interfering with religious belief or an affirmance of the pagan creeds.[12]

The court's conclusion that compelling a child to read the King James Bible is not an infringement of religious liberty contained a powerful message affirming majority control. The court declined to find interference with a religious right of conscience, because "the right as claimed, undermines the power of the State," and "then power ceases to reside in majorities, and is transferred to minorities." The deference to majority will barely concealed the moral judgment of the court, which surfaced at the end of the opinion. Shifting the issue from one of religious liberty to the importance of assimilation, the court implicitly accepted the argument that Protestantism served the goal of acculturation.

> Large masses of foreign population are among us, weak in the midst of our strength. Mere citizenship is of no avail, unless they imbibe the liberal spirit of our laws and institutions, unless they become citizens in fact as well as in name. In no other way can the process of assimilation be so readily and thoroughly accomplished as through the medium of the public schools, which are alike open to the children of the rich and the poor, of the stranger and the citizen. It is the duty of those to whom this sacred trust is confided, to discharge it with magnanimous liberality and Christian kindness.[13]

Whether in the streets, at the legislatures, or in the courts, the message to Catholics could not have been clearer. Jews and other minority religions received the same message. Protestantism dominated public school instruction.

Many Catholics abandoned the public system for the more compatible environment of Catholic education. Although Catholic schools existed even prior to American independence, the overt Protestantism of the common schools sparked the national expansion of Catholic schools. To aid that expansion, Catholics sought state funding for an alternative system, arguing that the state should support Catholic education if it was willing to support Protestant education in the public schools. New York, for example, adopted a law in the late 1830s authorizing state funds for "nonsectarian" schools, understood by everyone to include the generic Protestantism of the public schools. When Bishop John Hughes campaigned for public support for Catholic schools in 1842, a Protestant mob attacked his residence, smashing doors and windows and destroying furniture. The state called out the militia to protect the original St. Patrick's Cathedral on Mulberry Street in New York City. The New York legislature reacted swiftly, passing a no-aid law, prohibiting public funding of any school where "religious sectarian doctrine or tenet shall be taught, inculcated, or practiced." Since the courts had, overwhelmingly, already supported state claims that Protestant Bible reading constituted moral, not religious, education, public school funding remained unaffected. The no-aid legislative movement spread quickly to other states.

Catholics arguing for state funding of their schools met hostile audiences who charged the Roman Catholic Church with a conspiracy to destroy public education.[14]

Catholics won some battles, but in doing so, they lost the war. In 1872, local school boards in such religiously diverse communities as New York, Chicago, Buffalo, and Cincinnati, sympathetic to Catholic resistance to Protestant Bible reading in public schools, voted to ban Bible reading and religious exercises in public classrooms. In 1875, the public perception of growing Catholic influence spurred President Ulysses S. Grant to propose a constitutional amendment that would require the states both to provide public schools and to prohibit aid to sectarian schools. Only a week later, Congressman James G. Blaine of Maine, a Republican with presidential ambitions, sponsored the Blaine Amendment, which prohibited public funding of schools "under the control of any religious sect." Blaine failed in his bid to become the Republican nominee, losing out to Rutherford B. Hayes, but the Republicans did support Blaine's proposal as part of the party platform. When Congress voted on the Blaine Amendment before the election of 1876, the proposal passed the House, but in the Senate, it fell two votes short of the two-thirds supermajority required to pass a constitutional amendment.[15]

The strong support for the Blaine Amendment spawned a variety of no-aid legislation at the federal and state level during the late nineteenth century. Congress required new territories seeking statehood to include no-aid provisions in their state constitutions. Existing states rushed to amend their constitutions to add no-aid clauses, or "Baby Blaines." By 1890, 29 of the 45 states contained Blaine-type amendments in their constitutions. Catholics had lost their bid for parity in public education. Thwarted by public policy and the courts in their challenges to Protestant Bible reading and driven from the public trough, Catholics were left to construct and fund a Catholic education system.

The success of the no-aid campaign was owed in large part to Protestant fears of Catholic political ascendance. The hierarchical structure of the Roman Catholic Church appalled many Protestants, who were accustomed to a more egalitarian sectarian order and questioned Catholic political independence from the pope. Their concerns traced, in part, from the 1832 encyclical *Mirari Vos,* issued by Pope Gregory XVI, which rejected the separation of church and state. Many Protestant Americans viewed the Catholic perspective as profoundly un-American. They worried that Catholics would form a political faction to further the union of church and state. The visibility of Catholic leaders lobbying for parity in educational funding fueled Protestant apprehensions.[16]

Proponents of no-aid legislation revealed their hypocrisy by championing Protestant public education as nonsectarian, moral teaching. The Senate version of the Blaine Amendment, after an exhaustive list of prohibitions against aid, concludes, "This article shall not be construed to prohibit the reading of the Bible in any school or institution." The National Teachers Association resolved in 1869 both that "the appropriation of public funds for the support of sectarian schools is a violation of the fundamental principles of our American system of education" and that "the Bible should not only be studied, venerated and honored . . . but devotionally read, and its precepts inculcated in all the common schools of the land." The Know-Nothing Party argued in their 1856 political platform for a public school system unsullied by sectarian influence, where the Bible is recognized as "the depository and fountain of all civil and religious freedom."[17]

The triumph of Protestant "nonsectarian" public education backfired for advocates of Protestant assimilation. Catholic schools flourished despite the lack of public funding. By the mid-nineteenth century, Catholic education spread throughout many states. In response, patriotic societies, such as the anti-Catholic American Protective Association, founded in 1887 by Mason Henry F. Bowers, provoked fears of Catholic political conspiracies nurtured in parochial schools. In the 1890s, Illinois and Wisconsin passed controversial laws mandating instruction in English in all schools, as a way to accelerate assimilation in Catholic and Lutheran schools. The Bennett Law in Wisconsin allowed children to attend parochial schools only in their school district. In the rural, sparsely populated communities throughout Wisconsin, the Bennett Law effectively precluded children from access to religious schools. Although both states quickly repealed the English-only laws, the controversy profoundly impacted immigrant families and convinced the parochial schools that they should voluntarily move to English-language instruction.

Educational progressives also viewed the growth of Catholic schools with alarm. Educators like Horace Mann envisioned the public schools as the great social equalizer and guardian of democracy, stabilizing the country from "extremes of overgrown wealth and desperate poverty" by offering equal access to all.[18] Prominent intellectual and author Walter Lippmann voiced the concerns of many progressives when he denounced the religious "who flatly refuse to regard Pluralism as a way of life" and branded the Roman Catholic Church as "hostile to democracy and to every force that tend[s] to make people self-sufficient."[19] School Bill proponents had successfully exploited this assimilationist argument, invoking old tensions and intertwining anti-Catholicism with the case for progressive education reform. This strategy would emerge again, in the state's briefs defending the School Bill.

Defending the Faith

Despite the NCWC agreement with Archbishop Christie, it did not take long for Bishop Muldoon's apprehension about turf battles to become reality. The NCWC quickly became embroiled in a controversy over the selection of legal counsel. Archbishop Christie argued that the Oregon court would be more favorably disposed to local counsel, and he wanted Judge Kavanaugh to stay on the case. John Kavanaugh brought homegrown prestige and strong Republican credentials to the litigation. Appointed chief deputy city attorney in 1902, he served in that position for five years before being elected as Portland city attorney in 1907. Kavanaugh earned his "judge" title from years on the Multnomah County circuit bench before he returned to private practice. But Judge Kavanaugh made a less than favorable impression on some of the NCWC leadership, who wanted nationally prominent attorneys directing the litigation. Recommendations for counsel poured into the NCWC from bishops around the country. Roger Baldwin, founder of the American Civil Liberties Union, offered assistance in the selection of counsel. Father Hanna wanted his own attorney, Garrett McEnerney of San Francisco, as lead counsel. Father Burke remained convinced that Guthrie should be selected.

In late January, Archbishop Christie sent Kavanaugh to New York to retain Guthrie, leading Dowling, as chair of the litigation oversight subcommittee, to fret to Burke that Christie "seemed to feel himself in complete charge of the case."[20] On his way back to Portland, Kavanaugh reported to Burke that he and Guthrie were unable to reach an agreement because he found Guthrie "physically quite sick and very near a nervous breakdown." Guthrie left for the Mediterranean on February 7 for several months of rest and recuperation, and Kavanaugh offered his services to Burke, telling Burke that he was willing to devote extensive and exclusive time to the case. He assured Burke that he had begun "diligent investigation," and although he felt confident they would soon be ready to file suit, he promised he would not do so until the case was thoroughly prepared.[21]

Hanna and Burke remained determined to retain counsel outside Oregon. Hanna traveled to Portland to inform both Archbishop Christie and Kavanaugh that Guthrie would be named as chief counsel, with Garrett McEnerney, as associate counsel, directing the case until Guthrie's return. He authorized Kavanaugh to litigate the case in Oregon but made clear that Guthrie and McEnerney would handle the case before the U.S. Supreme Court. Kavanaugh wrote Father Burke that he would be pleased to work with any counsel selected by the NCWC's administrative committee and that he believed his views to be in complete harmony with those of the NCWC. In April, the committee, believing the matter settled, formally agreed to ask Guthrie to serve as chief counsel.

Despite his assurances to Father Burke, Kavanaugh was less than satisfied with the litigation arrangements, and he attempted to get Archbishop Christie to reopen the matter with the NCWC. In a letter to Christie, Kavanaugh complained that the decision to have outside counsel control the case was not acceptable. He insisted that it had been understood all along that one Oregon counsel would appear before the Supreme Court, because "no one outside the State of Oregon can visualize the situation we have here." Grousing that attorneys who conduct the litigation in the lower courts perform the "real services," by doing the bulk of the research and analysis, Kavanaugh claimed that he had not received one bit of useful information from outside attorneys. He was firmly convinced that they would not need "Eastern" counsel on the case. Clearly unhappy that he had been reduced to local counsel, Kavanaugh complained to Christie that McEnerney had failed to answer his last two letters. Kavanaugh stood to gain both personally and financially if he assumed the responsibilities of lead counsel. In June, he requested $10,000 for services rendered and informed Archbishop Christie that he could conduct the litigation all the way to the Supreme Court for $25,000, saving the NCWC the considerable extra expense of Eastern counsel.[22] Christie found Kavanaugh convincing and wanted to proceed with the litigation on the terms suggested by Kavanaugh.

Archbishop Dowling, distressed at the turn of affairs, wrote to Bishop Muldoon that while Guthrie had not yet been retained, he would never consent to being associate or assistant counsel to Kavanaugh. Dowling confided that he had received good advice on the importance of having a "man of address" argue the case to the Supreme Court. He remained convinced that an attorney of the stature of Guthrie or McEnerney would be indispensable to the case.[23] Dowling also expressed concern at the internal politics at the NCWC, frustrated that Christie was asking him for money when Hanna should be handling the financial arrangements. Dowling described the negotiations as "badly bungled" and expressed fears that "we are going to be made ridiculous."[24]

Archbishop Hanna described the situation in even bleaker terms, worried that the dispute would erupt into scandal. In a letter to Dowling, he admitted that "things are not satisfactory in Portland." After promising to give the NCWC full control of the case, Archbishop Christie had accepted the $10,000 from the Knights of Columbus "against his pledged word," Hanna wrote, and now wished to place the case in the hands of "second-rate Oregon lawyers." Hanna also advised Dowling that McEnerney found Kavanaugh's bill of $10,000 exorbitant and had laughingly dismissed Kavanaugh's labors as nothing more than opportunism. Hanna concluded by reminding Dowling, "I was afraid of a mess from the beginning and I was not far out."[25]

Not all the bishops on the NCWC administrative committee shared the concerns of Hanna and Dowling. Bishop John P. Carroll from Helena, Montana, spent two weeks in Portland trying to forge an agreement between Kavanaugh, Christie, and the NCWC. He found Kavanaugh and Christie's mutual desire to have Kavanaugh included as advisory or subordinate counsel to Guthrie quite reasonable, arguing that his knowledge of the case would be indispensable to a case where "we cannot afford to take any chances." Carroll urged Dowling to get the dispute resolved and move ahead with the litigation. He warned that the Knights of Columbus perceived the Oregon case as an opportunity to "save" the Catholic schools of the country and would like nothing more than to step in while the parochial schools' "God-appointed defenders were quarrelling about lawyers and haggling about the price."[26] Dowling made it clear to Archbishop Hanna that he did not want to lose control of the case.[27]

The conflicts over representation simmered through the summer, until Archbishop Hanna took action in late July to settle the matter. He rejected Kavanaugh's proposal for representation and offered him $15,000 for the litigation in trial court. Ultimately, Hanna agreed to $20,000, on the condition that "immediately upon the conclusion of the litigation in Oregon . . . the exclusive control of the litigation shall pass to William D. Guthrie, and he shall have the sole control . . . but you and your associates will render such services . . . as may be requested by Mr. Guthrie, but without any additional compensation."[28] McEnerney had urged even stronger language limiting Kavanaugh's authority, but Dowling rejected it as too harsh and belittling. On August 1, Archbishop Hanna telegrammed Dowling that Guthrie had been retained as chief counsel and, along with McEnerney, had agreed to work without compensation. With more than six months wasted bickering over legal representation, the NCWC was finally ready to turn its attention to preparing the case for litigation.

CHAPTER 11   A Perfect Storm

Although Guthrie did not finalize his agreement with the NCWC until September, his interest in the School Bill predated any formal contract. Sixty-four-year-old William Dameron Guthrie brought expertise, prestige, and connections to the School Bill case. Both legal scholar and successful attorney, he also brought a reputation as one of the leading architects of the antiregulatory judicial philosophy embraced by the Supreme Court since the turn of the century. The NCWC knew he would be a formidable advocate before the Court. More important, Guthrie had already devoted considerable thought to determining the legal arguments most likely to resonate with the Court. Guthrie's firm conviction that the primary challenge to the School Bill should be based on parental rights defined the litigation strategy for the NCWC. His certainty that the Constitution protected parental rights would prove persuasive to the Court.

Holy Warrior for the Constitution

Guthrie's life bore the marks of both privilege and hardship. Born February 3, 1859, in San Francisco, to a Scotch father and an Irish mother, he was the third of seven children in an affluent family. He spent his early years in California, England, and France. At 14, the start of the Franco-Prussian War forced his family from Paris to New York City, where the family suffered serious financial losses. Guthrie attended public schools for two years, until financial adversity forced him to work for five dollars per week as a messenger in the law firm of Blatchford, Seward, Griswold & Da Costa. In 1879, Guthrie, who never attended college, started Columbia Law School. He completed the coursework in just one year and was admitted to practice law in New York at age 21. In four short years, Guthrie became a full partner in the same firm where he started work as a messenger, which soon became Seward, Da Costa & Guthrie and eventually became Guthrie, Cravath & Henderson. In addition to their law practice, Cravath and Guthrie made fortunes speculating on real estate on Long Island, allowing Guthrie to maintain a country home in Locust Valley, along the Long Island Gold Coast, as well as a mansion on Park Avenue.

Guthrie became one of New York's most prominent attorneys, active in the city's legal, social, and political organizations. His philanthropy, as well as his appreciation of finely tailored suits, made him a well-known figure on the social circuit. He counted among his friends Henry W. Taft, the younger brother of former U.S. president Chief Justice William Howard Taft. His connections extended directly to Supreme Court justices. He attended receptions honoring Justice Rufus Peckham's appointment to the Supreme Court in February 1896 and maintained personal and professional relationships with a number of the justices who decided the School Bill case. Guthrie knew George Sutherland before Sutherland was appointed to the Supreme Court. When Guthrie left the Cravath firm in 1907, the firm replaced him with James Clark McReynolds, who was appointed to the Court in 1914. Guthrie and McReynolds, both active Republican conservatives, saw a great deal of each other in New York, and McReynolds ultimately wrote the opinion for the Court in the School Bill case.

Guthrie developed his professional reputation as an expert in constitutional law. In 1898, he published a collection of lectures on the Fourteenth Amendment that became one of the most influential treatises of the day. Named to the Storrs Lectureship at Yale, Guthrie taught at the university from 1907 to 1908. From 1909 to 1922, he served as the Ruggles Professor of Constitutional Law at Columbia University. He was elected president of the New York State Bar Association in 1921 and, later, president of the Association of the Bar of the City of New York.

Guthrie detested the Progressive movement. In 1912, during the keynote speech at the Republican State Convention, Guthrie described Theodore Roosevelt as "a Socialist at heart" and identified the most pressing concerns of the nation as "the constitutional right and power of Congress to protect American industries" and the "threatened overthrow of the representative system of government . . . by the introduction of the initiative."[1] Dismayed at the "anarchy" of pure democracy, he lobbied to dismantle New York's direct primary system and return it to the practice of selection by party conventions.

Guthrie fell prey to criticism, both public and private, that he was a snob with a "waspish" temperament. As president of the New York State Bar Association, Guthrie opposed compulsory Bar membership, arguing that it would bring in "undesirable" members, such as "immigrants and their progeny," who posed a "difficult and grave problem and menace" to "the elite of the Bar, the best of the Bar." He reversed the vigorous egalitarian recruitment policy of his three predecessors, preferring selective admission of attorneys based on their professional standing. Guthrie also alienated many members of the Bar when he canceled the association's scheduled performance of the musical spoof *May It Please the Court* because "the matter and form" of the play "were not compatible with the dignity of the Association."[2] The *New York World Telegram* criticized Guthrie for the haughty demeanor he projected as Bar president. Guthrie did consider most attorneys incompetent, and he bemoaned the absence of lawyers with sufficient business expertise and acumen to serve effectively as corporate counsels.

Complaints about Guthrie's elitism followed him from the corporate world to the ivory tower. Upton Sinclair, in his muckraking attack on education, singled out Guthrie's Columbia University professorship as an example of higher education's infatuation with the elite. Complaining that Guthrie received $7,500 per year for teaching once a week for half a semester, Sinclair charged that Guthrie did none of the work of an ordinary college professor but conferred on the university his "plutocratic prestige."[3] Guthrie's appointment as the Ruggles Professor at Columbia did in fact create a scandal, when his selection caused Dr. Charles A. Beard to resign from the faculty. Beard claimed that the Columbia trustees were reactionaries, appointing Guthrie only after they blackballed all progressive or liberal candidates for the chair. Guthrie's personal qualities did not advance his reputation at Columbia, where he was described as "not personally a likeable man. . . . highly irascible, increasingly inconsiderate and totally lacking in a sense of humor."[4] His disengagement from faculty life rankled his academic colleagues; he attended only four faculty meetings in his 13 years on the faculty, including one in 1917 to vote against the admission of women. Guthrie's skill as a scholar also received less than accolades from some colleagues at Columbia, because of an "ultra-legalistic mind which made him approach new . . . problems with stiff inflexibility."[5] A historian of the New York City Bar blisteringly assessed Guthrie as a "man driven and crippled by his ambitions which, for all his brilliance, he could never achieve because his temper, his selfishness and his snobbery always tripped him."[6]

In litigation, academic scholarship, and speeches, Guthrie established himself as one of the leading proponents of laissez-faire jurisprudence. In 1895, Guthrie served as lead counsel in the constitutional challenge to the federal income tax, *Pollock v. Farmers' Loan & Trust Company.* The challengers won the case before the Supreme Court after eight exhausting days of oral argument. The Court found the law unconstitutional, holding that any direct taxes levied by the federal government had to be apportioned by state population.[7] Populists reacted to the *Pollock* decision with deep hostility, and it was widely speculated that Guthrie had engineered the case so he could bring the tax before the Court. *Pollock* required passage of a constitutional amendment, the Sixteenth Amendment, to remedy the constitutional defect posed by a federal income tax, and Guthrie lobbied tirelessly, if futilely, against the amendment, which was ratified in 1913. He aggressively opposed the inheritance tax and other forms of progressive taxation, proclaiming that "the great danger" of all democracies is that one class votes the taxes for another class to pay."[8] In a speech before the Economic Club, Guthrie warned that "the moment you put the power with the majority to tax us, that moment you open the door to the ultimate destruction of the United States."[9]

His distrust of government regulation extended beyond taxation. As early as 1897, Guthrie argued that federal antitrust laws unreasonably restrained trade, violating individual liberty of contract and tending "towards centralization and socialism."[10] Historian Benjamin Twiss attributes to Guthrie the development of one of the most significant principles of constitutional law, "dual federalism," which posits the state and national governments as equal sovereigns with separate spheres of authority.[11] Dual federalism served Guthrie's laissez-faire philosophy because it severely restricted the permissible spheres of both state and federal regulatory authority. Under dual federalism, federal authority was limited by power reserved to the states, and state power was limited by federal constitutional protections for the individual.

In a series of landmark cases before the Supreme Court, Guthrie devised arguments for limiting the federal commerce clause and taxing authority over labor, manufacturing, and vice. In two cases in 1903 and 1904, the Lottery Case and the Oleomargarine Case, Guthrie argued unsuccessfully that Congress lacked the authority to prohibit the interstate transportation of lottery tickets or to tax oleomargarine, because such federal legislation intruded on state authority. By 1918, in *Hammer v. Dagenhart,* the Court came around to Guthrie's analysis when it struck down the federal Keating-Owen law prohibiting child labor, concluding that the law impermissibly regulated manufacturing, an activity reserved to the states under the Tenth Amendment. In 1922, when the Court struck down a federal tax on child labor in *Bailey v. Drexel Furniture Co.,* the Court's opinion read as though lifted from Guthrie's losing brief in the Oleomargarine case.[12]

Guthrie was no more enamored of state regulation. He publicly defended the hotly criticized Supreme Court opinion *Lochner v. New York,* which invalidated a New York law limiting the working hours of bakers. He viewed progressive legislation as little more than class warfare, "framed nominally for the benefit of labor but really for the purpose of serving a particular class against another."[13] Guthrie mistrusted the "despotism"of majoritarian politics, denouncing social policy as "the deadly weapon of socialism and communism," an evil that feeds the "superstition, so rampant, that legislation is a sovereign cure-all for social ills."[14]

Guthrie's views on limited government complemented his interpretation of the federal constitution as a broad and expansive framework for protecting individual rights. He argued that the Constitution was an organic framework that had to adapt to changing times and should be interpreted in the manner most conducive to the enhancement of liberty.[15] In his 1898 lectures on the Fourteenth Amendment, Guthrie claimed that the privileges and immunities clause of the Fourteenth Amendment was clearly intended to incorporate the Bill of Rights and make it applicable to the states, an argument rejected by the Supreme Court in 1873 in the *Slaughter-House Cases,* but one that would have dramatically expanded the scope of individual liberties protected by the federal constitution from state interference.[16] Guthrie took a broad view of the liberties protected by the Fourteenth Amendment, describing liberty as a "state of freedom existing under a republican form of government based on just as well as equal laws." "Just," rather than "equal," laws absorbed him. Equality, to Guthrie, functioned merely as an attribute of liberty, for "all may be equally degraded, equally slavish." Guthrie claimed that equality lacked intrinsic value and, unlike liberty, could be corrupted into a tool of oppression. He called communism and socialism examples of how equality degrades into despotism.[17]

Guthrie embraced judicial review as the guardian of individual liberties. The progressives during this period led a public assault on the courts for invalidating the social legislation Guthrie so despised. Guthrie viewed these attacks on the courts as one of the most significant threats facing the nation. His keynote address before the Pennsylvania Bar Association on June 25, 1912, decried progressives' impatience with constitutional constraints in their rush to champion the virtues of majority power. To the attorneys fell the role of educating the public on fundamental rights and political restraint, a task Guthrie embraced.[18] A colleague described him as a man driven by principles, who waged a "holy war" on behalf of his view of the Constitution.[19]

Guthrie's religion shaped his life. A devout Catholic, whose religiosity "filled his soul and colored all his life,"[20] Guthrie received numerous honors from the church, including the titles Commander of the Order of Saint Gregory, Master Knight of the Sovereign Order of Malta, and Grand Cross of the Order of Saint Lazare of Jerusalem. He represented the church in New York for many years and was well connected with the national Catholic hierarchy. Guthrie was a passionate defender of private religious schools, commending them for their expertise in teaching social morality through religion, and as early as 1915, he condemned the anti-Catholicism that questioned the patriotism of Catholic education.[21] He spoke out frequently against the Smith-Towner Bill of 1922, charging that federalization of education violated the rights of the states and would destroy education through standardization.[22]

The Oregon School Bill emerged as a perfect storm to Guthrie, roiling his deep religious convictions, his passionate belief in individual liberties, and his ardent distaste for progressive legislation. When the Oregon initiative passed, Guthrie moved to protect the interests of the Catholic schools long before he was formally retained by the NCWC. Proceeding on the instruction of Archbishop Dowling and on the recommendation of Thomas F. O'Mara, a respected Terre Haute attorney who occasionally advised the NCWC, Guthrie maneuvered to turn the attention of the Supreme Court to the School Bill before a challenge to the law had even been filed.

Meyer v. Nebraska: *The First Attack on State Monopoly of Education*

On February 20, 1923, Guthrie filed with the Supreme Court an amicus curiae (literally, "friend of the court") brief on behalf of "various religious and educational institutions," in the case of *Meyer v. Nebraska*. *Meyer* involved a challenge to a Nebraska law prohibiting instruction in any foreign language in public or private grammar schools, one of many "English-only" education laws passed during and after World War I.[23] Robert Meyer, a private school teacher, was convicted of teaching German during recess. Nebraska defended the English-language law as part of an assimilation program intended to "prevent children . . . from being trained and educated in foreign languages and foreign ideas before they have had an opportunity to learn the English language and observe American ideals." Nebraska argued that the English-only laws ensured that "the sunshine of American ideals will permeate the life of the future citizens of this republic."[24] Nebraska also claimed that foreign-language instruction posed a security risk to the state. Describing "isolated communities" where foreign languages are spoken as communities controlled by foreign leaders, Nebraska warned that "these communities are growing up as little Germanys, little Italys and little Hungarys."[25]

Meyer disputed the state's security concerns, arguing that the state failed to present sufficient evidence of a security threat to justify a prohibition on foreign-language instruction. He claimed that the law interfered with his ability to earn a livelihood, violating constitutionally protected economic liberties. Meyer did not dispute the state's interest in assimilation or in citizens proficient in English, but he charged that the state's methods violated the "spirit" of "liberty and toleration" that in other times has "prevented the efforts of tyrannical governments to suppress minority languages." Those tyrannical governments included Germany and Russia, which suppressed linguistic diversity.[26]

While the validity of the English-language laws arguably posed a narrower constitutional question than the issue of compulsory public education, Guthrie recognized immediately the impact the *Meyer* case could have on the School Bill case. The possibility of a ruling in *Meyer* upholding comprehensive state authority over education troubled Guthrie, who worried that something might be said in the argument or decision that would prejudice the issue in Oregon. The Nebraska law was in fact a compromise measure, enacted after a proposal for compelled public education failed by one vote. The Supreme Court would be briefed on the legislative history of the measure and likely would be aware of the passage of the Oregon law. Guthrie decided to use his amicus brief to alert the Court to the forthcoming School Bill. Guthrie thought the Court would be less likely to make expansive statements in *Meyer* about state authority over education if it anticipated an impending challenge to compulsory public education.

To that end, the short brief explicitly refused to take a position on the *Meyer* case and instead focused exclusively on informing the Court about the School Bill and persuading the justices to view *Meyer* from the broader question of state monopoly over education. Labeling the Oregon act "revolutionary," Guthrie charged that it "adopt[ed] the favorite device of communistic Russia—the destruction of parental authority, the standardization of education . . . , and the monopolization by the state of the training and teaching of the young." The brief excoriated the Oregon law as un-American, charging that state monopoly of education is "plainly repugnant to the spirit of Anglo-Saxon individualism." Guthrie conceded state authority to regulate education, but he contended that the elimination of private schools constituted "arbitrary, wanton ruthlessness," that violated fundamental rights without due process of law. Weaving together principles of educational autonomy, religious freedom, and parental rights, the brief argued that ceding monopoly power over education to the state was inseparable from the dogma of Sovietism.[27]

Guthrie knew that the Oregon case was likely to emphasize parental rights, not the economic liberties alleged by the plaintiff in *Meyer*. His amicus brief thus did not dwell on the individual liberties at stake; Guthrie instead focused the attention of the Court primarily on the permissible scope of state authority over education. He relied on one of the leading treatises of the day, written by Professor Ernst Freund, to argue that according to well-established law, the state lacked the power to interfere with the freedom of private instruction.[28] This principle held particularly true where religious freedom was at issue; because religious denominations rely on parochial schools to inculcate religious doctrine, the state could not suppress private schools.

Citing such diverse sources as John Stuart Mill and Herbert Spencer, the brief claimed that no modern educator of any stature advocated state monopoly of education. To the contrary, enlightened thinkers had "long ago" repudiated the "notion of Plato that in a Utopia the state would be the sole repository of parental authority and duty and the children be surrendered to it for upbringing and education." Parental prerogatives, not state power, constituted the "true rule" of constitutional law, Guthrie argued. He cited numerous precedents from state law that upheld the "God-given and constitutional right of a parent to have some voice in the bringing up and education of his children." The brief closed with a warning to the Court to exercise the "greatest caution" in reviewing sweeping restrictions on educational freedom, for such restrictions are typically driven by religious or political motives, not sound education policy.[29]

Guthrie's strategy succeeded. The Supreme Court heard oral arguments in the *Meyer* case on February 23, only three days after Guthrie filed his brief. Although Guthrie had departed for Europe earlier in the month and did not attend the oral arguments, the impact of his amicus brief became clear only moments into the oral arguments. As Meyer's counsel, Arthur F. Mullen, made the point that Nebraska acted arbitrarily by targeting language instruction in private religious schools, Justice McReynolds interrupted Mullen to clarify whether Nebraska prohibited private schools. Meyer's brief conceded the authority of the state to compel public school attendance: "That a law requiring that all persons within a certain age should be required to attend the public schools . . . would be a valid exercise of the police power . . . may be conceded." But Mullen was about to repudiate that concession at oral argument.[30]

Mullen replied that the state "could no more abolish private schools than they could . . . ," but McReynolds interrupted again to inquire, "I just wanted to see what you claim: What about the power of the State to require the children to attend public schools?" Mullen advised McReynolds that he would get to that question "in a moment." McReynolds demanded an immediate answer: "You will admit that, will you not?" Mullen refused to agree but said only, "I do not admit that." McReynolds pressed him again: "You do not admit that?" Mullen finally took the hint and offered the Court a lengthy rebuttal of state authority to "take complete control of education and give it a monopoly of education." Mullen argued that such power by the state is "not in accordance with the history of our people" and cannot exist in a constitutional government. He advised the Court that the issue "is one of the most important questions that has been presented for a generation; because it deals with the principle of the soviet."[31]

The justices questioned the parties primarily about the scope of government authority over education. Although Mullen argued vigorously that the language law violated an impressive list of liberties, including religious and economic rights, freedom of conscience, and the right of parental control over education, the Court showed little interest in debating constitutional rights. Near the end of the argument, Chief Justice Taft advised Mullen, "You know when we come to consider the question of the constitutionality of a law, we have, if we hold it invalid, to be able to put our fingers on the particular provision of the Constitution that is violated. Will you point out before you are through the particular provision which is violated?"[32]

Father Burke attended the arguments in *Meyer*. He wrote Kavanaugh in Portland that the Court's attention appeared clearly concentrated on government authority over education: "From the intense interest and attitude of the Justices, it was evident that they considered this question of education of primary importance." Burke noted that Chief Justice Taft made "some very pertinent inquiries on the history of education and the right of the State therein." Burke advised Kavanaugh that the oral arguments proved to him that "we have got to be very well informed when our case is presented."[33]

The Supreme Court handed down a decision in favor of Meyer on June 4, 1923, in a seven-to-two opinion that attests to the influence of Guthrie's brief. In holding that the English-language laws unreasonably interfered with liberty interests guaranteed by the Fourteenth Amendment, the Court articulated a definition of liberty extending far beyond economic interests. Justice McReynolds's opinion, while admitting that the Court "has not attempted to define with exactness the liberty thus guaranteed," proceeded to describe significant aspects of that interest. "Without doubt," he wrote, "it denotes not merely freedom from bodily restraint but also the right of the individual to contract, to engage in any of the common occupations of life, to acquire useful knowledge, to marry, establish a home and bring up children, to worship God according to the dictates of his own conscience, and generally to enjoy these privileges long recognized at common law as essential to the orderly pursuit of happiness by free men."[34] The Court concluded, "Corresponding to the right of control, it is the natural duty of the parent to give his children education suitable to their station in life." The Court held that the language laws impermissibly interfered with the plaintiff's right to teach and the parents' right to engage foreign-language instruction.[35]

The Court analyzed the relationship between state power and education in language remarkably similar to that of Guthrie's brief. The Court explicitly extracted Guthrie's argument that Anglo-Saxon society had repudiated the Platonic ideal of state control of child rearing and education. Justice McReynolds's opinion, in a powerful rejection of unlimited state authority over education, described Plato's Ideal Commonwealth as the prime example of "measures . . . approved by men of great genius" whose "ideas touching the relation between individual and state were wholly different from those upon which our institutions rest," measures that could not be imposed by an American legislature without "doing violence to both letter and spirit of the Constitution." Recognizing that "the state may do much, go very far, indeed, in order to improve the quality of its citizens, physically, mentally, and morally," the Court concluded that "a desirable end cannot be promoted by prohibited means."[36]

The Court's discussion of that "desirable end" provided insight into how the Court might evaluate the strength of the state's interest in using the public schools as a vehicle for assimilation. As Guthrie had hoped, the opinion suggested that assimilation could not be accomplished by state monopoly over education. Acknowledging that the "desire of the Legislature to foster a homogeneous people with American ideals prepared readily to understand current discussions of civic matters is easy to appreciate," the Court concluded that, in Nebraska, the "means adopted, we think, exceed the limitations upon the power of the state and conflict with rights assured to plaintiff in error."[37] The issue might be viewed differently when the country is at war, the Court suggested, but no adequate reason existed for the law during a time of peace and domestic tranquility.

Justice Holmes, an advocate of judicial deference to legislative judgment, dissented in a brief opinion joined by Justice Sutherland. Holmes saw the language laws as a reasonable means of achieving assimilation. He argued that the state had a valid interest in attaining a "common tongue" among all citizens and that the English-language laws did not pose an "undue restriction."[38]

Given the narrow issue presented in *Meyer*, the sweeping scope of the Court's language and its criticism of Platonic ideals seemed directed to a much larger question, a more fitting response to the question of the legitimacy of compelled public education than to the question of English instruction. In addition to the recognition of parental and economic rights, the opinion addressed an additional point potentially relevant to the Oregon School Bill challenge. Although it was the schoolteacher who challenged the Nebraska law, the Court found that the Nebraska law also violated the liberty interests of parents in educating their children and employing teachers to that end. The Court linked a parent's right to educate with an instructor's right to teach, implying they were interdependent. This linkage suggested that the Court might be receptive to challenges by the

Oregon private schools on behalf of not only their own economic interests but also the interests of parents in sending their children to private schools.

The Court, not surprisingly, appeared particularly concerned that the Nebraska law interfered with parental choices in the private market. Shortly after the opinion was issued, Chief Justice Taft explained to a friend that the problem with the Nebraska law derived from the state's efforts to prohibit parents from obtaining private language instruction. The state, Taft wrote, has extensive authority to dictate public school curriculum and mandate required courses in private schools. But the liberty secured by the Fourteenth Amendment "does prevent the Legislature from forbidding a parent to employ a private school or private school teacher to teach his child any subject matter which is not itself vicious."[39]

The expansive definition of constitutional liberty in *Meyer* derived, in large part, from the Court's willingness to "constitutionalize" the "privileges long recognized at common law as essential to the orderly pursuit of happiness by free men." The *Meyer* description boded well for the School Bill case. But *Meyer* did not squarely resolve the School Bill challenge. Despite the Court's broad definition of parental rights, the decision rested on narrower grounds—the right of parents to engage teachers for instruction in foreign languages. The Court linked parental rights to the economic liberties well established by precedent. The School Bill challenge could be reduced to the right of parents to contract for private education, but Guthrie sought broader protection for parental rights, protection not limited to economic transactions.

School Bill opponents were elated with the *Meyer* decision. The NCWC viewed the opinion as a significant foundation for a favorable outcome in the Oregon case. Garrett McEnerney advised Archbishop Hanna that he believed the constitutional question to be "fairly safe" and "almost decided" by the *Meyer* ruling. He even questioned the need to file an immediate challenge to the Oregon law.[40] Thomas O'Mara agreed that *Meyer* "practically settles" the matter. During July, Archbishop Hanna used these assessments to assist him in negotiations with Kavanaugh. In rejecting Kavanaugh's proposed fee arrangement, Hanna advised Kavanaugh that the NCWC understood that the Supreme Court had "in effect" declared the School Bill invalid and that "practically the only question . . . is whether the threatened danger is sufficiently imminent . . . to justify a present injunction." Given these circumstances, Hanna informed Kavanaugh that $15,000 would be very generous compensation for services rendered. Hanna emphasized his confidence in the outcome of the case primarily to reduce Kavanaugh's participation and compensation. He revealed his strategy when he concluded the letter by explaining that the NCWC chose Guthrie because it required the expertise of the most distinguished authority on constitutional law available.[41]

The *Meyer* decision finally prompted action in Oregon. In addition to the squabbles over attorney selection, the NCWC had been caught up in disputes about when to file the suit and whether to file it in state or federal court. Guthrie had reservations about challenging the law more than three years before it went into effect. The Court could dismiss the case if it found that the law could not be challenged until it was enforceable. In addition, if the NCWC wanted to seek an injunction against the law, the standard for injunctive relief required evidence of imminent danger of irreparable injury. Here, too, the Court could find insufficient evidence of imminence.

Guthrie recognized that the delayed effective date of September 1926 was intended to give public and private schools sufficient lead time to adapt to compulsory public schooling. The public schools faced the potential need to construct additional facilities, hire additional staff, and increase resources. For private schools, the School Bill meant either closure or replacement of full-day programs with after-school religious training. More immediately, the passage of the measure placed private schools under an immediate cloud of uncertainty. Parents would be unwilling to start their children in a school forced to close in less than four years. Many parents with children already in private schools would seek to transfer their children to public schools rather than have them educated in an environment disheartened by the threat of dissolution. The immediate economic displacement caused by the School Bill provided the challengers with a reasonable argument of imminent economic harm sufficient to justify an injunction against the law. *Meyer* also largely resolved the debate over whether to file the case in state or federal court. Not only would the federal court be more likely to be receptive to the case; a federal forum also eliminated the concerns of some members of the Catholic hierarchy that judges in Oregon state courts, elected officials subject to recall, might succumb to political pressure from the Oregon supporters of the School Bill. With these issues settled, only one key element remained missing from the NCWC litigation: a plaintiff.

CHAPTER 12   Delicate and Difficult Questions

To Archbishop Christie, the choice of plaintiff could not be more obvious. The Society of the Sisters of the Holy Names of Jesus and Mary maintained the oldest and most extensive system of Catholic schools in the state. The Sisters owned six schools throughout Oregon, including St. Mary's Academy in Portland, and schooled over 865 students. The Sisters also maintained, but did not own, six additional schools with over one thousand students attending. St. Mary's Academy, as the oldest, continuously operated Catholic high school in the state, bore a particularly distinguished history.

St. Mary's Academy opened its doors on November 6, 1859, the same year that Oregon became a state. Oregon archbishop Francis Norbert Blanchet found inspiration for the school while traveling by horseback to visit Catholics in small towns and wilderness throughout the state. Blanchet observed the poor or nonexistent education opportunities and encountered scores of orphans, the smallest victims of the harsh frontier existence. The archbishop purchased a block in bustling downtown Portland, which counted among its population of 2,900 many struggling families who came to Oregon after failing in the California goldfields. Archbishop Blanchet then set off for the village of Longueuil, Canada, near Montreal, to persuade nuns from the order of the Sisters of the Holy Names of Jesus and Mary to start a school in Portland.

The sisters responded to the archbishop's heartbreaking tales of homeless children orphaned in the wilderness. Although most of them did not know English, twelve sisters, led by Mother Superior Alphonse, embarked on September 15, 1859, on a monthlong journey to Portland. The sisters traveled by rail to New York City, where they stopped long enough to purchase a square piano and send it to Portland by way of Cape Horn. The nuns then boarded the steamer *Star of the West,* bound for the Isthmus of Panama. They crossed the isthmus by rail, then sailed for Portland, where they arrived, exhausted by seasickness and homesickness, on October 21. They spent their first night in Portland in a dilapidated frame house that was bordered by dense forest, filthy with garbage from vagabonds, drafty with chill autumn winds, and wet with leaks from the relentless rain. The Portland newspaper greeted their arrival by commenting, "What a foothold Romanism is gaining in our state!"

Only two weeks later, on a gray November 6, St. Mary's Academy welcomed its first six pupils—three Catholics, two Jews, and one Episcopalian. Thus started a tradition of administering to a diverse student body from varying religious and ethnic heritages, or as the *Portland Daily Herald* described St. Mary's students, "young ladies . . . of all European nations, making a most cosmopolitan throng . . . , all mingled together and making a most interesting study for the lover of ethnology."[1] Ten days later, the school brought in its first boarder, a seven-year-old orphaned girl. People in town peeked in the windows of the school and inquired if the sisters were Indians, for many had never seen a religious habit. The first harp and the first sewing machine in Oregon made their way to the school around Cape Horn. The curriculum spanned the full range of academic subjects, including sciences, art, and music. St. Mary's prospered and quickly became an educational force in the community. The order opened new schools throughout Oregon on almost an annual basis through the 1860s, including elementary and high schools and, eventually, a college.

Archbishop Christie claimed that the prominence and economic value of the educational network maintained by the Sisters would make the order an effective plaintiff. Judge Kavanaugh saw legal benefits to the selection. The order had filed articles of incorporation with the state on November 9, 1880. As a registered Oregon corporation, the Sisters stood in a contractual relationship with the state. Kavanaugh intended to argue that the School Bill caused the state to impair its obligation of contract—in violation of Article I, Section 10, of the federal constitution—by destroying the plaintiff's educational mission and economic worth. He explained to Mother Mary Flavia, "One of the arguments advanced . . . is . . . a contract cannot be annulled unless both parties consent to the act of annulling it." He argued that through the School Bill, "this contract has been broken without the consent of the Sisters, which is unconstitutional."[2]

Kavanaugh brought together a talented pool of local attorneys to assist him in developing the case. Kavanaugh's law partner, Jay Bowerman, was a well-known Republican who had briefly served as governor. Bowerman won election to the state senate in 1904 and became Senate president in 1909. When Governor Frank W. Benson was incapacitated by poor health in June 1910, he asked Bowerman, only 33, to become acting governor. Bowerman served only a year, losing the position to Democrat Oswald West. He moved to Portland and established a successful business law practice. Dan J. Malarkey, also a former Republican state senator and Senate president, was a widely respected trial attorney who had appeared before the U.S. Supreme Court in 1913. Two rising stars in Oregon law and politics completed the litigation team. Frank J. Lonergan, a former Notre Dame star halfback, went on to serve as a state representative, Speaker of the Oregon House, and Multnomah County Circuit Court judge. Hall S. Lusk, already a prominent and distinguished figure in the legal community, eventually became one of Oregon's most illustrious public figures. Lusk sat as a Multnomah County Circuit Court judge for seven years before he was elected to the Oregon Supreme Court. He would serve on the state Supreme Court for 31 years, including a two-year period as chief justice and an eight-month interruption when he was appointed in 1960 to fill the U.S. Senate seat made vacant by the death of Richard L. Neuberger. In late spring, Kavanaugh moved ahead with preparations for the case, despite his ongoing dispute with the NCWC.

Spring also brought Oregon the first adverse repercussions from the School Bill. The economy suffered from the negative national reaction to compulsory public education. Negotiations with a group of Lutherans from Wisconsin to settle lands as part of a new irrigation project in eastern Oregon collapsed when the families learned of the passage of the School Bill. A large Michigan furniture producer canceled plans to expand its operations to Oregon, as did a mining business from Spokane. A Massachusetts company broke off talks on a proposed purchase of Portland Woolen Mills, a deal that would have injected over a million dollars into the Oregon economy. All pointed to the School Bill as a factor.

Oregon endured national ridicule for its Klan-dominated legislature, but Klan influence actually proved to be more embarrassment than political upheaval. In addition to the law prohibiting religious garb in public schools, the legislature passed an anti-alien law on property ownership, directed at Japanese immigrants, and required an English literacy test for voting. But other nativist and anti-Catholic bills floundered. Bills repealing the tax exemptions for religious property, eliminating Columbus Day as a state holiday, banning the importation of sacramental wine, and prohibiting the hiring of aliens on public works projects all failed, as did a measure to require nonnative owners of businesses to post signs disclosing their nationality. Tensions over the School Bill remained high in Oregon. A speech given in Portland by Joseph Scott, a national official of the Knights of Columbus, caused considerable controversy when Scott encouraged Catholics not to comply with the School Bill because its proponents consisted of hypocrites and ignorant, unpatriotic scoundrels.

On June 21, Kavanaugh, frustrated at the extensive delays over the question of representation, wrote Archbishop Christie to advise him that there remained a great deal of work to be done before the case could be filed. Kavanaugh's letter constituted a long and impassioned pitch to Christie on the dedication and expertise of local counsel. Kavanaugh boasted that he and his legal associates knew they could prevail on the constitutional issue. He told Christie that he had closely followed *Meyer* and had predicted the outcome in that case. He had obtained the legal briefs from *Meyer* and corresponded extensively with counsel in the case, who, he reminded Christie, were local Nebraska attorneys. Kavanaugh insisted that the real difficulty in the case was not the constitutional challenge but the procedural question of whether an injunction could be sought more than three years before the effective date of the statute: "It should be understood that we have never from the beginning considered the constitutional question, the most serious question in these cases."[3]

Kavanaugh's assessment of the challenges facing the plaintiff served, not surprisingly, to highlight the importance of local counsel. Kavanaugh estimated that to show the imminent harm necessary to secure an injunction, attorneys would have to collect a "vast amount of statistical information" on economic loss to the private schools, information more readily accessible to local counsel, who were well connected with school administrators.[4] Kavanaugh advised Christie that his associates had, in fact, been accumulating this data for months. But the NCWC was adamant that Guthrie should direct all aspects of the litigation. Archbishop Dowling confided to Bishop Muldoon that he had been advised by an influential source that the Court may be disinclined to hear the case before 1926 unless it was argued by a respected litigator that had the "favor of the Court and their good will."[5]

As June drew to a close, events forced the NCWC to take action, despite Kavanaugh's warning that the case was not ready to be filed. In late June, Hill Military Academy made good on its postelection promise to challenge the School Bill and filed suit in federal district court in Oregon against Governor Walter M. Pierce, Attorney General Isaac H. Van Winkle, and Multnomah County district attorney Stanley Myers. The school asked the court to declare the law unconstitutional and issue an injunction restraining the defendants from "publicly threatening" to enforce the law. Represented by Portland attorney John C. Veatch, Hill Military alleged that the School Bill violated its constitutional rights by depriving the school of property without due process of law, denying it equal protection, and impairing the obligations of the school's contracts with parents and businesses.

Hill Military brought the plight of nonsectarian private schools to the School Bill challenge. The school combined Christian instruction with a military regimen, a popular educational model for young men. Founded in 1901 by Joseph Wood Hill, former headmaster of Portland's Episcopal Bishop Scott Academy, the school had struggled during World War I, with enrollment dipping to seven boys. To keep the school afloat, Hill took the unusual step of forming an honor guard of girls interested in assisting the war effort. Enrollment increased after the war, and Hill began an expensive expansion of the school to accommodate its elementary and college preparatory programs. Over 40 percent of the school's students attended its elementary school, which would be eliminated by the School Bill. The college preparatory program, although not directly affected by the School Bill, depended heavily on the patronage of students attending the elementary school. Enrollment in the school generally hovered around 100, the minimum Hill Military needed to stay in business, but applications dropped after passage of the School Bill, and some parents planned to withdraw their children prior to the start of the new school year. The principal of Hill Military, Joseph A. Hill, son of its founder, was well known in Portland and had worked tirelessly against the School Bill.

Who Should Be Plaintiffs?

The decision by Hill Military Academy to file suit did not take the NCWC completely by surprise, but it did complicate its litigation strategy. The Knights of Columbus had agreed to underwrite the litigation by Hill Military because it believed the lawsuit should include a nonsectarian plaintiff. As the Oregon state deputy of the Knights of Columbus explained, the challenge by Hill Military underscored the School Bill's threat to schools other than Catholic schools and served as "a very necessary auxiliary" to claims that would be brought by parochial schools.[6] The preemptive filing by Hill Military and the fact that the NCWC found out about the filing from the newspapers seemed to confirm Bishop Carroll's earlier fears that the Knights sought to control the case.[7] Kavanaugh had no choice but to act quickly. On July 19, Kavanaugh filed suit in federal court at the request of the NCWC, naming the Sisters as plaintiff.

Like the complaint brought by Hill Military, the Sisters' complaint alleged that the School Bill violated economic liberty interests, including property rights protected under the due process clause of the Fourteenth Amendment, and contractual obligations, prohibited from impairment by the state under Article I, Section 10, of the U.S. Constitution. Their complaint sought injunctive relief. The Sisters estimated the value of its six schools to be $595,000 and the equipment and personal property used by the schools to be worth $37,000. In addition to the concrete property losses threatened by the School Bill, the complaint also alleged that the law deprived the Sisters of the right to conduct their schools and deprived the teachers of their right to pursue their livelihood by teaching in private schools.

The Sisters' complaint went further than economic deprivation, charging that the law violated the right of parents to control and direct the education of their children and the right of children to attend private school, both personal liberties alleged to be protected by the Fourteenth Amendment. The complaint took an additional risk, asking the court to find that the School Bill interfered with the free exercise of religion protected as a "liberty" under the Fourteenth Amendment. The Supreme Court had held that the First Amendment limited only federal action and did not bind the states. The complaint did not specifically allege that the First Amendment's free exercise clause applied to the states. It instead asked the court to protect religious freedom as a "liberty" interest under the Fourteenth Amendment.

The filing of the complaint mobilized the Oregon Masons. Compulsory public education ranked as a national priority for the Masons, and they moved quickly to secure involvement in the case. Wallace McCamant, a highly respected former justice of the Oregon Supreme Court, represented the Masons. On August 24, he wrote to Oregon attorney general Isaac Van Winkle, attaching a copy of the Sisters' complaint. McCamant told Van Winkle that he understood the strategy of those attacking the School Bill. He anticipated that the Sisters would be adding as plaintiffs the name of "some parent who desires to send his children to parochial school" and the name of a specific teacher whose livelihood appeared threatened. McCamant recommended that they confer within two weeks and advised that "we should appear in one or more of these suits and move."[8]

Guthrie had his own ideas about the pleadings filed by the Sisters and by Hill Military Academy. He disapproved of Hill Military's narrow focus on property rights and advised Kavanaugh that the complaint filed by the military school was "not at all satisfactory." He wrote that Hill Military's filing left the Sisters little choice but to file an immediate pleading . Guthrie complimented Kavanaugh for moving so quickly to draft a complaint that "presents all the questions involved in the strongest aspect and in excellent form."[9]

Despite this praise, Guthrie directed Kavanaugh to amend the complaint. Guthrie shared Kavanaugh's concern that the court might be inclined to dismiss the suit as premature. Calling the issue a "quite delicate and difficult" question of procedure, he thought the Sisters should seek to persuade the court that the public interest would be best served by an early resolution. If the court delayed consideration of the law until its 1926 effective date, the private schools would have already suffered the loss of their pupils and the state and municipalities would have spent large sums to prepare the public schools for a large influx of students, expenditures that would be "wholly futile and wasteful" if the law was subsequently declared unconstitutional. Guthrie told Kavanaugh to collect data and statistics on the large public expenditures at stake and then file an amended complaint, which he believed would greatly strengthen the procedural argument and indirectly advance their arguments on the merits by demonstrating the substantial property interests impinged.[10]

Kavanaugh's amended bill of complaint, filed on December 22, detailed for the court the immediate harmful effects of the law, effects alleged to be directly injurious to parents, children, and private schools. The revised complaint asserted that the state already had threatened with prosecution any parents who continued to send their children to private schools after the effective date of the law. It also claimed that parents with children still in private schools suffered hostility and prejudice because the state implied these parents were unpatriotic for thwarting the spirit and intent of the law. Parents felt coerced to remove their children from private schools as soon as possible, to the detriment of the families and the schools. The economic harm resulting from this environment, the complaint alleged, had already injured parochial schools. The public reprobation dissuaded other parents from enrolling their children in private schools, as did the parents' quite reasonable anxiety that the prospect of having to change schools after three years would not be in the best interest of their children. In addition to the economic losses caused by parents abandoning the private schools, the Sisters also claimed that the law made it difficult to educate the students that remained, because banks were unwilling to loan money for essential repairs and equipment.

The economic adversity caused by the law extended beyond the private parties affected. The revised complaint alleged that the transfer of over 9,000 private school children into the public schools would cost the state over four million dollars in new expenditures.[11] The state, understandably, did not want this economic data as part of the record and moved to strike the information as irrelevant. After the filing of the amended complaint, Kavanaugh pushed Father Burke to generate publicity for the case. He particularly wanted the Associated Press covering the proceedings, to keep the case in the national spotlight.

The filing of the amended complaint sparked dispute within the NCWC over whether parents or teachers also should be included as plaintiffs. Without a parent in the suit the Court could refuse to hear the claim alleging violation of parental rights. The joinder of a teacher to the action would enhance the claim that the School Bill violated economic liberty. Father Burke, on his first reading of the amended complaint on January 3, 1924, wrote Guthrie immediately to question why the suit did not include a parent or a teacher. Burke assured Guthrie that he did not want to interfere with decisions involving legal strategy, but he inquired whether it would be safer to include an individual, a "human person, made by God," rather than to proceed with just a corporate plaintiff.[12]

Burke recommended that the litigation include a "human person" because he feared that without an individual plaintiff, the court would avoid the critical issue of the right to private education and instead render a decision based on the state's right to regulate corporations within its borders. Burke worried that a 1908 Supreme Court case, *Berea College v. Kentucky*, provided precedent for the court to uphold the state's extensive regulatory authority over its corporations and ignore the claims alleging deprivation of property or parental rights. In that case, Berea College challenged a state law that prohibited blacks and whites from attending the same school, whether public or private. The law clearly targeted the college, a private, racially integrated institution. The college argued that the statute unreasonably interfered with the economic rights of the school and its employees to earn a livelihood. The Court ducked the issue of economic liberty. It held that the law validly regulated the college because the school was created by state charter and could be regulated by the state as long as the state did not violate the original conditions of the charter.[13]

Guthrie, who left New York in early January for two weeks in Florida, asked Kavanaugh for an immediate opinion on the *Berea College* case. On January 5, Kavanaugh telegraphed Guthrie in Florida with his opinion that *Berea College* could be distinguished because, unlike Oregon law, the Kentucky Constitution reserved power to the state to alter the charter of any corporation.[14] Kavanaugh followed up with a lengthy legal analysis on January 8 that urged Guthrie to stay with the single, corporate plaintiff. Kavanaugh argued that the schools presented the strongest evidence of clear, existing, economic injury. He had been unable to find a teacher or a parent with a persuasive case for current injury, since the private schools still operated.

Guthrie agreed with Kavanaugh and, despite his conviction on the importance of parental rights to the case, concluded that the suit should be brought only by the Sisters. Guthrie's decision rested in part on his assessment that the Sisters suffered obvious economic harm. He also worried that the court could perceive the joinder of additional parties as an implied admission of legal weakness, a red flag that the private schools conceded expansive state authority over education and needed the presence of other parties to carry the challenge.[15] Arthur F. Mullen, who represented the schoolteacher in the *Meyer* case, strongly disagreed with Guthrie's strategy, publicly claiming that the failure to join individuals as plaintiffs weakened the case.[16] Kavanaugh, too, fretted about the wisdom of their decision.

The Masons' attorney, McCamant, surprised by the absence of parents as plaintiffs, recommended to Van Winkle that the state file a motion to dismiss the complaint, arguing both that the suit was premature and that the Sisters lacked the legal capacity to bring a claim on behalf of parents. McCamant had consolidated the Mason's influence on the case when the attorney general appointed him to assist in representing the state. The Masons agreed to continue to pay for McCamant's representation, relieving the state of any financial obligation and assuring protection of their interests.

Guthrie knew that the failure to join parents to the suit was risky, for any irregularities in the legal posture of that claim could give the Supreme Court an excuse to decide the case on other grounds. Guthrie recognized that the Court might be disinclined to look beyond well-established precedents protecting economic liberty. In a series of decisions, beginning in 1897 with *Allgeyer v. Louisiana* and reaching their apex with the era defining case *Lochner v. New York,* the Supreme Court, holding that the due process clause of the Fourteenth Amendment secured economic liberty, vigorously protected the right to contract, particularly the right to buy and sell labor, against state and federal efforts to regulate employment. The Court, hostile to efforts to restrict the free market, found most of the progressive legislation that came before it to be unconstitutional. It drew support for the constitutional protection of economic liberties from natural-law principles and from common-law precedents safeguarding economic interests.

The relationship between liberty and education was not a matter of first impression for the Court, however. Even before *Meyer,* as early as 1908, the *Berea College* case asked the Court to consider whether the Constitution protected the right of an individual to pursue literary and religious studies at the school of his or her choice.[17] Although the Court decided the case on other grounds, Justice Harlan, in dissent, chided the majority for avoiding the issue. He argued, "The capacity to impart instruction to others is given by the Almighty for beneficent purposes; and its use may not be forbidden or interfered with by government,—certainly not, unless such instruction is, in its nature, harmful to the public morals or imperils the public safety." Harlan identified the right to impart instruction as both a property right and a liberty "right of the citizen to be free in the enjoyment of all of his faculties." He described educational liberty as the right to impart and to receive instruction and argued that it was as significant as religious liberty. Justice Harlan concluded that interference with these rights would be an infringement of liberty "secured by the fundamental law."[18]

The Constitutional Argument for Parental Rights

The argument for specific constitutional recognition of parental rights stemmed from the same common-law and natural-law origins supporting economic liberties. Natural-law theory maintained that parents must be free to raise their children in order to assure the survival of the family, the core unit of society. Both John Locke and John Stuart Mill expounded on the obligation of parents to educate their offspring.[19] Blackstone described the duty and authority of parents under common law to maintain, protect, and educate their children.[20] English common law and early American law treated children as the property of their fathers, and fathers held rights, not only to the custody of their children, but also to their children's labor and earnings. As the patriarchal legal model receded, the common law continued to recognize the natural-law roots of parental duty and authority, including obligations to maintain, protect, and educate children. In 1870, in *People ex rel. O'Connell v. Turner,* the Illinois Supreme Court, in granting a father custody of his son who had been held in an institution for juveniles, observed,

> The parent has the right to the care, custody and assistance of his child. The duty to maintain and protect it, is a principle of natural law. . . . Another branch of parental duty, strongly inculcated by writers on natural law, is the education of children. To aid in the performance of these duties, and enforce obedience, parents have authority over them. . . . This power is an emanation from God, and every attempt to infringe upon it, except from dire necessity, should be resisted in all well governed States.[21]

Not all state courts held parental rights in such high esteem, however. The Supreme Court of Pennsylvania, in an 1839 case, *Ex parte Crouse,* rejected a father's claim for custody of his daughter detained in a juvenile institution, noting, "The right of parental control is a natural, but not an inalienable one. It is not excepted by the declaration of rights out of the subjects of ordinary legislation; and it consequently remains subject to the ordinary legislative power."[22] The Pennsylvania court's assessment highlighted the risk faced by advocates of parental rights. Even if common-law and natural-law principles supported parental rights, these rights could be subordinated to the state's considerable authority over children to protect their interests and secure their training. One court of the time described the relationship as follows:

> This rule is based upon the theory that the state must perpetuate itself, and good citizenship is essential to that end. Though nature gives to parents the right to the custody of their own children, and such right is scarcely less sa-

cred than the right to life and liberty, . . . yet among mankind, the necessity for government has forced the recognition of the rule that the perpetuity of the state is the first consideration, and parental authority itself is subordinate to this supreme power.[23]

In the Michigan campaign, the Lutheran leadership had acknowledged the absence of constitutional precedent protecting parental rights. In an internal memorandum, they outlined the risks of a court battle over the issue, concluding that the "situation would be different if parental rights were clearly outlined and guaranteed in the several Bills of Rights."[24]

Guthrie intended to rely on common-law and natural-law principles to convince the Court that *Meyer* should be solidified by a strong affirmation of parental rights. His predilection for parental rights was reinforced by his knowledge of Catholic canon, which articulated a divine and "inalienable" mission of parents to educate their children.[25] In December 1923, Father Burke wrote an enthusiastic letter to Guthrie, delighted that President Calvin Coolidge, in his first annual message to the country, on December 6, proclaimed that education "should always be pursued with the largest freedom of choice by students and parents." Burke was confident that the presidential declaration would help their case.[26]

CHAPTER 13   Take the Scholars

Just before Christmas, Kavanaugh telegraphed Guthrie that the federal district court had scheduled the hearing on the injunction for January 15, 1924. Guthrie, about to depart for Florida, replied by return mail with a lengthy letter outlining his strategy for the hearing. He expressed confidence that Kavanaugh would "comprehensibly and ably" represent the Society of the Sisters of the Holy Names of Jesus and Mary. But in the next line, he urged Kavanaugh to undertake exhaustive preparation and offered several recommendations on how the Oregon attorney could most fruitfully spend the long hours ahead. Guthrie's main concern was that Kavanaugh not overstate the limits on state authority over education. He believed the Sisters should not appear to be challenging the state's authority to regulate education but should stress only that the state lacked authority to prohibit all private education. This distinction was critical, Guthrie advised, because the courts had consistently upheld the authority of the state to compel school attendance and because the Supreme Court, in *Meyer,* reaffirmed that authority in no uncertain terms, stating that "the power of the State to compel attendance at some school, and to make reasonable regulations for all schools, . . . is not questioned." According to Guthrie, the Sisters should contest the "attempted *monopolization* of education by the State," which presents a "novel proposition in our day and in this country." Guthrie urged Kavanaugh to remind the court that "no government, however radical or revolutionary, has attempted to monopolize education except Soviet Russia."[1]

Guthrie counseled Kavanaugh to couple this carefully worded challenge with a vigorous defense of parental rights. Guthrie wrote that if the Sisters conceded the state's authority to reasonably regulate minimum educational requirements, the Supreme Court's decision in *Meyer* "is ample for our purposes," for the court "ought readily to accept" the parental liberty to choose private education as a logical result compelled by *Meyer*. Guthrie also wanted Kavanaugh to make clear to the federal court the potential national repercussions of upholding the School Bill. Kavanaugh had been busy collecting data on private schooling throughout the country, including statements from prominent educators on the significance of private education and the threat posed by the School Bill. That data could be used effectively to argue that the spread of legislation prohibiting private schools would impact far more than Catholic schools. Many of the great elite universities, such as Yale, Harvard, Columbia, and Princeton, not only selected their students primarily from private feeder schools but were themselves vulnerable to attack if the court upheld plenary state power over education.[2] As a matter of strategy, Guthrie believed that the "more we can show that Protestant and Jewish private schools will also be affected, the more persuasive our argument is likely to be."[3]

Guthrie followed up on this missive the very next day with highly positive legal developments that he believed resolved their pervasive anxiety about whether the court would find the lawsuit premature. Two recent Supreme Court decisions left him with far greater confidence about the outcome of the prematurity issue. In *Terrace v. Thompson,* issued only a week earlier, the Court held that an injunction could be sought to challenge the constitutionality of a law prior to the enforcement of the law where threatened enforcement infringed on the property rights of the plaintiff.[4] This case followed *Pennsylvania v. West Virginia,* a June decision from the Court that found that a request for an injunction against a state law was not premature where the injury was impending, for "one does not have to await the consummation of threatened injury to obtain preventive relief."[5] Guthrie advised Kavanaugh that if he relied on *Terrace* and *Pennsylvania,* "there ought to be no difficulty in meeting the question of alleged prematurity of the suit."[6]

Nonetheless, as the hearing approached, Kavanaugh continued to worry about this issue and the question of the Sisters' standing to bring claims on behalf of parents. He queried Guthrie on whether he knew of "any reason" why a corporation could not bring the claim. He fretted to Father Burke that he had learned that the Scottish Rite Masons intended to appear at the hearing as amicus curiae, complaining that it "is difficult to understand fully the relation of this body of Masons to this measure," particularly since the Masons he knew disavowed any knowledge of Mason involvement and, in fact, opposed the law.[7]

The Arguments for the Plaintiff

The Sisters' trial brief incorporated the points developed by Guthrie and Kavanaugh into a two-prong attack that challenged the constitutional legitimacy of the law and asserted the plaintiff's right to bring suit. The brief acknowledged the state's legitimate interests in regulating education and protecting children. But this authority, the brief argued, coexists with the rights of parents to educate their children and the rights of teachers and private schools to pursue their livelihoods. The School Bill failed the constitutional test of reasonableness because it eliminated private education.

The distinction drawn between the state's authority to regulate matters affecting individual liberty and its lack of authority to prohibit the exercise of rights found wide support in existing precedent. In numerous decisions protecting economic liberties, the Supreme Court repeatedly drew the line between permissible regulation and impermissible prohibition of economic activities. The Sisters' brief argued that the *Meyer* case made clear that the same principle limited the state's authority to prohibit parental access to private education.

The success of this argument rested on whether the Sisters could convince the court that the School Bill truly prohibited private education. Their brief admitted that the law did not explicitly ban private schooling, but it argued that the effect was the same. The brief contended that the School Bill "permits the schools but prohibits them from having scholars" and that by "taking the scholars the Act has effectively taken the schools."[8]

The Sisters' claim that the School Bill impaired the obligation of contract between the corporation and the state, in violation of the contracts clause of the federal constitution, also turned on similar questions. Impairment of contract could be found, based on precedent like *Dartmouth College v. Woodward,* if state legislation substantially interfered with the ability of a corporation to fulfill its chartered purposes and if the state lacked sufficient justification for the interference. The Sisters' alleged that the School Bill destroyed their status as an educational corporation. The court's decision on that issue would depend, in large part, on how it assessed the burden imposed by the law on the Sisters' educational mission. An impairment of contract claim, although a common challenge to economic legislation, generally proved to be more difficult to establish than a violation of economic liberty under the due process clause. So while the Sisters' brief developed the impairment argument, the heart of the case against the School Bill lay with the due process claims. To support the due process claims, the Sisters' brief drew heavily on *Meyer*'s recognition of parental rights and the economic interests of educators. Arguing that "there is no occasion to cite further authority" than *Meyer*, the Sisters claimed that the decision "is, therefore, conclusive on the points that the right to teach or conduct schools and the rights of parents to employ teachers or schools for their children are rights guaranteed ... by the Constitution."[9]

The brief also urged the court to view the state's justifications for the law with suspicion. Without specifically mentioning anti-Catholic sentiment, the brief nonetheless implied that prejudice fatally tainted the School Bill. It described as irrational the state's claim that the School Bill aided the enforcement of mandatory attendance requirements. The private schools already enforced mandatory attendance laws. This cannot be the real reason for the law, the brief suggested, and "perhaps the real reason is so clearly unlawful that counsel have not deemed it wise to put it forward." As to the melting-pot justification, the Sisters argued that the elimination of private schools would do little to achieve this goal, because "it is well known that the foreign emigration to this country is of the poorer classes whose children will and do attend the public schools, because they cannot afford to pay the tuition at the private schools." According to the Sisters, a true melting pot in education could only be achieved by establishing "certain quotas from all races and creeds to each public school; or by compelling certain quotas of people from all races and creeds and conditions in life to make their residences in each public school district." *Meyer* rejected the melting-pot argument, the brief explained, when the Court, despite its acknowledgment of the importance of assimilation, concluded that the state lacked the authority to prohibit German-language instruction. If *Meyer* holds that German-language instruction cannot be banned in the furtherance of assimilation, the Sisters argued, surely the more drastic step of eliminating private schools must also fail. Why, the brief asked, is the patriotism of the private schools now questioned when private school students so valiantly served their country? The compulsory public education movement, the Sisters concluded, "does not spring from patriotic motives; it is based on motives less noble, and no pretense can obscure its real purpose."[10]

Meyer also formed the core of the Sisters' argument on their right to bring suit. In *Meyer,* the teacher successfully claimed not only that the Nebraska law violated his economic liberty but also that it deprived parents of their rights to employ him. The rule established in *Meyer* and numerous other cases, the Sisters argued, permitted an individual, including a corporation, to question a law that violated the constitutional liberties of another person, as long as that violation resulted in injury to the complainant. They contended that the School Bill, by penalizing the parents rather than directly closing the private schools, was "an attempt to accomplish by indirection what could not be directly done." On the question of whether the timing of the suit was premature, the Sisters admitted that "there is no exact precedent," but they then claimed, "neither is there any precedent against it." The threat of imminent harm required to bring suit and seek an injunction was a "relative" term, the brief asserted. Arguing that the "enforcement of this law, unless restrained, is as certain as anything in human affairs ever is," the Sisters declared fanciful the state's insistence that there was still time for the legislature to meet and repeal the law before it went into effect. The legislature had met in 1923 and had not even considered repealing the law. The brief claimed that the "gradual process of decay contemplated for the private schools" had already commenced, rendering them "moribund institutions" with a "sentence of death" hanging over their heads.[11]

The brief closed by linking the School Bill case to profound political issues. Claiming that "no case of greater moment was ever heard in an Oregon Court, and, few, if any, in any court of this country," the Sisters urged that far more was at stake than the fate of private schools in Oregon. Basic questions of liberty and human rights were "as surely up for determination here as in the celebrated case of Dred Scott," because the court must decide whether the "Government is instituted for the people, or the people are here simply for the exaltation and greater glory of the Government." With a thinly veiled reference to the nationalist fervor sweeping the country, the brief concluded that the country was facing a parting of the ways, where it must choose between "Spartan ideals" and the ideals of a free republic.[12]

Hill Military Academy submitted a short brief that, for the most part, replicated the economic harms alleged by the Sisters. It disputed the state's claim that assimilation goals justified the School Bill, pointing out that over

85 percent of Oregonians were native born. Of the remaining 15 percent, over half of the foreign-born residents were already citizens. Since over 95 percent of Oregon schoolchildren already attended public schools, even if all the children of the foreign-born went to private schools, far more of these children would still be in public schools. The academy's brief argued that mandatory public education would not break down social barriers and improve tolerance, because "antagonistic groups" based on wealth, creed, or social status are not formed in elementary school, where "the banker's son will wrestle with the garbage man's boy . . . and will play with the little negro or Chinaman without a thought of his ancestry." It is only later, after childhood, contended the brief, that "we . . . draw a line between the white and black, the rich and the poor, and those who look at life from our viewpoint and those who have the temerity to take another view."[13]

The State Response

The state filed a brief arguing that the plaintiffs had failed to establish the imminent harm necessary to obtain an injunction. The state also moved to dismiss the complaint filed by Hill Military, asserting that the academy had not alleged sufficient facts to support its claim. In its brief, the state argued that the School Bill affected the plaintiffs only "indirectly and collaterally." The state maintained that the plaintiffs had "no right to complain" about the School Bill, because they suffered only minimal or indirect harm from the law. This "incidental harm," the state argued, did not violate economic liberty or impair contract obligations. The state invoked federalism, urging the federal court to refrain from deciding the constitutionality of the law until Oregon state courts had reviewed it.

The state defended the School Bill primarily by asking the court to defer to the will of the Oregon voters, who had decided that compelled public education promoted assimilation and good citizenship. Their decision was sound, the state argued, because "there is no neighborhood in or about the city of Portland in which the children of the poor and of the rich will not mingle in the public schools." The state claimed its authority over curriculum and teacher qualifications justified compelled public schooling. Not all private schools may be as competent as those run by the plaintiffs, the state insisted. Nor can private educators be controlled as thoroughly as public schools, where if "a vicious textbook finds entrance to them there is an easy remedy." The state failed to respond fully to the parental rights claim. Instead, it discussed numerous cases, unrelated to education and typically involving challenges to protective labor legislation, where courts found the rights of parents to be subordinated to the "supreme" right of the state as guardians, or *parens patriae*. The brief offered scant consideration of *Meyer,* with the state simply asserting that the case did not control because, unlike the law in *Meyer,* the School Bill did not prohibit the teaching of any subject.[14] When the state saw how extensively the plaintiffs relied on *Meyer,* it submitted a supplemental brief arguing that *Meyer* should be distinguished because the law in Nebraska was already in effect. The state never squarely addressed the significance of *Meyer*'s limitation on state authority over education. That oversight weakened their argument.

The state took the unusual step of raising the religious liberty argument in its brief against Hill Military, even though it was the Sisters, not Hill Military, who claimed the School Bill violated religious liberty. The state first argued that the First Amendment protection of religious liberty did not apply to the states. It then launched into an extensive discussion of the meaning of religious liberty, citing state cases that unsuccessfully challenged Sunday closing laws and those that upheld restrictions on polygamy and wearing of religious garb in public schools. The government, the state argued, may limit religious conduct, so long as it does not interfere with religious belief. No malevolence, religious hatred, or prejudice animated the measure, the state insisted.[15] But in its brief against the Sisters, the state undermined its purported neutrality, arguing that the electorate could legitimately conclude that "children of every form of religious belief will be more tolerant . . . if they mingle with children whose religious beliefs are different from their own."[16] With this provocative statement, the state submitted the School Bill to the federal court.

CHAPTER 14   An Extravagance
in Simile

A three-judge panel, required by federal law when an injunction was sought against a state law on the grounds of unconstitutionality, convened the morning of January 15, with both the Sisters and Hill Military Academy present through counsel.[1] The panel consisted of Ninth Circuit judge William B. Gilbert and district judges Charles E. Wolverton and Robert S. Bean. Wolverton and Bean, both in their seventies, had been friends for over 50 years. Their friendship began in college and flourished when they served together on the Oregon Supreme Court. Wolverton was appointed the federal district judge for Oregon in 1905, and when Congress added a second U.S. district court seat in 1909, Wolverton welcomed his friend Bean, who was confirmed for the new position.

The judges had consolidated the Sisters' case with the complaint of Hill Military Academy. They combined the hearing for the injunction with the hearing on the state's motion to dismiss, so that all the challenges could be heard together. As it turned out, while the state had filed a motion to strike part of the Sisters' complaint and had advised Kavanaugh that it would file a motion to dismiss, it ultimately chose to file a motion to dismiss only against Hill Military, claiming that Hill Military failed to allege facts demonstrating the harm required for equitable relief.

The hearing did not get off to a good start for the Sisters. Wallace McCamant stood immediately to address the court. Kavanaugh expected the esteemed McCamant to appear as amicus curiae on behalf of the Masons, but McCamant had other plans. Although he informed the court, "I should say prefatory to my argument that I appear here primarily as the representative and at the instance of the Scottish Rite Masonic bodies," McCamant disclosed that he was "relieved from the necessity of appearing as a friend of the Court," because he had been asked to represent Governor Pierce, the attorney general, and the district attorney at the hearing. He offered the court two letters from these officers, appointing him as counsel for the state and the county district attorney.[2] McCamant's appointment as government counsel allowed him to move beyond the limited participation allowed to an amicus curiae and to enter fully into the case as counsel for the defendants.

Judge Gilbert accepted McCamant's appointment and asked him to address first the motion to dismiss against Hill Military. The motion to dismiss went to the heart of the prematurity problem, with the state claiming that the case should not proceed because Hill Military had failed to demonstrate how the School Bill caused them present, as compared to future, harm. Judge Gilbert's decision meant that the Sisters would not be heard on this pivotal issue. Kavanaugh rose to his feet, interrupting McCamant, and requested the court to postpone consideration of the motion. Citing a recent federal case, Kavanaugh asked the court to defer substantive challenges to the case until the court decided whether to grant a temporary injunction against the law. Judge Bean was unimpressed, pointing out, as did McCamant, that the issues on the motion to dismiss were similar to those on the preliminary injunction and directly concerned the court's jurisdiction to hear the case, for "if the Court does not have jurisdiction it will have to take note of that fact." Judge Gilbert agreed. "It may be that this is a case in which there is no jurisdiction to proceed," he told Kavanaugh. "If so, we want to know that first."[3]

McCamant presented the state's case precisely as Guthrie and Kavanaugh anticipated. He argued for dismissal on two grounds: the court lacked authority to determine the constitutionality of a statute before it goes into effect; and Hill Military failed to allege current harm from the law. McCamant told the court that the Supreme Court had never ruled on constitutional challenges to a statute before its effective date. He distinguished *Terrace* and *Pennsylvania,* the two cases that so impressed Guthrie, as involving statutes that were legally in effect but not yet enforced.

Judge Gilbert offered McCamant an easy opening on the factual dispute, asking whether Hill Military's complaint alleged "any facts, or any acts that are being done by the defendants?" The sloppy pleading by Hill Military, short on factual details, allowed McCamant to contend that the school failed to state facts showing real, as opposed to speculative, harm to contracts, property, or enrollment. Although the Sisters were not part of the motion to dismiss, McCamant did admit that their complaint included more detailed, but still insufficient, allegations of harm. Even if the court found the factual allegations adequate, the injury asserted was not actionable, he argued, because the School Bill did not directly regulate the plaintiffs; it did not close the private schools; it did not take their property. The plaintiffs, to the extent they could factually support any harm, suffered merely "a diminution of their patronage, and that is all."[4]

McCamant closed his argument with an attack on both plaintiffs, disputing the standing of the schools to raise claims concerning the rights of parents, economic or otherwise. He offered the court a long list of Supreme Court cases limiting standing to those parties who suffer the constitutional harm alleged. McCamant concluded by advising the court that the prospect of a ruling allowing corporations to bring claims on behalf of parents "is beyond my comprehension."[5]

John C. Veatch, attorney for Hill Military, moved immediately to counter the prematurity claim, arguing that "it makes no difference whether it is two days or two years" before a law goes into effect, as long as present damage can be shown. He contended that the school's ongoing decline in enrollment, alleged in the complaint, sufficiently demonstrated existing harm to its property rights. Veatch spoke briefly, using far less time than the one hour allowed each party. Kavanaugh rose as soon as Veatch sat down, asking the court for an opportunity to speak, insisting his client "ought" to be heard because any ruling on the motion against Hill Military could affect the Sisters' case. Without waiting for the court's response, he plunged into his rebuttal of McCamant's argument.[6]

The three-year delay before the effective date of the statute presented a "novel" question for the court, Kavanaugh admitted, but one that he thought equity could address. He asked whether the schools were "obliged to wait until some one chooses to violate that law before they can have redress from a clearly unconstitutional statute." Kavanaugh turned to Judge Gilbert and Judge Wolverton, reminding them of a recent case where they had enjoined a statute several months before the law became effective, because they concluded that real and imminent injury existed. No enterprise, claimed Kavanaugh, that depends on public patronage could survive with the "sword of Damocles" hanging over its head. Equity jurisdiction allowed the court wide discretion, and it should not delay judgment on a law that is unconstitutional and, by a delayed effective date, "may bleed a plaintiff white" before judgment is rendered.

Kavanaugh disputed McCamant's contention that the law did not directly injure the schools. The only reason for the suspended effective date, Kavanaugh insisted, was to give the public schools time to prepare for the influx of new students. Equity "is not afraid of new questions," he argued, contending that the court has a duty to consider the impact of the law prior to its effective date. Kavanaugh spoke at length about the "appalling" injury done by the Oregon law to the great institution of private schooling, which was older than the nation and responsible for educating and inspiring its founders. As the afternoon session drew to a close, Kavanaugh concluded by asking the court to deny the motion to dismiss filed against Hill Military, for although "the motion is not directed against our complaint, if you sustain, it will have an effect upon ours that would be detrimental."[7]

The Plaintiffs Argue against State Monopoly of Education

The court adjourned until 2:00, when it returned to hear the challenge to the constitutionality of the School Bill. Kavanaugh heeded Guthrie's advice and began with a vigorous defense of the state's authority to regulate education: "And let me say here that we favor distinctly compulsory education; we favor state regulation; we invite the fullest inspection and regulation, and the fixing of minimum standards in the education of the young and in all forms of education." But the School Bill, argued Kavanaugh, did not constitute legitimate regulation, because there existed no evidence that the private schools failed to provide competent, patriotic education. "There is no evil to be remedied," Kavanaugh contended, and without evidence of harm from private education, the law arbitrarily and unreasonably interfered with certain "natural and inherent rights."[8] These natural-law rights, which "existed before constitutions were made," included the rights of parents to direct the education of their children, the rights of teachers to pursue a livelihood, the rights of children to receive an education, and the rights of the schools to pursue education as a business. The Fourteenth Amendment protected these liberties, Kavanaugh claimed, and precedent made clear that the state police power must yield to the Constitution. Otherwise, the Constitution "would be a light extinguished, a broken shield and a scrap of paper."[9]

Kavanaugh drew extensively from a wealth of Supreme Court precedent grounded in *Lochner,* quoting long passages from opinions supporting economic liberties against state regulation. State regulation of economic rights, to survive constitutional challenge, he argued, must be justified by a necessity, by an evil that Oregon had failed to prove. The School Bill reached beyond regulation to prohibition, for the sole purpose of giving the state a monopoly of education. Drawing from Guthrie's notes, Kavanaugh advised the court that a ruling upholding the School Bill threatened the great private universities, such as Yale and Harvard, for state monopoly power over education must rationally include authority over higher education. Linking state monopoly of education to tyranny, in what would become a recurring theme of the case, Kavanaugh charged, "There is no country of the world, save one, which undertakes to have a monopoly of education, . . . and that is soviet Russia." Courts can be trusted not to "look through a glass darkly," he claimed, and not to be "confused or deceived" by prohibitions masquerading as regulation.[10]

Kavanaugh shifted his argument to *Meyer,* telling the court that "there is one recent decision . . . which sets at rest, and forever, all questions urged in favor of the constitutionality of this act." He began to read aloud the Supreme Court's opinion. Judge Gilbert finally interrupted, requesting he refrain from taking the court's time to read the opinions "in extenso," because the court "would prefer to read them itself." "Then I shall refrain from reading that," Kavanaugh announced, moving on to the merits.[11]

Kavanaugh drew from *Meyer* what he argued was a simple and undebatable principle: by protecting the right of private schools to teach in a foreign language, the Court necessarily implied that it supported the right of private schools to exist. Kavanaugh questioned whether the district court wanted to risk challenging the analysis of the Supreme Court: "Does it need any argument to convince you that where the highest Court of this land prohibits . . . regulation as a violation of the constitutional right of that institution, that a State can, then, in the light of that decision, prohibit the existence of that institution entirely?"[12] He closed his argument with an appeal to the wisdom of the judges before him, who had spent their "fruitful years" in the "temple of justice" and who had "grown gray" in their "sanctuary." The judges know that alarms about patriotism "come and go" in waves, but why, Kavanaugh implored, aim this fear "at the little ones," whose natural impulse, in all innocence, is to love their country. The danger comes not from the children, he concluded, but from persons far older in years, who present a "blight upon our civilization."[13]

Veatch rose to speak for Hill Military, arguing that the court should find the law unreasonable; the state offered no evidence that private schools failed either to educate or to produce good citizens. Walking the court through the official ballot explanations for the initiative, Veatch disputed that Oregon struggled with assimilation. Oregon "has no foreign born problem," he said, because 45 percent of the population are white natives. The state, Veatch pointed out, presented no evidence that the children of the foreign-born even attend private school, and since 95 percent of Oregon children already go to public schools, the 5 percent forced into the public system by the law were unlikely to advance assimilation. Whatever deficiencies in instruction existed in the private school—and Veatch once again noted that the state had failed to introduce any evidence of inadequate instruction—should be addressed, said Veatch, by reasonable regulation, not destruction of private education. Veatch, too, willingly conceded the extensive power of the state over education. He went further than Kavanaugh, suggesting that the state could prescribe the textbooks used in private schools. Veatch did, however, urge the court not to draw parallels between the School Bill and laws mandating school attendance, commenting that "everybody believes in compulsory education, and it [the School Bill] has nothing to do with it at all."[14]

The State Has the Power

McCamant spoke first for the state, and he surveyed the packed courtroom before he began. McCamant strategically sought to shift the court from thinking about constitutional rights to focusing on the justifications for the law. To this end, he sought to minimize the impact of the law on the private schools, while at the same time arguing that the state's comprehensive authority over education, as well as its substantial interest in assimilating immigrants, warranted whatever intrusion on the schools the state deemed appropriate. The plaintiffs' arguments are irrelevant, McCamant told the court, because they suffer from a misapprehension about the School Bill: the initiative could not reasonably be construed as prohibiting the operation

of private schools, since they were "nowhere mentioned in the statute."
Children could attend private school after they completed their day at public school, he argued, or before they reached age eight. He concluded that the "indirect" impact on the plaintiff did not constitute a legal injury.[15]

McCamant delved extensively into the history of the Fourteenth Amendment, arguing that the Constitution does not protect parental rights. He relied heavily on the analysis in the *Slaughter-House Cases,* which found the Fourteenth Amendment was intended primarily to prevent discrimination against the newly emancipated "Negro." Although McCamant acknowledged that the Supreme Court had since extended the reach of the amendment beyond racial discrimination, he insisted that the court must "inevitably" recognize the "utter impossibility" that the framers of the Fourteenth Amendment intended that the "hand of the State should be stayed" from requiring children to attend public schools.[16] *Meyer,* McCamant argued, should not be viewed as expanding the meaning of the Fourteenth Amendment to protect parental rights. *Meyer* protected the contractual rights of the teacher to pursue a living by teaching in German; it thus fit neatly within precedent protecting economic liberty. The Court's discussion of parental liberty in *Meyer* constituted no more than dicta, unessential to the holding and of no significant weight.

McCamant pressed his argument on state authority, telling the court that the proven right of the state to insist on mandatory school attendance ineluctably led to a ruling upholding the School Bill. The state, McCamant contended, has wide discretion in selecting the most appropriate means of exercising its authority over education: if the state concludes that public schools provide the best means of assuring that children receive the kind of education envisioned by the state, the state is within its police power to mandate public education. The educational vision of the state should be accorded particular deference in this case, McCamant claimed, because of the patriotic necessity for the law. The School Bill, he warned in closing, was intended "to meet one of our great national dangers. . . . the great danger overshadowing all others which confronts the American people is the danger of class hatred." To McCamant, the state's response to this danger should be clear and unequivocal, because "history will demonstrate . . . that it is the rock upon which many a republic has been broken."[17]

Stanley Myers, district attorney for Portland's Multnomah County and himself a named defendant in the case, stood to ask the court's permission to speak, prompting Judge Bean to ask Myers who he represented. After

Myers identified himself, Judge Bean gave him permission to close the government's argument. Myers's summary, offered without consultation with the state, damaged McCamant's carefully constructed argument. The court should be tolerant in its review of the School Bill, Myers urged, because the initiative was not prepared by experts. Myers claimed that the law represented the will of the people to consolidate all education into one public system. By admitting that the School Bill was intended to consolidate all schooling into the public system, Myers contradicted a key point in McCamant's argument, for McCamant had insisted that the law did not eliminate private schooling.

Myers asked the court to be lenient also in evaluating whether the School Bill actually furthered assimilation. This argument brought Dan J. Malarkey, part of Kavanaugh's team, to his feet. Claiming to speak not only for the Sisters but for the millions of patriotic American parents who want the best for their children, Malarkey suggested that the court should review the initiative with less, rather than more, deference, because the "waves of intolerance and bigotry passing over this country" created a greater danger of unconstitutional acts undertaken by the people at large rather than by the legislatures.[18]

Malarkey, the last to speak, waited until the end of his argument to raise the *Meyer* decision. He bluntly suggested that the Supreme Court was well aware of the School Bill case when it decided *Meyer*. Beginning, "Now don't forget . . . ," he reminded the court that *Meyer* was decided only last June, after passage of the School Bill, and that Supreme Court justices "are men as well as judges." If the Supreme Court believed that the state had the power to abolish private education, it would have decided *Meyer* differently, Malarkey insisted: it would have held that the greater authority to abolish private schools included the lesser power of prohibiting foreign-language education in private schools. But the language in the opinion repudiating the Spartan model of plenary state authority over children made clear, according to Malarkey, that the Supreme Court rejected state monopoly of education. Malarkey closed the hearing by suggesting to the court that the "flames" of class hatred would only be fueled if a "dominant majority undertakes to compel parents to surrender this right that they have exercised since the dawn of history."[19]

Guthrie reviewed the transcript from the hearing as soon as it was prepared, and he wrote Kavanaugh that he was pleased with the presentation on behalf of their client. He complimented both Kavanaugh and Malarkey for their excellent arguments, which "fully covered" the controlling aspects of the case. Guthrie remained convinced, however, that Veatch was not up to the task, finding his oral presentation as disappointing as his complaint, especially when he conceded the state's authority to dictate textbook selection to private schools, which Guthrie thought went too far. Guthrie expressed great relief that Kavanaugh had taken the "laboring oar" and put the Sisters in control of the case. He found the government's presentation weak. For Guthrie, the high point of the hearing occurred when Myers contradicted McCamant on the critical issue of whether the law would eliminate private education.[20] Father Burke also reviewed the transcript and accompanying briefs. Confiding to Guthrie that he concurred with Guthrie's assessment, Burke noted in particular that he believed Myers "gave away his case."[21]

The District Court Ruling

Ten weeks after the hearing, on March 31, the district court convened to announce its decision. Kavanaugh moved to the counsel table through a courtroom "crowded to suffocation." Among the crowd, he felt a "tensity of feeling that cannot well be described," of which he later said, "In all of my years in Portland I have never seen its like." Multiple conversations blended into an "irritating" noise and then dissipated to silence when the judges entered the courtroom.[22] The Scottish Rite Mason leaders who sponsored the School Bill sat confidently in the front row. Their faces hardened when Judge Wolverton read the court's unanimous opinion aloud, declaring the School Bill unconstitutional and granting the request for an injunction. Shocked at the decision, the Masons quickly left the courtroom. Oregon newspapers rushed out special editions, carrying the full text of the decision, and the story flashed all over the country.

The court sided with the plaintiffs on all points. Judge Wolverton's opinion readily found that the equitable jurisdiction of the court to issue an injunction extended to instances of threatened enforcement that would cause irreparable harm. The question of whether the threatened harm justified an injunction more than two years prior to enforcement, however, presented one of the most "searching" issues for the court. The court accepted the plaintiffs' argument that despite the remote effective date, the "work of destruction of complainants' occupation has already set in." Noting that "parents are looking to the future," the court found that the School Bill imposed direct and immediate consequences on the plaintiffs through the loss of patronage, which will continue with "increased progression until the day when all will be lost."[23] Equity, the court stated, exists precisely to protect parties from threatened irremediable injury and does not require delay until consummation of the harm. The government in fact admitted the likelihood of serious harm, the court determined, by setting the effective date several years away.

The court struggled far less with the issue of whether the schools had standing to raise the constitutional rights of the parents. It found the constitutional rights of the schools and the parents integrally connected, because the schools were dependent on the support of the parents to sustain their businesses. The court thus deemed it appropriate to look not only at whether the schools suffered infringement of their constitutional rights but also at whether the parents incurred constitutional injury, for an injury to the parents would adversely affect the schools. The court concluded that the harm to the schools could occur from invasion of their constitutional rights, from invasion of their patrons' rights, or from invasion of both.

Although the court recognized the legitimacy of parental rights throughout the opinion, the decision rested primarily on the safely grounded precedent of economic liberties. Relying on *Meyer,* the court described the parental rights at stake primarily as economic ones—the right of the parents to contract with the schools to educate their children. The court took no risk with precedent, ignoring the Sisters' claim that the School Bill violated religious liberty.

The court conceded the state's authority to require mandatory attendance. But the power to compel attendance did not include the authority to compel public education. The state had failed to present evidence justifying the elimination of private schools. As Guthrie had argued, the court found that the state may regulate business but not destroy it. Concluding that the School Bill was intended to destroy private education and would achieve that goal, the court stated, with some sarcasm, that the "act could not be more effective for utterly destroying the business and occupation of complainants' schools . . . if it had been entitled 'An Act to prevent parochial and private schools from teaching the grammar grades.'" Suggesting that one need look no further than the official ballot statement in support of the School Bill— "A divided school can no more succeed than a divided nation"—to understand the destructive intent of the measure, the court held that the state had abused its regulatory authority by prohibiting the exercise of a legitimate business.[24] Private schools, existing from time immemorial, have an absolute right to conduct their business, the court found, unless the state could prove they constituted a menace. The state's assimilation argument utterly failed to impress the court. While the state may have a legitimate interest in assimilation, the means adopted—the elimination of private education—was arbitrary and unreasonable, given the small number of children who were foreign born or of foreign-born parents. The court concluded with a withering critique of the School Bill, dismissing the melting-pot justification for the law as "an extravagance in simile."[25]

The next day, April 1, McCamant wrote to Assistant Attorney General Willis Moore that he was "of course greatly disappointed" by the decision. McCamant had already researched the deadline for an appeal to the U.S. Supreme Court. Federal law authorized a direct appeal to the Supreme Court, allowing an appellant to bypass the circuit court of appeals in certain cases, including cases in which a state law is claimed to violate the federal constitution. Acknowledging that the state would have to weigh the merits of an appeal, McCamant nonetheless suggested that the state had a "duty owing to the Oregon electorate to carry a matter so important as this through to the court of last resort."[26]

The Oregon press generally greeted the decision with a belated righteousness. Those papers that had been reluctant to attack the School Bill now rushed to call the decision "expected." The *Oregon Journal* relaxed its grudging opposition to the measure. Admitting that the problem of illiteracy in America raised questions as to whether the country could afford to "lock the door of any schoolhouse," it concluded that the lower court "probably" got it right. The *Oregonian* stuck its neck out to predict that the schools also would prevail at the Supreme Court.[27] But not all papers supported the decision, and their criticisms were infused with bigotry. The *Riddle Enterprise* ceded the first round to the "Holy Names" but predicted that the majority would prevail. An editorial in the *Grants Pass Spokesman* wondered "why foreign minorities in America are ever listened to by our courts, when they endeavor to cancel issues Americans vote in."[28]

The decision garnered nationwide attention. The story made the front page of the *New York Times* on April 1. That paper's April 2 editorial typified the national response, casting the decision as the victory of individual liberty over statism. Claiming that "one finds no precedent for this law in the statutes of other American States," the editorial identified the Soviet Russian system as the nearest analogy. Despite the importance of assimilation, it argued, a policy of compulsion violates the "very first principle of individual freedom." Describing the district court decision as "so sound as to make unlikely any reversal," the editorial concluded by observing that the decision, if sustained by the Supreme Court, "will have its greatest value in protecting the parental right against a socialist invasion."[29]

The newspapers were not alone in their belated condemnation of the School Bill. The decision profoundly affected the people of Oregon. Kavanaugh described the relief and goodwill generated by the decision as unlike anything he had ever experienced. The ruling punctured the aura of Klan power in Oregon, and the public mood shifted from fear to optimism. Kavanaugh saw fellow Catholics raise their heads with a confidence missing since the passage of the School Bill. He wrote to Guthrie early in April that he believed the Oregon era of pandering to the Klan was ending.[30]

By April 21, Guthrie had written an analysis of the Oregon law and litigation for *Columbia Magazine*. In it, Guthrie blamed anti-Catholicism for the success of the initiative and expressed profound regret that the great Masonic fraternity aligned with the Ku Klux Klan. He cautioned citizens throughout the states to resist the pernicious advance of intolerance and bigotry and to take from the Oregon experience a lesson of the dangers of assuming that one religion or one race has a monopoly on patriotism or virtue.[31]

A tone of finality ran through Guthrie's article, as if the case truly had been resolved. But Guthrie knew, as did everyone involved in the School Bill litigation, that the district court decision played only as a prelude to the final coda. In April, Willis Moore informed McCamant that the state had decided to appeal.[32] On June 30, Oregon filed an appeal with the U.S. Supreme Court.

CHAPTER 15   Final Duty and Power

In an impassioned letter to Gaetano Cardinal DeLai, secretary of the influential Consistorial Congregation, Archbishop Hanna apprised the Vatican of the significance of the School Bill litigation before the Supreme Court: "No matter has presented such a critical issue in the well-being of the Roman Catholic Church in the United States as the legislation successfully enacted by the State of Oregon." Hanna assured the papacy that the NCWC had "labored unceasingly" on the case.[1] Guthrie had already met with the papal secretary of state, Pietro Cardinal Gasparri, in Rome to convey the same message.

The NCWC, cautiously confident after the Oregon district court's decision, had not lost sight of the implications of an adverse decision by the Supreme Court. With efforts to enact laws compelling public education already underway in Washington, Michigan, Nebraska, and Indiana, the NCWC predicted that these states, in addition to Oklahoma, Texas, and Illinois, would be the first to legislate. Maine, Colorado, Iowa, Missouri, the Dakotas, and Montana also seemed likely to adopt compelled public schooling. The NCWC worried that a ruling upholding the Oregon law would embolden Protestants to push for greater presence of a "Protestant form" of religion in the public schools. A memo to NCWC general secretary Father Burke even recommended that the church consider whether it could accept readings of portions of the Old Testament in public schools. A change of church position on this bitterly contested matter would create goodwill with the Protestants and perhaps deflate campaigns for compulsory public schooling.[2]

Guthrie urged the NCWC to launch a national, but quiet, publicity campaign favorable to the School Bill challenge. He claimed the country should be informed about the significance of the case. Guthrie worked closely with the NCWC to orchestrate public relations prior to the Supreme Court hearing. At his request, the NCWC printed and widely distributed pamphlets containing the Oregon law and the lower court's decision. Guthrie insisted that the pamphlet contain no references to the NCWC or arguments against the law. He wanted people around the country to read the district court's opinion, but he did not want to give the opposition reason to print their own pamphlet.

Guthrie also knew how easily public opinion could turn sour. He cautioned the NCWC to keep tight control on public statements made by Catholics. Referring to a letter from Kavanaugh filled with bitter comments about Oregon Masons, Guthrie urged Father Burke to ensure that the contents remained confidential. Worried that hostile words by Catholics would inflame the many prominent Masons throughout the country, Guthrie warned that Catholics should be careful not to arouse enmity while the suit was pending before the Supreme Court. The time would come, Guthrie assured Burke, for expressing "just resentment" against the School Bill sponsors, but any confrontation at this stage would be "wholly unnecessary" and damaging to their case.[3] In several additional letters and telephone conversations, Guthrie reiterated to Burke the importance of avoiding public comment until completion of the oral argument, lamenting that they had "surely suffered enough in the past from the writings and sayings of indiscreet and incompetent advocates."[4] Guthrie's orchestration of public relations was fairly novel for the times and became a model in litigation concerning public policy.

Preparations for the Supreme Court

Despite the early disputes over Kavanaugh's role in the litigation, he remained on the appellate team, responsible for preparing the Sisters' brief against the Oregon attorney general. Kavanaugh, who would be making his first appearance before the Supreme Court, applied to be admitted to the Supreme Court Bar. Guthrie communicated frequently with Kavanaugh, peppering him with questions about Oregon. Not content to rely solely on Kavanaugh's expertise, Guthrie immersed himself in the state's history and politics. In a letter to Father Ryan, Guthrie revealed his limited understanding of Oregon politics when he requested Ryan to verify whether Governor Pierce was elected as the Klan candidate. Guthrie's inquiry was, however, surprisingly pertinent. Pierce's relationship with the Klan—rocky from the last days of the 1922 campaign, when he distanced himself from the School Bill—had soured dramatically. Late in 1923, the Klan and a number of leading businessmen organized a movement to recall Pierce. Both groups charged Pierce with "bad faith" for repudiating campaign promises. By January 1925, the *Oregonian* would report on a confrontation between Pierce and Klan Grand Dragon Fred Gifford, where Gifford returned honors awarded by Pierce to fourteen Klansmen for service to the state and informed Pierce that he was "through" with him.[5]

Van Winkle asked McCamant to help with the state appeal, but only if the Masons would continue to pay for his services. McCamant acknowledged in June that his client, the Supreme Council of the Scottish Rite, was "deeply interested in the litigation and will undoubtedly put forth some effort in the Supreme Court."[6] The Masons wanted McCamant to remain part of the litigation team, but they had not yet decided whether they wanted their counsel to be listed publicly as attorney of record for the defendants. McCamant agreed to participate but, for the time being, keep his name off the legal documents. He reached an agreement with Governor Pierce to split the costs, with the state bearing the expense of preparing and printing the record on appeal while the Scottish Rite covered the cost of the Supreme Court briefs.

Events outside Oregon influenced the legal preparations. During the summer of 1924, a wanton murder by two sons of privilege, Nathan Leopold and Richard Loeb, obsessed the nation. As Clarence Darrow waged a battle in the press and the courts to save the young defendants from execution the public debated the social and genetic sources of criminal behavior. The "trial of the century" surfaced in the briefs of both the Sisters and the state, as each side sought to use the controversy to its advantage. Guthrie, arguing that religious schools provide moral education essential to good citizenship, wrote that "only recently a revolting murder was perpetrated for sport and in cynical disregard of all that was right by two educated young sons belonging to respectable families," who, despite being "amply educated . . . by parents of large means, had no religious or moral training worthy of the name."[7] His argument backfired, however, when the governor closed his supplemental brief by quoting this passage and pointedly concluding, "The fact was that these young men had been educated in private schools." Guthrie, now worried that the education of Leopold and Loeb might be raised by the state at the Supreme Court hearing, asked Father Burke to seek information about the defendants' academic records from Rev. Leo Kalmer, Catholic chaplain of the prison in Joliet, Illinois, where the youths were imprisoned.[8]

Public relations occupied others interested in the School Bill case. The Lutheran Schools Committee, embroiled in an ongoing debate, dating from the early days of the litigation, on whether it should participate in the case, finally decided in the summer of 1924 not to seek intervention. Advised by counsel that they could only participate at this late date by submitting an amicus brief, the committee concluded that they would gain little from the expense they would incur. But more than financial concerns affected their decision. The committee had considered engaging Arthur F. Mullen, lead counsel in the *Meyer* case, to represent them, going so far as to draft an employment agreement. But the negotiations fell apart when the committee learned that Mullen was a Catholic. Unwilling to be perceived as "making common cause" with the Catholics, the committee agreed that retaining Mullen would offend prominent Lutherans, some of whom took umbrage when the Lutherans simply borrowed lists of registered voters from the Catholics during the School Bill campaign. Despite cordial relationships during the campaign, the Lutherans sought to distance themselves from public alliance with the Catholics and they rejected a Catholic offer to underwrite litigation expenses if they would agree to join a Lutheran school as a party to the case.[9]

In the summer of 1924, with preparations for the Supreme Court hearing underway, Guthrie sailed to Europe for an extended rest. His friend, Justice Sutherland, was already in London and Guthrie hoped to see him. On July 9, before Guthrie departed, he cabled the clerk of the Supreme Court, William R. Stansbury, to request the London address of Sutherland. Stansbury telegraphed Guthrie that same day with instructions to contact Sutherland through the bankers Brown, Shipley & Co.

Guthrie returned from Europe at the end of September, and on October 1, he wrote Stansbury to inquire when the Court would hear the School Bill case. Stansbury replied that the Court was unlikely to hear the case for another year, even though the case was docketed for the October 1924 term. Stansbury's response spurred both sides of the dispute to action, and on December 8, they filed a joint motion to advance the case on the Court's docket. The motion urged the Court to hear the case as expeditiously as possible, so that the people of Oregon would know the fate of the private schools and could plan accordingly. Stansbury arranged for a Washington, D.C., attorney, Robert Ash, to argue the motion on behalf of the parties. The Court granted the motion on December 16 and assigned the case for argument on February 24, 1925.

The state intended to file two briefs with the Court, one on behalf of the governor and the second in the name of the attorney general. In December, the Masons retained Washington, D.C., attorney George Chamberlain to represent Governor Pierce. Chamberlain, widely respected in both Oregon and Washington, was a veteran of 12 years in the U.S. Senate, a former two-term governor of Oregon, and a former attorney general of Oregon. Chamberlain disliked Governor Pierce, but he was a Mason, and the Masons brought him into the litigation and paid for his services. Some initial confusion existed between Chamberlain and Attorney General Van Winkle as to Chamberlain's role. On December 10, Van Winkle wired Chamberlain a note explaining his understanding that the Masons hired Chamberlain to appear on the state's behalf and prepare an amicus brief. Van Winkle made a point of confirming that his office was in charge of preparing the official briefs for the state. Chamberlain responded by return mail, "Am I to understand from that, that you will object to my appearance with you as one of the attorneys for the State." Chamberlain explained that he had only agreed to represent Pierce because he "assumed of course that it would be agreeable to your office."[10]

Van Winkle did not reply, and Chamberlain sought clarification again in early January, writing that his brief was ready to go to the printer. Van Winkle wrote immediately, attributing the previous delay to political considerations; Governor Pierce had been conferring with Mason leader P. S. Malcolm on Chamberlain's role. Van Winkle proposed that Chamberlain appear only on behalf of the governor, "so long as no financial liability . . . attaches to the State of Oregon." He assured Chamberlain that "it is personally a pleasure to me to have your association and assistance in this important and somewhat loaded litigation."[11] This arrangement proved acceptable to Chamberlain, who told Van Winkle, "It has not been my purpose to look to the State of Oregon for compensation in this matter." Chamberlain wrote that his brief explored the constitutional issues in depth and that he had concluded that if the Supreme Court did not reverse the trial court, "the effect will be to deprive the States of one of their most important reserve powers."[12] Van Winkle approved of Chamberlain's brief, writing his congratulations on the expertise with which he presented the law.

Guthrie saw little to appreciate in Chamberlain's brief, describing it as the most "objectionable" of those submitted by the state. Guthrie took offense at what he perceived as anti-Catholic statements, where Chamberlain suggested that voters might reasonably perceive religious schools as a threat to domestic security. Guthrie asked Father Ryan to investigate Chamberlain further, particularly any connections Chamberlain might have to the Klan. Ryan's sources advised him that Chamberlain abhorred the Klan and maintained excellent relations with the Roman Catholic Church. Chamberlain, Ryan believed, had not penned the offending language but had included arguments in his brief prepared by less-judicious Oregon attorneys.

National interest in the case kept the Supreme Court clerk, Stansbury, busy responding to numerous requests from members of Congress, attorneys, and the general public on the date scheduled for the hearing. Stansbury also fielded letters from various people inquiring as to how they could submit arguments to the Court on the case. He gave all the same advice: they could seek to appear as amicus curiae through the consent of all the parties or through the approval of the Court. One supporter of compulsory public education from the Michigan campaign, E. W. Cornell, skeptical that all parties would consent to his request, asked Stansbury to suggest how Cornell could "get around" that requirement. Stansbury's polite reply declined to offer the assistance Cornell requested, and Cornell, like most who sought to "do my bit," dropped the matter.[13]

Stansbury won the appreciation of Guthrie for the "many courtesies" received from the clerk's office. On January 13, 1925, Guthrie sent Stansbury two volumes of Guthrie's collected speeches, which he hoped Stansbury would accept as a "memento." In the cover letter, Guthrie also asked Stansbury how to respond to the numerous requests Guthrie had received regarding submission of amicus briefs. He closed his letter with a more personal request. Explaining how he had been "favorably impressed" with the young clerks in Stansbury's office, who seemed "unusually alert, willing, accurate and courteous," Guthrie asked Stansbury to recommend a "young man between twenty and thirty" willing to relocate to New York to work for Guthrie with an "idea of studying law here."[14] Stansbury's response, thanking Guthrie for the gift and outlining the procedure for obtaining consent to submit an amicus brief, offered an insider's advice: "While the Court apparently obeys the admonition of St. Paul to suffer fools gladly, it does recognize the right of counsel to resent the intrusion of strangers and self-constituted advisers of the Court." Stansbury ended his letter with regrets that none of his current clerks were "so situated" to take advantage of Guthrie's "very advantageous offer of employment."[15]

At the end of January, the parties received notice that the case had been delayed until the March 2 calendar, where it sat as the thirty-sixth case for consideration by the Court. The uncertainty as to when the case would be heard caused concern among Oregon counsel, particularly the attorney general, who was in the middle of a legislative session. Stansbury estimated that the case would not be heard before March 9 and would probably be heard later. Guthrie used the additional time to refine his brief and argument. Although he included in the brief a thorough discussion of Oregon schools, including Catholic institutions, Guthrie omitted many of the statistics collected by the NCWC on Catholic education around the country, concluding that it was unwise to chart the "phenomenal" national growth of Catholic schools, which served over a million and a half students and held millions of dollars in property. Guthrie feared that this data might, "unconsciously to them, touch upon some latent apprehension on the part of some of the Justices" that such growth should be "checked, for fear of ultimate domination of Catholic influences."[16]

Guthrie also ultimately excluded from his brief an argument that he had drafted asking the Court to review an initiative measure with closer scrutiny than it would a statute passed by the legislature. He thought he could convince the Court that the deference it normally accords a legislative enactment, which is presumed the product of research and deliberation, should not apply when it reviews initiatives. But he ended up rejecting this argument as "dangerous," deciding it could backfire if the Court took it as a concession that laws compelling public education were valid as long as they were passed by a legislative body. Private schools would be protected, Guthrie concluded, only if the Court found that compulsory public education was unconstitutional, regardless of the process by which it was adopted.[17]

The Taft Court

Guthrie's successful amicus brief in the *Meyer* case dictated the Supreme Court litigation strategy for the Sisters. By persuading the Court to view state restrictions on foreign-language teaching in the broader context of state efforts to monopolize education, Guthrie believed he had laid the groundwork to convince the Court to reject compelled public schooling. His assessment of the Court and the predilections of the justices merited credibility, for even as Guthrie prepared the brief for the Sisters, President Calvin Coolidge was considering him for a seat on the Supreme Court. On January 5, 1925, Justice Joseph McKenna retired from the Court, and President Coolidge sought recommendations for McKenna's replacement from his friend, Columbia University president Nicholas Murray Butler. Butler recommended as candidates Columbia Law School alumni Guthrie, state appellate judge Benjamin Cardozo, and former Columbia Law School dean and then U.S. attorney general Harlan Fiske Stone. Coolidge rejected 66-year-old Guthrie as too old and passed over Cardozo because the Court already had one Jew, Louis D. Brandeis. He nominated Stone, who was confirmed and took the bench on March 2, in time to hear the oral arguments in the School Bill case.[18] The replacement of the Catholic and pragmatic centrist McKenna with the more liberal Stone marked the latest shift in a Court adjusting to five new members in as many years, beginning with President Warren G. Harding's appointment of Chief Justice William Howard Taft in 1921.

President Harding survived only two short years of his presidency, but in that brief time, he made his mark on the Supreme Court, with the appointment of four justices, including Chief Justice Taft. Harding, a Republican who swept the 1920 presidential election in a massive landslide, promised a country weary from war and political turmoil a "return to normalcy," and his appointments to the Supreme Court reflected his desire to move the country away from the intrusive presence of government necessitated by the war. Taft, who bears the unique distinction of being the only former president to serve also as chief justice, saw his lifelong ambition realized when he became chief justice, for he coveted that position more than the presidency. According to Felix Frankfurter (then a professor and later a justice), Taft, who came to the Court "a very rusty lawyer indeed," exercised strong leadership.[19] He assigned to himself many of the Court's major constitutional decisions. Taft, like Harding, distrusted progressive legislation as "socialistic raids upon property rights." He had argued, prior to the 1920 election, "There is no greater domestic issue than the maintenance of the Supreme Court as the bulwark to enforce the guaranty that no man shall be deprived of his property without due process of law."[20]

Taft was soon joined on the Court by three new justices with well-established conservative credentials, George Sutherland in 1922 and Pierce Butler and Edward Terry Sanford in 1923. Justices Sutherland and Butler joined with sitting conservatives James C. McReynolds and Willis Van Devanter to form an antiregulatory voting bloc. Criticized as the "Four Horsemen of the Apocalypse" because of their persistent admonishments that progressive legislation threatened democracy, they controlled the outcome of most of the major cases before the Court. Justice McReynolds, who wrote both the *Meyer* and *Pierce* decisions, had a reputation for disagreeableness. He was also an infamous anti-Semite, who refused to speak to Justice Brandeis. The appointment of Justice Stone in 1925 did little to shift the balance on the Court, leaving Stone generally in the minority, with Justices Louis D. Brandeis and Oliver Wendell Holmes, Jr. To Taft and the other conservative justices, the "return to normalcy" meant a reinvigorated commitment by the Court to Lochnerian principles of limited governmental power over the individual, particularly in economic regulation.

The Taft Court zealously embraced these precedents, and it invalidated social and economic legislation with an enthusiasm missing during the prewar and war years. Felix Frankfurter parsed the Court's precedents during the years of Woodrow Wilson's presidency (1913–21) and the tenure of Chief Justice Edward D. White as a "period in which the Court was more tolerant toward legislation, less prone to write its own social-economic views into the Constitution."[21] But the war rekindled "the fear of change, the fear of new ideas," and from 1920 to 1926, the Court struck down legislation in a significantly higher percentage of cases than in the entire previous 52 years since the ratification of the Fourteenth Amendment.[22] Taft and his fellow conservatives argued that an expansive reading of liberty was consistent with "the highest and most useful functions of courts," because "it is the exercise of a sound judicial discretion in supplementing the provisions of constitutions and laws and custom, which are necessarily incomplete or lacking in detail essential to their proper application, especially to new facts and situations constantly arising." As Taft explained, the Supreme Court bore the ultimate responsibility for preventing the majority from committing the fundamental error of seeking "quick action in making changes of policy," which could lead to "disastrous changes in which the proposed remedy may be worse than the evil." The Constitution entrusted the Court with the "final duty and power" to protect the individual against the sovereign people.[23]

The Court's nearly obsessive constitutional focus on contract and property rights was due, in part, to the elitist predilections of its conservative members, who viewed progressive legislation as little more than abhorred efforts to redistribute wealth. Influential scholar Roscoe Pound, writing in 1909, typified many critics of the Court's *Lochner* doctrine when he depicted the Court as beholden to "an individualist conception of justice, which exaggerates the importance of property and of contract, [and] exaggerates private right at the expense of public right."[24] This image, although accurate, depicts only part of the larger canvas painted by the Court.

The Court's zealous protection of economic liberties evinced a broader constitutional concern. Its aggressive deployment of contractual liberty derived primarily from its deeply antistatist perspective. To the Taft Court, the protection of liberty served a normative function, assuring that the individual retained the autonomy essential to democratic governance. The danger of the developing regulatory state lay in its power to standardize personal relations, jeopardizing individuality. This antipathy toward government regulation took on sharpened focus during the 1920s. The international spread of communist and socialist doctrine gave the conservative justices a heightened political sensitivity to the attributes of state autocracy. Justice Holmes perceived a Court preoccupied with the fear that the expansion of government authority into everyday life imperiled democracy. He criticized the conservative majority on the Court for allowing its hatred of socialism to drive constitutional doctrine: "When twenty years ago a vague terror went over the earth and the word socialism began to be heard, I thought and still think that fear was translated into doctrines that had no proper place in the Constitution or the common law."[25]

The Taft Court found particular reason to be hostile to the growth of regulatory power. State and federal legislation had increased dramatically during the Wilson presidency and World War I. That growth, coupled with the spread of labor unrest and domestic radicalism, troubled the conservative bloc, who saw the constitutional framework endangered by social "experimentation." Taft argued that the "very purpose" of the Constitution was "to prevent experimentation with the fundamental rights of the individual."[26] In *Adkins v. Children's Hospital,* where the Court invalidated a law setting a minimum wage for women, Justice Sutherland explained how limiting state power served the constitutional design: "To sustain the individual freedom of action contemplated by the Constitution is not to strike down the common good but to exalt it."[27] By the 1920s, the surge of the regulatory state threatened to become a torrent, and the Court conservatives saw the Court positioned as the bulwark between democracy and socialism.

The ideological divide on the Taft Court derived from dramatically different views on the constitutional legitimacy of the regulatory state and the dangers posed by legislative "experimentation." The conservatives on the Court, as around the country, often saw little difference between progressive legislation and socialist policy. The common conservative criticism of progressive proposals sought to align even modest reforms with radicalism. Playing on national fears, they ridiculed them as "socialist, progressive, bolshevist," a chant occasionally heard from Chief Justice Taft. By contrast, Justice Brandeis claimed that democracy needed experimentation to thrive. Brandeis and his colleague Justice Holmes embraced a more limited role for the Court, stressing deference to reasonable legislative policy. As Brandeis explained, "the rights of property and the liberty of the individual must be remolded from time to time, to meet the changing needs of society."[28] For this position, he earned Taft's disdain for being a "muckraker, . . . a Socialist."[29]

The progressive imprint on federal and state education policy made education reforms a particular thorn in the side of antistatists. *Meyer* revealed the Court's skepticism of the progressive agenda for education. Both the opinion and the oral argument demonstrate the antistatist predilections of the Court. The *Pierce* case offered the Court an opportunity to define more clearly the limits of state power over education.

Fourteenth Amendment Liberty and Parental Rights

Guthrie remained convinced that the success of the Sisters' suit could rest on the Court's willingness to protect parental rights. Since the lower court found that the School Bill violated economic liberties, the Sisters, along with Hill Military, fully addressed the economic injuries they suffered as a result of the law. But Guthrie did not want a decision from the Court that could leave the church in the position of fighting a state-by-state battle against compulsory public education, with the outcome dependent on the parochial schools proving economic harm. A decision based on parental rights would destroy the movement for compulsory public education.

Guthrie believed that the Court stood poised to constitutionalize parental rights. *Meyer* may have marked the first time the Court had extended Fourteenth Amendment liberty beyond economic concerns. But the

Court had never specifically limited its definition to economic rights. To the contrary, the Court typically embraced an expansive definition of liberty. In one of the earliest cases interpreting the Fourteenth Amendment, *United States v. Cruikshank,* the Court concluded that the Fourteenth Amendment "furnishes an additional guaranty against any encroachment by the States upon the fundamental rights which belong to every citizen as a member of society."[30]

The Court's interpretation of the Fourteenth Amendment was not always so generous. Only two years earlier than *Cruikshank,* in the *Slaughter-House Cases,* the Court rejected the argument that the privileges and immunities clause of the Fourteenth Amendment protects fundamental rights from state interference.[31] Over time, the Court compensated for its stunted view of the privileges and immunities clause with a far more sweeping construction of the due process clause. In *Allgeyer v. Louisiana,* the Court described the liberty protected by the Fourteenth Amendment in expansive terms, as "not only the right of the citizen to be free from the mere physical restraint of his person" but also "the right of the citizen to be free in the enjoyment of all his faculties; to be free to use them in all lawful ways."[32] In *Meyer,* the Court expanded this definition to include the right of the individual "to acquire useful knowledge, to marry, establish a home and bring up children."[33] But the decision in *Meyer* ultimately rested on the teacher's right to contract and on the right of parents to engage the teacher for foreign-language instruction. *Meyer* left unclear how far the Court would be willing to go to protect parental liberty, particularly whether the Court would be willing to hold that a statute specifically violated constitutionally protected parental rights, quite apart from any economic liberties involved.

Guthrie's litigation strategy shrewdly sought to appeal to the conservative Court's respect for traditional family relationships. Guthrie explained to Father Ryan that he found it "extremely important that the writings of philosophers and pedagogues should be carefully examined and extracts made wherever they deal with the subjects of parental control over the education of children and state monopoly of education." Guthrie had already discussed and distinguished Plato in his amicus brief in *Meyer,* but he wanted the Sisters' brief to examine the modern pedagogical and philosophical essays. He intended to "lay before the court the consensus of opinion on this subject as it may have crystallized through the years." The weight of such evidence, Guthrie was convinced, would "be of great, if not controlling, importance."[34]

The key element of their strategy lay in persuading the Court that parental rights possessed a long and distinguished common-law pedigree worthy of constitutional recognition. The Fourteenth Amendment's protection of "liberty" offers no textual insights into which interests qualify as constitutional liberties. The Court often looks to history and tradition as a guide in this difficult interpretive exercise. It is not unusual for the justices to rely on common law to determine whether an alleged liberty deserved constitutional protection. As the Court explains in *Meyer*, liberty includes the right of an individual "generally to enjoy those privileges long recognized at common law as essential to the orderly pursuit of happiness by free men."[35]

Indeed, the Court's seeming willingness to "constitutionalize" common-law rights proved to be the source of some its most fervent criticisms. Contemporary scholars, such as Roscoe Pound, argued that the Court engaged in a profoundly misguided interpretation of the Constitution when it was willing to elevate the broad range of common-law property rights into constitutional liberties. Pound perceived this error as due to a "deep conviction by American lawyers that common law doctrines are part of the universal jural order." To Pound, the Court misused common law in constitutional analysis and compounded this folly by insisting that its interpretation was justified by the natural-law foundations of the Bill of Rights. Natural-law rights, as Pound argued, had no discernible limits, and the extensive domain of natural-law and common-law rights, if constitutionalized by the Court, left scant room for valid legislation.[36]

Guthrie, who had won several cases on economic liberty before the Court by emphasizing common-law and natural-law principles, was confident he could persuade the Court to consider the substantial common-law heritage supporting parental rights. Thus, the Sisters' Supreme Court strategy rested on the same essential arguments made at the trial court: that the law was arbitrary because the state lacked sufficient justification for the measure and that the School Bill unreasonably interfered with parental rights and economic liberties protected by the Fourteenth Amendment.

CHAPTER 16   The Little Red Schoolhouse

While the schools stayed with the strategy that had proved successful at the district court, the state's appellate case departed dramatically from its position at trial on two major issues—that the schools lacked standing to assert parental rights and that the case was premature. After vigorously insisting at the trial court that the case should be dismissed because of these flaws, and after including these issues as part of the state's assignments of error to the Court, the attorney general's brief inexplicably waived standing and prematurity arguments, advising the Court that the "manifest interest" of all would best be served if the Court disregarded all "technical questions" and focused on the constitutional liberty question.[1] The brief for the governor did not specifically waive these challenges. It did, however, omit any argument about prematurity of the case. It did not emphasize the dispute over standing. The governor took less than two pages to argue that the schools lacked the capacity to bring arguments on behalf of the parents.

Why the state decided to omit or minimize the standing and prematurity challenges is not clear. Existing precedent offered reasonable arguments for both the state and the schools. The district court had in fact admitted that its finding that the suit was not premature was one of the most difficult in the case. The state's waiver or de-emphasis of these issues did not change their relevance to the case. Perhaps the state concluded its strategy would shift the Court's focus away from the economic harm suffered by the schools. If so, the state miscalculated. The Court's equitable jurisdiction to issue an injunction against the School Bill existed only if the Court found that "irreparable harm" would occur without the injunction. This analysis required the Court to consider both the question of prematurity of the suit and the question of who will be injured by the law. Similarly, the Court could assert jurisdiction to resolve the constitutional challenge to the School Bill only if at least one of the schools had standing to sue. Thus the state's decision not to emphasize standing or prematurity did not dissuade the schools from addressing these issues in their briefs. Both Guthrie and Kavanaugh developed the issues at length, and Hill Military Academy argued that the state's threatened enforcement of the law disposed of any questions of prematurity.

The State's Position before the Court

The state's omission of any serious consideration of standing and prematurity meant that its briefs focused almost exclusively on two points: that the School Bill did not violate any protected rights of the schools or the parents and that the Court should defer to state authority over educational policy. The brief for the governor began by asserting that the corporate status of the schools precluded any claim to constitutional liberty. It argued that the question of the schools' liberty interests "is very quickly disposed of," because the Fourteenth Amendment protects only natural, not artificial persons. The argument made by the governor had some merit, although the trial court had rejected it. The Court had vigorously protected personal economic and property interests, but it had not addressed explicitly the scope of corporate liberty. The brief for the governor relied on two Supreme Court cases that flatly stated that Fourteenth Amendment liberty is guaranteed only to natural persons. But these cases involved corporate claims to be free from allegedly burdensome regulation and did not directly concern economic or property interests. As Guthrie responded in the brief for the Sisters, one of the plaintiffs in the cluster of cases decided by *Meyer* was a corporation. In *Meyer*, the Court did not discuss the school's corporate status, but it also did not distinguish the corporate plaintiff from the individual plaintiffs when it found that the English-only laws violated their constitutional rights.

The governor's brief spent little time on parental rights, calling the Fourteenth Amendment's due process clause the "most overworked portion" of the Constitution. Acknowledging that parents may have some liberty interest in the education of their children, it insisted that parental rights were subordinate to the "paramount" right of the state to exercise control over minors. The brief gave scant credence to the language in *Meyer* substantiating parental rights. Instead, it argued that the "dicta in this case would appear to be somewhat broader than can be supported by the previous decisions of the United States Supreme Court." The *Meyer* dicta should not be taken too seriously, the brief asserted; elevating parental rights to constitutional status would allow federal courts to intrude into the sphere of domestic relations clearly assigned by the Constitution to the states. No prior Supreme Court decision, the governor's brief claimed, contained "any expression of opinion that the Fourteenth Amendment gives the Federal Courts any power to interfere between a state and its citizens relative to questions of religion, education, or domestic relations including the question of the division of the power of control over children between their parents and the state." To further neutralize *Meyer,* the brief for the governor emphasized the well-established precedents validating state authority over education, maintaining that the School Bill was simply another example of a law consistent with the dictum in *Meyer* recognizing the "power of the state to compel attendance . . . and to make reasonable regulations for all schools." This power, the governor argued, prevailed over personal liberty interests.[2]

In its briefs, as it did at trial, the state argued that the School Bill did not cause legal harm to the schools. The law does not prohibit private schools from operating, the state claimed, it merely deprives them of some prospective students. Even if economic injury occurs, concluded the state, due process is satisfied when the state acts within the sphere of its legitimate regulatory authority over education.

Van Winkle filed a supplemental brief, on the advice of McCamant, to argue specifically that the Court should defer to the state's judgment on educational policy. McCamant, after reviewing the state's initial briefs, urged Van Winkle to stress that compulsory public education constituted a permissible means for the state to assure educational quality. He wrote to Van Winkle that "there can be no doubt that if the state has the power to require the education of all children within its bounds, it has the right to adopt such regulations as will make this education effective." McCamant had submitted a supplemental brief to the trial court on precisely this point, and he recommended that Van Winkle revise the earlier document and submit it to the Court. McCamant thought this reasoning would appeal at least to Justices Holmes and Sutherland, who dissented in *Meyer*, and he told Van Winkle, "I believe there are men on the supreme court who would be interested in this argument."[3] The supplemental brief filed by the attorney general tracked McCamant's recommendations, arguing that it is the legislature's prerogative to determine how the state will assure satisfaction of minimum education requirements and that without this authority, mandatory school attendance would be a "farce."

The heart of the case lay in persuading the Court where the state's authority over education should end. Both sides understood this, and they made the relationship between education and democracy a central theme in their briefs. Both sides invoked the threat posed by radical, antidemocratic isms—socialism, communism, bolshevism, syndicalism. They cast these political themes into the language of constitutional conflict, with each side invoking a different constitutional crisis. The state claimed that public school indoctrination furthered the government's substantial interest in assimilation. The schools, in turn, argued that such indoctrination destroyed essential democratic values. The governor asserted that the state's interest in "Americanizing its new immigrants and developing them into patriotic and law-abiding citizens" justified the law. Reminding the Court that the vast majority of private schools maintain religious affiliations, the state asked the Court to contemplate not only existing private schools but private schools that might flourish in the future if the School Bill was held unconstitutional.

> They may be followed, however, by those organized and controlled by believers in certain economic doctrines entirely destructive of the fundamentals of our government.
>
> If the Oregon School Law is held to be unconstitutional it is not only a possibility but almost a certainty that within a few years the great centers of population in our country will be dotted with elementary schools which instead of being red on the outside will be red on the inside.
>
> Can it be contended that there is no way in which a state can prevent the entire education of a considerable portion of its future citizens being controlled and conducted by bolshevists, syndicalists and communists?[4]

The governor's brief made clear the risk to national security presented by an educational system unfettered by state control, arguing that there would be "nothing to prevent the establishment of private schools, the main purpose of which will be to teach disloyalty to the United States or at least the theory of the moral duty to refuse to aid the United States even in the case of a defensive war." The damage to democracy could be substantial, the state cautioned, for "it is hard to assign any limits to the injurious effect, from the standpoint of American patriotism, which may result."[5] The brief dramatically invoked national security but offered no evidence that private schools posed any risk to political stability.

Taken together, the state's briefs made a vigorous defense of plenary state authority over education. But the state underestimated both the significance of *Meyer* and the antistatist predilections of the Court. *Meyer* had already undermined the state's assertion of sweeping and comprehensive power over education. The state misjudged the Court's enthusiasm for protecting liberty by its dismissive treatment of the due process clause and parental rights.

The Sisters' Argument from Democracy

Not surprisingly, Guthrie's brief for the Sisters presented a very different picture of the threat to freedom confronting the Court. It expanded on the themes of democracy and parental liberty developed by his amicus brief in *Meyer,* arguing that state monopoly of education jeopardized democratic principles. The Sisters did not dispute the state's legitimate authority over many aspects of education, including mandatory school attendance, curriculum, and teacher credentials. Guthrie included with the brief an exhaustive appendix summarizing state laws regulating education, including mandated patriotism instruction. But the brief flatly denied that subversive or inferior education by private schools justified the School Bill. The state failed, the Sisters argued, to provide any evidence that private schools teach "disloyalty and subversive radicalism or bolshevism." Even if the risk of such "evil" was real and not merely a "chimera" conjured by the state, they contended, there was no justification for destruction of private schools: patriotism could be ensured by regulating curricula and by proper licensing of schools and teachers. The message of the *Meyer* case was that educational diversity should be regulated, not prohibited. Compulsory public education, the brief insisted, crossed the line into autocracy.

Guthrie marshaled writings in philosophy, history, law, and education to support the Sisters' depiction of democracy, and he quoted at length from such scholars as John Stuart Mill, Chancellor Kent, and Herbert Spencer. The brief denounced the Oregon law for embodying the "pernicious policy of state monopoly of education" and argued that this policy met with "universal condemnation," for "except in Soviet Russia, there has been none in modern time so poor as to do that discarded doctrine of tyrants any reverence." Playing on the comparison between Russia and the Oregon law, the brief claimed that before Oregon enacted the School Bill and before Soviet Russia embraced state monopoly of education, the "total absorption of the individual in the body politic and his entire subjection to the state" would have been politically unacceptable.[6]

The Sisters' specific comparison of the Oregon law to Sovietism provoked an angry response from the state, submitted in a supplemental brief. Oregon disingenuously complained that "the cry of Bolshevism" had been overused by special interests, invoked to stigmatize almost any unpopular policy or person. The state claimed that national security would suffer, like the little boy who cried wolf, because the "great mass" of people in the country would come to lose their fear of Bolshevism.[7]

Guthrie focused the core of his brief on persuading the Court of the link between democracy and parental rights. Claiming that "children are, in the end, what men and women live for," Guthrie portrayed parental rights as "the essence of liberty." His brief contended that America treasured this liberty, exalting the family, and that Americans understood that "in this day and under our civilization, the child of man is his parent's child and not the state's." Guthrie continued to press the contrast between American democracy and autocratic forms of government. Describing Plato's ideal commonwealth as creating a "state-bred monster," he argued,

> It need, therefore, not excite our wonder that today no country holds parenthood in so slight esteem as did Plato or the Spartans—except Soviet Russia. There children do belong to the state. . . . In the final analysis, it is submitted, the enactment in suit is in consonance only with the communistic and bolshevistic ideals now obtaining in Russia, and not with those of free government and American conceptions of liberty.[8]

What a counterpoint Russia was to America, Guthrie claimed, where "children mean everything" and parents live "under the blessings of free institutions and of the Constitution which guarantees them." In America, he wrote, it is natural for parents to be "tenderly solicitous" about their children's education and "keenly zealous" of their own right to guide and control it. Guthrie closed his argument on parental rights by offering the Court a justification for extending constitutional liberty beyond economic concerns. After quoting extensively from the Court's cases concerning economic liberty, Guthrie argued that the Court should find parental rights protected by the Constitution because "the right to engage in a business, to teach, to acquire knowledge, to contract . . . verily shrink into relative inconsequence" when compared to parental rights.[9]

The briefs prepared for the Sisters demonstrated the depth of Guthrie's expertise, both in his command of constitutional doctrine and in his knowledge of the Court. Guthrie's attack on state monopoly of education played directly on the Court's hostility toward intrusive government regulation. He also understood that *Meyer* clearly opened the door to parental rights. Guthrie used the Sisters' brief to convince the Court that the rich common-law history of parental rights justified constitutional protection.

Delicate Questions of Religious Liberty

Religion and religious intolerance surfaced in the briefs, baring the subtext of bigotry underlying the School Bill. Guthrie's brief for the Sisters avoided a specific argument that the School Bill violated religious liberty. Guthrie thought that the Court was unlikely to rest the opinion on religious liberty; there was no precedent holding that the federal constitution restrained states from interfering with religious liberty. With the secular Hill Military Academy a plaintiff, the Court would not be forced to consider the issue. Guthrie doubted that the Court would address such a controversial matter unless it had no choice.

Prior to the ratification of the Fourteenth Amendment in 1868, the Supreme Court had been very clear that the First Amendment restricted only the exercise of federal power. In *Permoli v. Municipality No. 1 of the City of New Orleans,* the Court held it lacked jurisdiction to resolve the plaintiff's claim that a municipal ordinance prohibiting Catholics from displaying corpses in church violated religious liberty under the federal constitution. Dismissing the claim, the Court concluded that the Constitution "makes no provision for protecting the citizens of the respective states in their religious liberties." The Court explained that "this is left to the state constitutions and laws," adding, "nor is there any inhibition imposed by the Constitution of the United States in this respect on the states."[10]

After ratification, advocates for federal constitutional protection of religious liberty from state interference argued that such protection could be found in the language of the Fourteenth Amendment prohibiting a state from depriving a person of "liberty" without due process of law. However, the Supreme Court cases offered little support for federal nullification of state laws that burdened religion. As recently as 1922, in *Prudential Ins. Co. v. Cheek,* the Court had rejected an argument that the Fourteenth Amendment imposed on states any restrictions concerning the freedom of speech. The Court had shown little inclination to make the significant shift in constitutional doctrine necessary to decide *Pierce* based on religious liberty. Guthrie knew that attacking the School Bill as a violation of religious liberty presented risks; if the Court adopted a narrow construction of religious liberty, it could have consequences far beyond education.

The Sisters' brief instead addressed religious liberty by arguing that religious choice was an essential aspect of parental rights. Describing parents' "tenderly solicitous" feelings about their children's education, the brief claimed, "What more natural, also, than that we should desire them to be taught our own faith, to cherish whatever religion we accept, to hold fast to the moral precepts taught with or in our own creed, and to learn these things from teachers of our own choosing?" Such instruction, the brief explained, is "not to be found in the public schools."[11] Indeed, the Sisters argued, the parental interest in guiding children both intellectually and religiously is the heart of parental choice. Educational choice is essential to freedom of religion, the brief insisted, for free exercise "implies teaching as well as worship."[12] The brief turned the state's argument about patriotism on its head, arguing that the moral instruction important to a law-abiding citizenry is best attained through religious education. References to religious freedom appeared throughout the brief, describing the connection between religious tolerance and democratic principles.

The key argument about religious liberty arose defensively. George Chamberlain's brief for the governor asserted that the School Bill legitimately eliminated the religious divisiveness fostered by private education. The governor's brief claimed that Oregonians may have passed the School Bill because they were properly alarmed by an educational system that fomented "religious suspicions" by allowing children to be separated into religious schools during the most susceptible years of their lives. The School Bill ensured that a portion of a child's education could occur without "class or religious bias." Public education, the governor argued, provided the best "safeguard" for the community against "foreign dangers."[13]

The governor's brief pushed this point further, warning that private religious schools posed a particular danger to the state because they may teach impressionable children greater allegiance to their religion than to their country. Guthrie, furious at this disparagement of the patriotism of parochial schools, fired off an angry response in his brief for the Sisters. He opened the brief with an examination of the history and significance of private religious education in the United States. Denouncing the assertion in the governor's brief as "inexcusable and cruel . . . libel," the Sisters' brief insisted that "patriotism, obedience to the law and loyalty to the Constitution are taught" in parochial schools, "not merely as a patriotic duty, but a religious duty as well," and that "the best and highest ideals of American patriotism and citizenship are exalted" in them.[14] The brief contended that any attempt to invoke patriotism as a justification for destroying religious education could only be viewed as a deliberate interference with religious liberty. The state responded disingenuously, denying it had made religion an issue, because "no charge against any religion" could be found in its briefs.[15]

The Oregon attorney general also could not resist bringing religion into his brief, even when it contradicted one of his own arguments. He first contended that claims based on religious liberty did not present a federal question for the Court, because the First Amendment did not apply to the states. He then went on to argue that religious schools threatened the separation of church and state, because they used religious instruction to fulfill the state's curriculum requirements. This ill-supported argument provoked a lengthy response in Kavanaugh's brief for the Sisters, on the state's frank and "astonishing confession" that the School Bill was enacted to prevent private schools from providing religious instruction.

Both sides included brief arguments on whether the School Bill impaired the obligation of contract in violation of Article I, Section 10, of the federal constitution. The trial court had shown little interest in the issue. A similar reaction was expected from the Supreme Court. The Court's robust protection of economic liberties under the due process clause resolved most cases without resort to the contracts clause.

Several amicus curiae briefs completed the record. The Episcopal Church and the Seventh-Day Adventists documented the damage that compulsory public education would wreak on their schools and religious training. The Episcopal Church claimed that the moral training achieved through parochial education enhanced social order. The Seventh-Day Adventists traced the natural-law foundations of parental rights, disputing the authority of the state, as *parens patriae*, to "step into the family circle as a supplanter while the parents perform their natural duties."[16] Louis Marshall, one of the leading constitutional litigators of the day, a New York colleague of Guthrie's, and a founder of the American Jewish Committee, filed a brief, on behalf of the American Jewish Committee, that argued the connections between democracy, educational choice, and religious liberty. He, like Guthrie, equated state monopoly of education to the tyranny of communism, condemning the religious intolerance of the educational system in Russia, where parents were forbidden by law to impart religious instruction to their children. Marshall argued that an inseparable link exists between liberty and freedom of education. Liberty, he claimed, depends on freedom of thought, which, in turn, can only be assured when learning is unrestricted. State monopoly of education, he concluded, would impose on American children "an undeviating rule of uniformity" that would render them "mechanical Robots and standardized Babbits."[17]

As the parties completed their briefs in February, Guthrie worried that he would not be able to present the Sisters' case fully in the one hour of oral argument allowed by the Court per side. He wrote Stansbury for advice on how to apply for extra time, declaring that the issues raised by the School Bill case "are, in my judgment, more important than any other case in my day, if not in the history of the court." Guthrie made it clear that he did not want to do anything "out of the ordinary" and asked Stansbury whether the request for more time should be made privately to the chief justice or in open court.[18] Stansbury advised that Guthrie do both, saying that it would be "entirely proper, and might tend to clear the atmosphere," for Guthrie to speak with the chief justice prior to the hearing.[19]

Politics, both local and national, sharpened the focus that spring on the questions of tolerance debated in the briefs. On February 9, Governor Pierce signed into law Senate Bill 19, which allowed any child, upon application of the child's parent or guardian, to be excused from public school for 120 minutes per week to attend schools providing religious instruction. The timely passage of this law, just prior to the Supreme Court hearing, benefited the state, which could use the law both to dispute the Sisters' charges of religious bigotry and as evidence that the School Bill would not eliminate parochial schools. Calvin Coolidge, in his inaugural address on March 4, asked the country to embrace religious and ethnic diversity, declaring, "The fundamental precept of liberty is toleration." America, he claimed, "cannot permit any inquisition either within or without the law," for "the mind of America must be forever free."[20]

Anxieties surfaced as the hearing approached. Father Burke urged Guthrie and Kavanaugh to expand their arguments to include claims that the School Bill violated intellectual and religious liberties. He told them that a decision based on these interests would insulate Catholic schools from government regulation better than parental rights. Parental rights could protect private schools from closure but would not prevent state intermeddling in Catholic education. Burke's efforts proved unsuccessful. Kavanaugh claimed that he did not have time to rework his argument; Guthrie, restive as the hearing approached, simply ignored Burke's recommendation.[21] Guthrie had staked the Sisters' case on parental rights. More than two years after the passage of the School Bill, he was ready to persuade the Court that he was right.

CHAPTER 17   Last Refuge

The Court finally called the case for Monday, March 16. Prior to the hearing, Guthrie did get an opportunity to speak with the chief justice about additional time for argument, and the conversation yielded an unexpected boost for his client. As the attorneys for the Sisters and Hill Military Academy—Guthrie, Kavanaugh, Veatch, and Lusk—gathered in a small conference room at the Court to discuss strategy, Chief Justice Taft poked his head in, declaring the assembled attorneys "a formidable array." When Guthrie asked the chief justice if the Court would be willing to allow additional time for oral argument, the chief justice hinted at victory for the schools when he replied, "I don't see why you want any more time. In principle, this case is simply the *Meyer* case over again."[1]

The hearing started late in the day, at 3:30. Chief Justice Taft announced that Justice Holmes would not be attending that afternoon. The chief justice "assumed" there would be no objection if Justice Holmes participated in the case and the opinion through the briefs alone, and the parties readily agreed. Taft commented that Justice Holmes would hopefully be present for the conclusion of the hearing on Tuesday.

The Court scheduled only one hearing for the two cases involving the Sisters and Hill Military. The hearing began with Guthrie's expected request for additional time to present "this extremely important case." Guthrie advised the Court that it would be "practically impossible" to present the Sisters' case in less than an hour and a half. His argument required an hour,

Guthrie told the justices, and he recommended that Judge Kavanaugh speak for at least half an hour. Chief Justice Taft granted Guthrie's request and also awarded the state an extra 30 minutes. Hill Military was not as fortunate. After inquiring about the overlap between the two cases, Taft concluded that the Sisters and the state would discuss most of the issues in the case during the first part of the hearing. Hill Military would have to be content with the regular one-hour argument.[2]

Willis Moore, assistant attorney general, spoke first on behalf of the Oregon attorney general. He began his argument, as he had his brief, by advising the Court that the attorney general waived the standing and prematurity challenges raised by the state at the trial court. Moore insisted that the attorney general's waiver was because of his desire to have the Court focus solely on whether the School Bill was constitutional. Unfortunately for Moore, the attorney general's brief inappropriately raised an issue concerning state constitutional law, and the justices spent the first part of the hearing questioning whether the Court should hear the case.

One section of the attorney general's brief argued that the ballot title of the School Bill initiative satisfied a provision of the Oregon Constitution requiring that the subject of each law be clearly expressed in the ballot title. The justices immediately questioned Moore on this issue; the Court would dismiss the case if it could be resolved on state constitutional grounds. Justice McReynolds interrupted Moore's summary of the constitutional issues to inquire, "Is there any State constitutional question injected in it?" McReynolds asked Moore to explain the state laws involved in the case, and Justice Sutherland wanted to know, "Is that the thing that was complained of in this suit?" Moore seemed perplexed by the justices' continuing questions concerning state law, until Justice Sanford asked him, "Well, there was a question raised originally about the title under the Constitution of the State, was there not?" When Moore started to explain that the attorney general did not intend to rely on that argument, Justice Sutherland interrupted to ask if any of the parties were raising the state constitutional issue. Moore clarified that the parties were "in accord" that the case should be submitted on the federal constitutional claims. Justice McReynolds asked Moore to move on, but not before he pointedly observed that he hoped Moore understood that the "sharp" issue presented is whether the state can require a child to go to public school.[3]

Moore's argument rested on one straightforward point: the law was a reasonable exercise of the state's legitimate police powers. He began by reminding the justices of the well-established principle that the Court should presume that a state law is constitutional. That presumption applies, Moore insisted, unless the challenger can demonstrate that the law is arbitrary and unreasonable. Moore argued that the schools had failed to meet their burden. The School Bill, Moore claimed, was a permissible exercise by the state of its extensive authority over education. In *Meyer,* the Court explicitly acknowledged the state's authority to compel school attendance and regulate education. Whether the state compelled attendance at public or private school was a matter of educational policy to be left to the discretion of the state. The Court should defer to the judgment of the people of Oregon, Moore claimed. He distinguished *Meyer* by claiming that, in *Meyer,* the Court was faced with a simple question within their judicial knowledge—whether the teaching of German was so inherently injurious as to justify a ban on instruction in any school. The Oregon law, by contrast, involved factual determinations on education policy that should be decided by Oregonians.

Moore moved early to deflect any claims that the School Bill was the product of religious intolerance, shifting the discussion from education to religion. He advised the Court that he felt compelled to raise the issue of religious intolerance, not because the state thought it relevant, but because he was certain the other side would make much of it. Moore argued that neither the ballot title nor the text of the School Bill made any reference to religion. Oregonians, Moore insisted, are a "religious people," who are "liberal and just and generous" in the support of religious tolerance.[4] Evidence of that tolerance, Moore claimed, could be found in a law passed only a month earlier by the Oregon legislature, allowing a public school student to be excused from school for up to 120 minutes per week to attend schools offering religious instruction. The newly enacted law also demonstrated that the state did not intend to interfere with religious instruction or the operation of religious schools.

Moore's argument that the School Bill did not interfere with religious education did not satisfy the justices. Justice McReynolds wanted Moore to discuss the "practical effect" of the law on religious schools.[5] Moore admitted it required all children to attend public school. He insisted that state authority over educational quality justified the law. Private schools, Moore argued, could not prove they provide an education superior to that of public schools. The sole issue in the case, Moore told the Court, was whether the Constitution guaranteed the private schools the right to impart religious instruction. Moore claimed the answer was no, for having religious schools fulfill state curriculum requirements violated principles of separation of religion and state.

Justice McReynolds wanted to hear more on the specific impact of the School Bill. He asked Moore how many hours, days, and months children would be required to attend public school. Moore explained that children are generally in school Monday through Friday from nine to four, provoking a question from Justice Sutherland as to whether children "kept" in the public schools could attend any other school during those periods. Moore argued that with the passage of the new law by the Oregon legislature, religious schools could continue because children could attend them for religious instruction for two hours per week.

Justice Sutherland was not convinced, responding, "It would not be any use to keep up the private schools if the children could not go to them?" Moore replied that compulsory public education was a reasonable extension of the established authority of the state to mandate school attendance, but Justice McReynolds interrupted to inquire, "Well, we do know, do we not, . . . that this act, if it is put in force, will shut up every parochial school?" Moore finally conceded that it would.[6]

Justice Sutherland told Moore that his position inevitably led to the conclusion that the state could control the activities of every private school in the state, including prohibiting enrollment at private institutions and imposing criminal penalties on parents. Moore insisted that education is a police power reserved to the states. When Moore claimed that the details of education policy should be left to the state, Chief Justice Taft broke in to ask whether the state could enact laws that violate rights secured by the Constitution. Moore did not concede the point, arguing that the Fourteenth Amendment did not limit police powers reserved to the state.

Throughout his argument, Moore repeatedly described the School Bill as a "compulsory education law." During Moore's summation, Justice Sanford finally corrected him, noting that the law "is not compulsory education, as I understand, it is compulsory public school education." Moore agreed and sat down.[7]

Guthrie followed Moore. He had only 10 minutes left before the Court adjourned at 4:30, so he opened with a summary of the Sisters' arguments. The attorney general's attempted waiver of standing and prematurity challenges was irrelevant, he began, because the jurisdiction of the Court could not be established by waiver or consent. The Court must decide these questions. The Sisters, Guthrie argued, were entitled to relief. The law caused them direct and immediate harm, forcing parents to remove children from their schools and teachers to leave their employ. Contrary to the assertion in the brief of the governor, Guthrie argued that corporations were entitled to liberty and property rights under the Fourteenth Amendment. Any other result was "untenable" and not supported by precedent.

Guthrie's initial comments outlined the essence of the Sisters' case. He conceded the state's extensive powers to regulate education, including mandating school attendance and directing the curriculum of private schools and the qualifications of their teachers. The state's authority did not extend, however, to prohibiting or destroying private education, nor could the state destroy the economic livelihood of the schools and the teachers. Substantial economic harm suffered by the schools constituted only part of the case, Guthrie explained, for the School Bill violated the "fundamental, natural and sacred right" of parents to send their children to private schools.[8] Despite the limited time before adjournment, Guthrie repeatedly reminded the Court of the *Meyer* decision, quoting from Justice McReynolds' opinion three times within 10 minutes.

Guthrie saved his most controversial argument for the last few minutes of the day. Moore had accurately predicted that the Sisters would raise the issue of religious intolerance early. Guthrie closed his summary by claiming that the "true and real motive and intent" of the School Bill, as "deliberately disclosed and confessed" by the state is to deny the religious liberty of parents who wish to send their children to parochial schools. The Fourteenth Amendment protects this religious liberty, Guthrie argued. Departing from his brief, he invited the Court to hold that the Fourteenth Amendment's liberty clause made the protections of the First Amendment applicable to the states, a holding he argued was ordained by the Court's discussion of liberty in *Meyer*.[9]

At noon the next day, Tuesday, March 17, Guthrie began again, walking the Court through the substance of the argument he had outlined the previous afternoon. Justice Holmes did not make it to the hearing on Tuesday either. Also absent was Justice Stone, who had been called away by the death of a close friend. Guthrie spoke virtually without interruption, the justices questioning him only about where to find specific documents in the record. He laid the groundwork for his argument by emphasizing that every state except Oregon allowed children to attend private schools, including parochial schools. Guthrie spoke to the justices about the paramount importance of education and detailed the many legitimate regulations of education undertaken by the states. None of these regulations, he argued, prohibited or destroyed private education. The destructive impact of the School Bill, by contrast, was indisputable. On Monday, the justices had responded with some skepticism to Moore's argument that the School Bill would not shut down private schools, and Guthrie now pushed the point anew: "I shall not argue the obvious: that the effect as well as the intent of this statute was to prohibit and destroy religious and other private schools." The School Bill "suppressed" these schools, he argued, "no matter how superior their instruction, . . . no matter how desirable and necessary for certain children."[10]

If the bill were held constitutional, Guthrie contended, legislatures across the country could act to shut down private schools, putting at risk the great private schools, such as St. Paul's and Groton. The great tradition of private education extended back to the founders of the country, including in its ranks nearly every attendee at the Constitutional Convention in 1787 and the signers of the Declaration of Independence. Most significantly, Guthrie insisted, the consequences of recognizing such formidable state authority would not be limited to elementary and secondary education, as private colleges also would be vulnerable.

National security did not justify the School Bill, Guthrie argued. Quoting from the governor's brief, he told the justices that if they upheld the School Bill, the state could eliminate all private schools simply because they "may possibly teach prejudicial, unpatriotic, or subversive doctrines"; because they may become "red" and teach revolution; or because there simply is no way to be certain private schools are not being "controlled and conducted by bolshevists, syndicalists and communists."[11] The mere possibility of harm, he asserted, did not justify eliminating private education.

Guthrie lamented that "time did not allow him to address fully" all the arguments raised by the briefs. He then turned to the heart of his case: the claim that the School Bill violated the constitutionally protected liberty and property interests of parents, children, teachers, and owners of schools. Guthrie brought the weight of common law and history to his argument, claiming that "first and foremost," the law interferes with the "sacred rights of parents," recognized by Blackstone over 150 years ago and by Puffendorf centuries earlier. He even raised a liberty claim not well recognized at common law: the limited right of a child to make a choice about education, even if that choice is ultimately subordinated to parental decision. As to the rights of teachers to pursue their profession, Guthrie argued that *Meyer* resolved any doubt as to the validity of that claim. Finally, he urged the Court to recognize the rights of school owners and managers because of the historical importance of private education. The significance and sweep of these varied interests led Guthrie to conclude this part of his argument by insisting that he did not exaggerate when he urged the Court that "no more far-reaching and momentous question, or one more closely affecting American institutions . . . or a greater number of people . . . , or one more deeply reaching to the very roots and springs of American constitutional liberty, . . . has ever been submitted to this Court for decision."[12]

The remainder of the Sisters' argument illuminated the significance of the broader principles at stake. The liberty interests at risk, while substantial, represented only part of the constitutional equation. The Court also had to evaluate Oregon's claim that "exceptional circumstances" justified the law. To Guthrie, those exceptional circumstances amounted to no more than the state's efforts to use nationalism as an excuse for religious and ethnic intolerance. Complaining of his "great apprehension and disappointment" in having to "gallop" through the case in the limited time allotted, Guthrie charged that the state sought to assimilate all children into one belief and one religion when it claimed that children must not, "under any pretext," be separated into "antagonistic groups" to "absorb the narrow views of life as they are taught." He overtly ridiculed the state for raising the issue of religion in their briefs—even though it had not been raised in the trial court—and then protesting that it had no intention of bringing religion into the case because the people of Oregon are a "religious people." The state's inconsistency provided Guthrie with the opportunity to speak at length on the harm caused by religious intolerance. The Court did not discourage him; when Guthrie explained that he intended to use the remaining nine minutes of his time to discuss religious liberty, Chief Justice Taft replied that Guthrie was not giving himself enough time.[13]

Guthrie responded with a passionate defense of religious liberty. He read a statement by Presbyterian ministers, who denounced the School Bill, calling it an autocratic law born of the philosophy that children belong primarily to the state. He read passages in the state's briefs that showed, he argued, that the School Bill was fatally tainted by religious intolerance. The state, Guthrie insisted, had confessed that the underlying motive for the School Bill was to eliminate religious schools, when the attorney general concluded his brief by claiming that the School Bill protected the separation of church and state The state's position made clear the antireligion purpose of the School Bill, Guthrie claimed, "as much so as any atheistic or sovietic measure ever adopted in Russia."[14]

The governor's brief only compounded the attack on religious liberty, Guthrie insisted, by suggesting that religious schools do not teach patriotism. Guthrie quoted from part of the governor's brief, which claimed that private schools teach children that "the claims upon them of the religion to which they belong are superior to the claims of the United States." It also claimed that children in private schools "may be intentionally mistaught as to the true character of the Government and history of the United States." At this point, Guthrie incredulously reminded the Court that the afternoon before, the state had insisted that the case presented no religious issues. Guthrie drew one more argument from the state's briefs, quoting the governor's warning that if the Court strikes down the School Bill, a "bitter question" will spread throughout the country, which could lead to a federal constitutional amendment. Although the governor claimed that this warning concerned the more general question of state control over education, Guthrie insisted that the "bitter question" could only be the historically divisive conflict over parochial education.[15]

As the clock ran down, Guthrie asked the Court's forgiveness for "how inadequately" he had presented "this great question." He regretted not having the time to discuss fully "this cant of Americanization on the part of the promoters of this un-American measure." Imagine, he put to the Court, destroying the right to religious liberty and freedom of education "on the pretense of Americanization with the wickedly false cry that they who seek to close all private and religious elementary schools are the only true Americans." The whole history of the country, Guthrie argued, "cries out against this pretense." Guthrie was not above injecting his own religious commentary, when he reminded the Court of the many Catholics who had served and died in World War I, while many "loudly canting on Americanization" remained "safely at home."[16]

The School Bill case, Guthrie concluded, lifted the Court into the "highest plane and realm of constitutional jurisprudence." What could be more fundamental, he asked, than religious liberty, freedom of conscience, freedom of education, and the rights of parents to bring up their children "in the faith of their fathers." An adverse decision, he concluded, would be the death knell of these quintessential American values.[17]

Judge Kavanaugh finished the last half hour for the Sisters. He devoted his time to the economic issues, describing the "inherent" rights of private schools and teachers to pursue their livelihoods as natural rights that predated formal law and were rightly secured and protected by the Constitution. The School Bill, Kavanaugh told the Court, never was intended to improve education or resolve deficiencies in private education; its only purpose was to shut down the private schools.

Kavanaugh rapidly let his argument drift into a comparison between public and private education in Oregon, inviting sharp questioning from Justice McReynolds. When Kavanaugh described the deficiencies in some of the rural public schools, Justice McReynolds interrupted to inquire, "Suppose they had the best public schools that could be obtained, and had all the money they needed behind them?" Justice McReynolds pushed Kavanaugh to see whether he would concede that the School Bill could be justified if private education was clearly inferior to public schooling. Kavanaugh did not concede the point, insisting that superior public schools "would not make any difference" to his position. Justice McReynolds pressed him, asking again, "I was trying to find out if it would make any difference."[18]

Kavanaugh's long answer—touting the benefits of private schools, including the availability of religious education, and denouncing the School Bill for destroying private education—provoked further questioning from Justice McReynolds on the same point. Kavanaugh failed to answer the question directly, arguing instead that "no emergency justified the legislation," because the foreign-born population in the state "is small, and is quite negligible," and because very few students attended private schools. Justice McReynolds, still not satisfied with Kavanaugh's answer, inquired, "I will ask again, if you think that affects this question?" "Not at all," replied Kavanaugh. Justice McReynolds sought one final clarification, "As I understand you, you argue that this thing cannot be done under any conditions." "Not under any conditions," Kavanaugh concluded. Kavanaugh took a few minutes to argue that the School Bill violated the contracts clause by unreasonably interfering with the corporate franchise. He finished his presentation by reminding the justices that the Constitution protected minorities: "We repair with confidence to the Constitution. It was the first hope of the Fathers. It is the last refuge of the persecuted and the oppressed."[19]

Senator George Chamberlain, representing Governor Pierce, opened his argument by bringing the justices back to the questions of religious intolerance raised by Moore and Guthrie. Although he denied any intent by the state to libel the Roman Catholic Church or to bring religion into the case,

Chamberlain's argument undermined the neutrality he asserted. The Sisters, not the state, Chamberlain insisted, sought to inject religion into arguments "without religious significance." "I am not a member of any church, . . . and I have no animosity toward any church," Chamberlain explained. But, Chamberlain advised the justices, "I shall undertake to be frank with the Court; and I may be led, possibly, to make some criticisms of church methods and church laws. . . . I feel it is my duty to do that under the circumstances, and to talk plainly to the Court."[20]

Chamberlain then proceeded to argue that the parental rights argument was a sham, because Catholic parents cede control over the education of their children to the Roman Catholic Church. The Sisters' claim that the School Bill violates the rights of parents to educate their children is in "direct opposition" to Catholic canon law, Chamberlain contended. In particular, canon 1374 prohibits Catholic children from attending non-Catholic schools unless the local bishop decides that attendance "may be tolerated without danger of perversion of the pupils." How can the parents assert a liberty interest, Chamberlain questioned, if the church canons take away the authority of the parents to control the education of their children and "absolutely dictate" what school a child shall attend? Violation of the Oregon law is punishable as a misdemeanor, but what punishment is meted out to parents who violate the laws of the church? Control by the church is "certainly asserted and asserted most strenuously," Chamberlain claimed.[21]

Chamberlain argued that the School Bill challenge really was about whether the rights of parochial schools, not parents, prevailed: "I question the right of the Catholic, or any other church, to insist that its communicants and adherents have the absolute right to send their children wherever they please." Chamberlain spoke "plainly" when he concluded, "I challenge the statement, that there is any liberty to the parents or to children under the rules of the church." Between church and state, Chamberlain argued, "we insist that the state has the prior and paramount right to direct the education of the children in the state." Chamberlain took the argument one step further, reminding the Court that parents who fail to fulfill their duty of control over their children lose their rights. The law recognizes the liberty of children, Chamberlain contended, and the state may "assert the custody and control of the parent to be an illegal restraint" on a child's liberty, for the "rights of the father and mother are both subject to the still higher right of the child to have its welfare guarded."[22]

The state's authority over children and their education must be particularly respected here, Chamberlain claimed, because the School Bill embodies the direct, unfiltered will of the people. Chamberlain asked the Court to disregard the Sisters' efforts to depict the state as a potentially dangerous usurper of liberty. The threat of tyrannical state power raised in alarm by the Sisters' brief, with its comparisons to Plato's Ideal Commonwealth, Prussia, and Bolshevik Russia, arises, he claimed, only in states conceived as autocratic authorities. A "state" under the American Constitution, by contrast, is defined by the control of the people themselves, and nowhere is that control more directly manifested than through the initiative process that produced the School Bill. Chamberlain suggested that if the Sisters strike from their briefs all references to the state deriving from the autocratic model, "there will be very little left of their argument."[23]

Chamberlain's reference to the Oregon initiative process sparked the interest of the justices. Justice Sutherland interrupted Chamberlain to ask whether the Supreme Court had approved the initiative process. "Yes," responded Chamberlain. "It was submitted and argued and the question of its constitutionality was decided by this Court, and it was sustained." Justice Sutherland was not certain: "I thought the Court declined to consider that question; but I was not sure about it." The case they sought to remember, *Pacific States Telephone & Telegraph Co. v. Oregon,* was decided in 1912, 10 years after Oregon amended its state constitution to authorize the initiative and referendum. The case concerned a challenge to a corporate tax established by initiative. The plaintiff did not attack the tax directly but instead claimed that the process of direct legislation violated the guarantee clause of the federal constitution, Article IV, Section 4, which requires the United States to "guarantee" each state a republican, or representative, form of government. The Court did not decide whether the initiative and referendum violated the guarantee clause; instead it held that challenges brought under that clause constituted a nonjusticiable political question.[24]

Justice Sutherland and Chamberlain continued their efforts to recall the case, with Chamberlain advising the justices that he believed that the initiative was upheld by the Court. Justice Sutherland did not agree, responding, "The Court did not consider the political question, as I remember; I may be wrong." Chamberlain admitted that he had heard the case argued before the Court but had "forgotten" the exact holding, remembering only its "general effect." Chief Justice Taft interrupted at this point, offering his opinion that the case was argued "on the objection that it was not a republican form of government" and that "that question was a political question which this

Court could not consider." Chamberlain agreed with this assessment of the case and proceeded to address the justifications for the School Bill.[25]

Chamberlain invoked a decidedly progressive defense of the School Bill by arguing that public schools provide an education in democracy antithetical to the elitist tendencies of private schools. Mandatory public education serves democracy, he argued, because it eliminates the risk of religious indoctrination. Chamberlain insisted that there can be but one answer to the question of why parochial schools "insist on depriving these children" of a public school education: "It is to stamp upon its children a distinction which is to set them apart during the rest of their lives, and to make them other than they would be if they grew up in the atmosphere of the democracy of the public schools." Chamberlain described his own six children, who attended public school to be in contact with "rich and poor alike" and to learn tolerance.[26]

Chamberlain, admitting, "who knoweth the mystery of the human will?" offered his "candid opinion" that the voters of Oregon approved the School Bill because of "an intense feeling" that there should be "greater democracy cultivated amongst the people." The School Bill represented democratic values, not nationalism, he concluded; it was adopted "not to Americanize particularly, but to democratize the children, and to cut out this social and group class feeling that exists when they attend any sectarian or private school." He contended that the law exemplified the progressive legislation for which Oregon was famous. Mandatory school attendance laws originally encountered opposition, Chamberlain reminded the Court, because "not a single progressive movement has been taken in the cause of education, or any other great cause, without protest." Oregon, he boasted, "has been doing a good deal of thinking for itself during the past ten or fifteen years, and her progressive steps have been followed, in a great many instances, by the older states, which have been too busy to do their own thinking."[27]

Chamberlain returned once again to the issue of religious liberty at the end of his argument. He protested the Sisters' charge that the School Bill interfered with religious freedom. How could public schooling interfere with religion, Chamberlain argued, for certainly the Court knows that "the religion a man has he learns at his mother's knee." Chamberlain urged the justices to reflect on their own experiences, for they learned their religious views at home, not at school or college.

Chamberlain's associate, Albert Putney, planned to address economic liberty during his argument in the *Hill Military* case, but Justice Sutherland wanted to hear Chamberlain's position on whether the right to conduct a school should be considered a property right.[28] Chamberlain did not answer Justice Sutherland directly; he insisted that the schools could still be used outside of regular school hours or with children younger than 8 or older than 16. Justice Sutherland pushed Chamberlain to see if he would admit that the School Bill caused a partial deprivation of property. Chamberlain held his ground, reminding Justice Sutherland that the Court had held in a number of cases that a slight loss of revenue resulting from a state's exercise of its police powers does not constitute an unconstitutional deprivation of property. Chamberlain closed his argument by explicitly refusing to concede that the Oregon law effected a partial taking of property. On this point, the Sisters' hearing on the School Bill ended.

Father Burke, general secretary of the NCWC, and Father Ryan, NCWC education director, attended the oral arguments. Their reactions were mixed. Father Burke found that the Court treated Guthrie with the "utmost" respect, in marked contrast to what he perceived as the rather brusque treatment of the other attorneys. Kavanaugh and Guthrie, he thought, presented a more persuasive case to the justices. As soon as the hearing ended, Burke wrote to Cardinal Dougherty that "nothing occurred to lessen our confidence in a favorable decision."[29] But Burke still was not convinced that they had put forth the best arguments to protect Catholic education. Confiding in attorney Thomas F. O'Mara, Burke again suggested that a decision based on intellectual liberty offered the greatest security to Catholic schools: "I am more convinced than ever, after hearing the oral arguments, that a magnificent opportunity was presented to us to have intellectual liberty of education definitely written into a decision of our Supreme Court." Burke expressed doubt that Guthrie and Kavanaugh had devoted sufficient attention to that point: "I still pray that we have not altogether missed the opportunity."[30]

While Burke was optimistic that the Court would invalidate the School Bill, he was less certain about what impact the case would have on other education battles the church faced. Even a favorable decision, if written to emphasize state authority over education, could spur further legislation and create a future "full of rough places" for the church. With the hearing behind them, Burke admitted to O'Mara that the management of the case had been difficult. He wrote that the bishops should have strongly exercised their authority at the beginning of the litigation. That failure was "one misfortune in this case," he said, because it allowed conflict and competition to develop between the NCWC, Archbishop Christie, the Knights of Columbus, and the various attorneys. Given all the turf battles over counsel and case strategy, Burke was "thankful" that "everything has come out as well as it has."[31]

Father Ryan shared similar observations with O'Mara. He praised Guthrie and Kavanaugh for their "excellent" arguments, but Ryan, like Father Burke, expressed disappointment that Guthrie did not devote any of his oral argument to intellectual liberty. Ryan wrote to O'Mara that he had tried to convince Guthrie the night before the hearing to emphasize freedom of thought but that Guthrie was "so nervous and excited . . . that it was impossible to get anything to him." Ryan found the Court attentive to the issues, writing that the justices, particularly Justice McReynolds, showed by their questioning that they "understood the situation perfectly." The attorneys for the state performed poorly, according to Ryan, saying "nothing at all," other than to "constantly" assert that the Court should presume the School Bill to be valid because it reflected the will of the people. The justices, with the exception of Justices Brandeis and Butler, reacted to that argument with considerable skepticism, Ryan observed.[32]

Ryan ultimately found the oral argument frustrating, writing that the hearing failed to explore fully the threat to private education posed by restrictive state regulation like the Oregon law: "The pity of it all was that the real problems, both in their educational and constitutional aspects, were merely touched upon, while a lot of irrelevant stuff took up the time of the court." The failure of Guthrie and Kavanaugh to argue more broadly for protection of private education from state regulation troubled Ryan. He thought the Court seemed disinclined to address the general question of state regulation of private schools, writing that "from what I could get of the atmosphere of the situation, I do not think the court will say anything specifically about regulation of schools." Ryan also expressed confidence that "we have little doubt about what the ultimate decision will be." But he worried about the direction the Court would take, confiding to O'Mara that the "possibility, however, remains that they may state this power of regulation in such wide terms as to cause us trouble in the future."[33]

Father Burke's and Father Ryan's concerns understandably reflected a desire to see the Court issue an opinion that offered the greatest protection to Catholic education. Guthrie's focus on parental rights had not been completely satisfactory to them, but it represented a sound litigation strategy. Guthrie recognized that the precedent established by *Meyer* enabled the

Court to find in favor of the schools without breaking substantial new constitutional ground. By contrast, if Guthrie had pushed the claim of intellectual liberty, he would be asking the Court either to expand its interpretation of liberty or to take the significant doctrinal step of applying the protections of the First Amendment to the states. Contrary to Father Burke's and Father Ryan's wishes, the Court was not likely to be persuaded to curtail substantially the state's extensive powers over education, given the delicate federalism issues involved any time a federal court limits a state's traditional police powers.

Less than a week after the hearing, Guthrie, mindful that Justice Holmes had been absent from the hearing and that Justice Stone attended only on Monday afternoon, sought and received the permission of the Court to submit copies of his and Judge Kavanaugh's oral argument on behalf of the Sisters. He obtained the Court's permission to file the transcript as part of the record and distribute copies to all the justices, ensuring that Justices Holmes and Stone would have a full record of his client's argument.

The completion of oral arguments marked the official submission of the School Bill case to the Court. But supporters of compulsory public education made one last attempt to influence the Court. On April 9, the Public School Defense League, the Klan-affiliated organization driving the Michigan school campaign, submitted an amicus brief to the Court. The president of the league was none other than James Hamilton, Michigan Klan leader, politician, and leader of the Michigan movement for compulsory public education. Stansbury, the Court clerk, refused to file the brief, informing the league that it would have to obtain the consent of the parties or the express leave of the Court. On April 23, more than one month after the *Pierce* oral arguments, the league filed a motion with the Court seeking permission to submit its brief. Guthrie, suffering from exhaustion, received the motion just one day before he set sail for a two-month rest in France. His brief objection, filed on April 25 on behalf of the Sisters and Hill Military Academy, called the league's untimely request "unprecedented."[34] Unable to procure the consent of all the parties, the league made an unsuccessful plea to the Court on May 11. Michigan attorney George William Moore represented the league and argued so vigorously in support of the petition that Chief Justice Taft "had difficulty" convincing Moore that it was too late to file the brief.[35] With the dismissal of the petition, the School Bill case was in the hands of the Court for decision.

CHAPTER 18   A Mere Creature of the State

Pierce arrived at the Court during a time of great national debate on the very principles of democracy argued in the School Bill case. The country's antipathy toward immigrants and radicals lingered after the war, justified, argued many, by national security. With the war and the Red Scare still permeating the mood of the United States, the country was rethinking fundamental questions about the appropriate balance between national security and individual liberty. But as the war years receded, so did the public hysteria over national security. With this shift came an increasing public perception that intolerance toward nonconformity and dissent was itself undemocratic. The rise of fascism in Italy provided one powerful example to the country of how intolerance breeds repression.

Political leaders who, after the war, had proclaimed that unquestioning loyalty exemplified "Americanism" now warned that an "intolerant spirit" blew ominous winds across the country. In 1923, Charles Evans Hughes, secretary of state under President Harding, was one of many politicians who vigorously insisted that a true patriot would never question America's policies. But by 1925, Hughes, as president of the American Bar Association, cautioned that America's institutions "were not devised to bring about uniformity of opinion." Instead, Hughes stressed, "the essential characteristic of true liberty is, that under its shelter many different types of life and character and opinion and belief can develop unmolested and unobstructed."[1] The wartime intolerance of Bolshevist ideas, while still present in 1925, met increasing resistance from liberals who proclaimed the virtues of tolerance and diversity and who argued that free expression offered the best avenue for defusing radicalism in America.

The Court mirrored the mood of the country, as it, too, struggled to define the proper balance between personal liberty and nationalism. Its wartime cases upholding convictions under the Espionage Act made clear that the First Amendment offered scant shelter to those who advocated radicalism when weighed against the exigencies of war. But as the aura of emergency that colored the war years faded, so, too, did the Court's justification for punishing dissent. Both sides of the *Pierce* dispute played the radicalism card, gambling that the Court, like the rest of the country, had not reached a consensus on when liberty could be restricted to advance national security. The debate within the Court emerged most clearly not in the *Pierce* decision but in *Gitlow v. New York,* decided one week after the *Pierce* decision came down. In *Gitlow,* the Court once again upheld the conviction of a member of the Socialist Party for the preparation and distribution of radical literature and for advocating revolutionary "mass action" against the government. In deferring to the state's decision to punish simple advocacy of revolution, the Court concluded that the state's assessment of the dangers "must be given great weight," with "every presumption . . . indulged in favor of the validity of the statute."[2]

Justice Holmes's prescient dissent in *Gitlow,* joined by Justice Brandeis and echoing his 1919 dissent in *Abrams* v. *United States,* most vividly demonstrates the tensions within the Court, as well as the First Amendment analysis that eventually would be embraced by a majority of the Court. Justice Holmes insisted that suppression of radical speech by the government, absent immediate incitement, is inconsistent with democratic principles. Invoking one of the fundamental justifications for the protection of speech, the marketplace of ideas, Holmes argued, "If in the long run the beliefs expressed in proletarian dictatorship are destined to be accepted by the dominant forces of the community, the only meaning of free speech is that they should be given their chance and have their way."[3] For Holmes and Brandeis, radicalism posed less of a threat to democracy than did the danger of tyranny from state suppression of speech.

The School Bill case posed a comparable dilemma for the Court, requiring the justices to weigh the national interests in assimilation and patriotic indoctrination against the prospect of state monopoly of education, a system vigorously assailed as antidemocratic. The religious and ethnic bigotry infusing the School Bill's history forced the Court also to contemplate the relationship between intolerance and tyranny. The Court already had emphasized the connection between education and liberty in *Meyer*. Observing that "the American people have always regarded education and acquisition of knowledge as matters of supreme importance which should be diligently promoted," it had quoted the language of the Northwest Ordinance of 1787, declaring education to be essential to good government and personal happiness. Justice Brandeis, in particular, had spoken extensively about the importance of education, describing it as a fundamental interest, much like speech and critical to democratic governance. Brandeis had long argued that every citizen should receive a thorough education, for "the educational standard required of a democracy is obviously high."[4]

Chief Justice Taft had made his opinions known on a number of issues germane to the School Bill case, but Taft's public comments did not necessarily foretell his vote on the precise question before the Court. A strong supporter of economic liberty and religious training, Taft also advocated the importance of public education, particularly to advance assimilation. Taft abhorred Bolshevism and perceived it as an ongoing threat to American democracy, insisting that radicalism is "noisy" and "needs watching."[5] Taft also described public education as essential to breaking down the feelings of class consciousness that foment Bolshevism. Yet he viewed the moral training received through religion as the country's chief weapon against Bolshevism, claiming that as "long as the United States remains a religious nation, there is no danger of the corrosion of Bolshevism, Communism or any destructive and cruel cult."[6] Taft's position on the School Bill also was likely to be affected by his disgust for the initiative system, which he described as a failure of "so-called 'purer' democracy."[7] Although the Court had never specifically considered whether the state could compel children to attend only public school, the fundamental issues underlying the School Bill were not unique or novel to the justices.

On June 1, the Court found the School Bill unconstitutional, in a unanimous opinion that is striking in its brevity. Chief Justice Taft's prediction to Guthrie that the Court would find little difference between the School Bill case and *Meyer* proved accurate. The opinion, written by *Meyer* author Justice McReynolds, ruled that the Oregon law violated constitutionally protected parental rights. The doctrine of *Meyer*, Justice McReynolds wrote, made it "entirely plain" that the School Bill "unreasonably interferes with the liberty of parents and guardians to direct the upbringing and education of children under their control." *Meyer* may indeed have provided the precedent for the Court, but the School Bill decision expanded the constitutional status of parental rights. *Meyer* recognized the liberty interest of parents in raising and educating their children; *Pierce* made that interest the central holding of the decision.[8]

In five scant pages of opinion, the Court showed no interest in precisely defining the scope of parental rights. It was content merely to assert that they deserved constitutional protection. The Court did not address explicitly the intolerance that drove the passage of the School Bill and pervaded the litigation. Nor did the Court address the issues of religious liberty that were so central to the political and legal conflicts. Instead, the analysis of the School Bill, limited to a few short paragraphs, confirmed that the Court remained deeply absorbed in delineating the relationship between individual liberty and state power. The Court relied on *Meyer*, rejecting expansive state authority over education in the name of enhancing citizenship and nationalism. The opinion went further than *Meyer* in describing the threat to democracy posed by state monopoly of education. Like *Meyer*, the decision acknowledged the state's extensive control over education, noting that "no question is raised concerning the power of the state reasonably to regulate all schools, to inspect, supervise and examine them, their teachers and pupils; to require that ... certain studies plainly essential to good citizenship must be taught." In even more comprehensive language, the Court confirmed the authority of the state to assure that "nothing be taught which is manifestly inimical to the public welfare."[9]

The Court recognized that the law undoubtedly would destroy private education in Oregon, a business "not inherently harmful, but long regarded as useful and meritorious." The state, the Court concluded, offered no reasonable justification for eliminating private education. There was no evidence that the schools had failed to discharge their educational responsibilities. While leaving the door open to the possibility that extraordinary circumstances could warrant uncommon measures, the Court found that the state failed to show any evidence of exigencies requiring the state to eliminate private education.

The Court soundly rejected the state's claim that assimilation of immigrants constituted a valid political emergency. What remained, the Court concluded, was a choice by Oregon to pursue a policy that bore "no reasonable relation to some purpose within the competency of the state." State monopoly of education overstepped the permissible reach of state power, because, as the Court explained in the passage quoted in newspapers throughout the country, "the fundamental theory of liberty upon which all governments in this Union repose excludes any general power of the state to standardize its children by forcing them to accept instruction from public teachers only." The Court's language is revealing; *standardization* was a term commonly used to describe the goals and practices of autocratic governments. Parents, the Court concluded, have the right to choose private school for their children: "The child is not the mere creature of the state; those who nurture him and direct his destiny have the right, coupled with the high duty, to recognize and prepare him for additional obligations."[10]

The Court dismissed the argument that the suit was premature, finding that the injury to the schools "was present and very real, not a mere possibility in the remote future." The Court's equity jurisdiction supported action, for to wait until the effective date of the law would make the injury "irreparable."[11] The challenge to the schools' standing to bring the suit also failed. The Court made no distinction between the rights of parents and the schools' ability to raise those rights. For the first time, the Court explicitly held that corporations could claim the protections of the liberty clause of the Fourteenth Amendment. The Court cited numerous precedents recognizing the right of a business enterprise to seek an injunction to prevent the arbitrary and unreasonable interference with their business and the patrons of their business. The Court thus concluded that the Oregon law also interfered with the economic liberty of the schools. Missing from the opinion was any specific discussion of religious liberty, particularly the Sisters' claim that the Fourteenth Amendment protected religious freedom from state interference. The Court ignored the issue, resting the decision solely on parental and economic rights. In doing so, the Court protected all private education, religious and secular. Thus Hill Military Academy also could claim victory.

The opinion, like *Meyer* and like many of the Taft Court's precedents concerning economic due process, reflected a vision of democracy that embraced extensive protection by the judiciary of liberties essential to political and economic autonomy. The Court's protection of parental rights demonstrated its broader concern with the impairment of liberty wrought by legislative intrusion into fundamental individual choices. To this end, it mattered little to the Court whether the liberty in question was "economic" or "personal" in character. To focus on the "economic" as compared to "personal" distinction is to obscure the powerful antistatist message of the Court.

The unanimity of the Court notably distinguished *Pierce* from the *Meyer* decision, where Justices Holmes and Sutherland dissented. Either these two justices found the School Bill a more draconian intrusion than the Nebraska language law, or they concluded that stare decisis required the Court to adhere to the precedent of parental rights established in *Meyer*. Justice Sutherland wrote early in June that the decision was an easy one for the Court, but he did not explain why: "The decision of our Court in the Oregon School law case . . . was the only possible one. There was never any division of sentiment in the Court from the beginning."[12] Chief Justice Taft apparently did not share Sutherland's perspective. Taft, too, wrote to a friend early in June about the *Pierce* decision. He agreed with Sutherland that "we had no difficulty after we had decided the Nebraska language case." But he also wrote, cryptically, "I can tell you sometime about how we made the Court unanimous."[13] Thus, while Sutherland may have readily joined the majority in *Pierce,* Taft's comments suggest that Justice Holmes may have taken some convincing.

The unanimity of the Court may also reflect the reality that the decision issued in 1925, not 1923. By 1925, the nativist hysteria had subsided, national public opinion was clearly against the School Bill, and public discourse emphasized tolerance more frequently than nationalism. Harvard Law professor Felix Frankfurter, who would be appointed to the Court in 1939, claimed that Supreme Court opinions, "under the guise of constitutional interpretation," often reflected the "disposition of the justices." The Court, Frankfurter charged, serves largely as a "reflector of that impalpable but controlling thing, the general drift of public opinion."[14]

Frankfurter's criticism of the Court's jurisprudence oversimplifies the relationship between constitutional interpretation and popular will. The debate undertaken by Oregonians exposed their struggle to define the relationship of public education to democratic principles. The School Bill forced Oregonians, who took great pride in their progressive policies, to evaluate both the antielitist appeal of mandatory public education and the obvious intolerance that drove many of its supporters. It also pushed an independent-minded citizenry to decide whether they were willing to embrace educational conformity because they so abhorred the threat of socialist or communist influence.

As for the Court, it, too, perceived the School Bill case as a debate about fundamental principles—namely, the relationship between education and democratic self-governance. Through education, the state decides whether to help prepare its citizens for liberty or for dependence. Informed governance disappears if the state dictates what people learn. The *Pierce* opinion rests on the premise that freedom of thought and, ultimately, democratic governance require that parents be able to teach their children according to their beliefs. Without this liberty, the state has the power to "standardize" its citizens, forcing them to conform to an identity forged primarily by government.

The Court's emphasis on personal liberty captured the shifting political mood of the country. The intolerance and nationalism that marred postwar America may have influenced the Court, as well as the public. This congruence does not mean that the *Pierce* decision merely reflects public consensus. The social and political forces that shape public opinion also may impel the Court into new insights about fundamental constitutional guarantees. The judicial resolutions gained from these insights may be consonant with public consensus, but they result from constitutional analysis, not public opinion. The perceived parallels between Court decisions and public opinion also can be misleading. The *Pierce* decision may be viewed as a victory for tolerance, but the Court's rejection of state monopoly of education more aptly reflects the determination by a conservative court to protect traditional parental prerogatives from encroaching state control.

News of the decision reached Portland by telegraph and telephone. St. Mary's students and teachers rejoiced at the decision. Sister M. Benildis, like many in the Catholic community, walked through Portland "hardly able to see through my tears." Telegrams, phone calls, and letters poured into the school, celebrating the "splendid triumph." One congratulatory message rejoiced, "You have more than pioneered!"[15]

The decision captured the attention of the nation, with excerpts from the opinion appearing in newspapers across the country. The *New York Times* devoted front-page coverage to the case, writing that "few decisions in years have attracted as much attention as the present one."[16] Indeed, many of the articles described the case as one of the most important decided by the Supreme Court in a generation. Editorials praised the opinion as a triumph for liberty and a defeat for statism. Louis Marshall, author of the amicus brief for the American Jewish Committee, wrote to Father Burke that the case would prove to be a "landmark in our constitutional history."[17] Religious and education leaders hailed *Pierce* as the "Magna Charta" of education.

Members of Congress, attorneys, educators, politicians, and religious leaders flooded the Court with requests for copies of the opinion. Within three days of the decision, the Court professed to have no opinions left, although it did manage, throughout the summer and fall, to find some copies in response to requests by senators and other public notables. An Ohio businessman, William Clerkin, sent Chief Justice Taft, a fellow Buckeye, a copy of an editorial in the *Akron Beacon Journal* lauding the opinion as a triumph of liberty over the "vicious" Prussian law. Clerkin's cover letter concluded with praise for the Court's role in undoing the "wrongful" laws enacted by "the howling chimpanzees; orangoutangs [*sic*]; and slabbering-mouthed demigods with their patriotism in their shoe soles."[18] Neither the chief justice nor the Court clerk responded to his letter.

Not everyone found cause to celebrate the decision. Some supporters of compulsory public education, dismayed at the decision, vowed to seek an amendment to the federal constitution. Michigan Klan leader James Hamilton sought to keep the case alive. Two days after the decision, he wrote to Oregon attorney general Isaac Van Winkle, asking Van Winkle to seek a rehearing before the Court and offering the assistance of his attorney. Van Winkle's response made clear that the state did not intend to pursue the case further.[19]

Felix Frankfurter published an unsigned article in the *New Republic* describing the decision as "just cause for rejoicing." Frankfurter expressed relief that the Court terminated the country's experiment with compelled public education: "Thus comes to an end the effort to regiment the mental life of Americans through coerced public school instruction." But Frankfurter's assessment of *Pierce* was mixed and ultimately unfavorable. He warned, "In rejoicing over the Nebraska and Oregon cases, we must not forget that a heavy price has to be paid for these occasional services to liberalism." Frankfurter argued that the *Pierce* decision necessitated "a more rigorous appraisal of the actual encouragement to liberalism afforded by judicial nullification of anti-liberal legislation." He worried about the "gains and losses to our national life due to the Supreme Court's control of legislation by the states." On balance, he concluded, "we regard the cost of this power of the Supreme Court on the whole as greater than its gains."[20] Frankfurter's objections to the Court's broad reading of the due process clause proved to be more substantial than his editorial disclosed. He did not treat *Pierce* kindly during his years on the Court, and the vitality of *Pierce* suffered from his opposition.

Oregonians greeted the decision primarily with relief. In the two and a half years since the passage of the School Bill, the influence of the Klan had waned, as had the postwar fear of radicalism. By the time the case concluded, Oregonians, like the rest of the country, were ready to view the decision as a victory for individual liberty and were eager to put a disquieting period of intolerance behind them. The *Oregonian* called the result "wise" and recommended that the state move on to other political issues. Claiming that the outcome was predictable and "foreseen by many including this newspaper," the paper failed to acknowledge that it had waited until late in the campaign to oppose the School Bill.[21] The *Corvallis Gazette-Times,* one of the few newspapers that had vigorously opposed the measure, was less sanguine. It opined that history would brand the School Bill as a "typical" instance of "mob rule" that "elected a governor, defeated and killed an Oregon Congressman, alienated forever friends of many years standing and created animosities and hatred which will not die in their generation."[22] Assistant Attorney General Willis S. Moore made clear that the state viewed the decision as conclusive on the matter of compulsory public education, claiming that the unanimous opinion of the Court "settles the fate of the law."[23]

Not all in Oregon government were ready to close the door on state monopoly of education or on the use of public schools as a tool of nationalism. On the day after the opinion issued, Governor Pierce, who agreed that the Court's decision ended the state's official involvement, announced his support for a federal constitutional amendment mandating public schooling. Even before the decision, the Oregon legislature had taken steps to advance assimilation through public education. The 1925 legislature created a department of Americanization, a state commission empowered to devise a "standardized course of study of Americanism" and to used the public school system to "promote and advance the work of Americanization."[24]

The NCWC had cause to celebrate, for the Court had embraced the parental rights so critical to the future of Catholic education. But the opinion was not the complete triumph they sought. While the NCWC publicly extolled the Court's decision for its endorsement of parental liberty, they privately expressed concern that the Court's affirmation of the state's considerable power over education would stimulate legislative efforts to regulate religious schools. The Court's sweeping articulation of parental rights left a great deal of ambiguity about where state power ended and parental liberty began. Given its confirmation of substantial state authority over education, the Court's failure to draw a more precise line separating state and parental prerogatives left considerable unresolved tension as to how that line would be drawn in future cases. Felix Frankfurter, in his editorial in the *New Republic*, described the Court's nod to state authority over education as "loose phrases" that left "ample room for the patrioteers to roll in their Trojan horses," because it "temptingly indicated to those bent on coercion how much room for mischief there is still left under the aegis of the Constitution."[25]

Father Burke shared Frankfurter's concerns. He confided to Kavanaugh his fears that the opinion left Catholic schools vulnerable to considerable meddling by the state: "A careful reading of the decision should sober those who are inclined to be drunk with enthusiasm over this decision."[26] Burke sought the counsel of O'Mara, who assured him that the opinion protected Catholic schools. O'Mara explained that the Court's reliance on the natural rights of parents was "the most satisfactory basis" possible for the decision because it confirmed a "political philosophy above the written constitution." O'Mara predicted that the decision "forever bars the abolition of the private school." He also believed that the opinion promised private schools additional autonomy. The language used by the Court rejecting state authority to "standardize" children impressed O'Mara as a powerful indicator that the Court would not allow states to mandate uniformity in textbooks or curriculum. Overall, he found that the decision "leaves the matter safe and secure." O'Mara best captured the sentiments of the inner circle of the NCWC when he concluded that he found the Court's opinion "not as comprehensive in some respects, and . . . not, perhaps, as satisfying in others, as we desired, [but] it affords less ground for misgiving than might be at first perceived." He also revealed, perhaps, the depth of his and Father Burke's disquiet with the presentation of the Sisters' case. Guthrie's willingness to concede extensive state control over education troubled O'Mara. Referring to the opinion's affirmation of expansive state authority to regulate education, he concluded his letter to Burke: "At least we can congratulate ourselves that the court did not state these powers of the state were conceded by counsel for the appellee."[27]

Guthrie had little opportunity to bask in his success. News of the decision reached him at Aix-les-Bains in eastern France. Bernard Hershkopf, Guthrie's New York associate on the case, sent Guthrie a copy of the opinion the day it issued. Guthrie, taking treatment in sulfur springs for his exhaustion, hoped to recover sufficiently to give the keynote address at the annual American Bar Association meeting in early September. Charles Evans Hughes, president of the ABA, had invited Guthrie to discuss *Pierce,* calling the case a landmark decision for constitutional liberties. Guthrie wanted to avoid any discussion of religious education. He thought it "essential" to avert "anything that would be likely to stir up a controversy in the American Bar Association on the subject of the public schools." Guthrie warned Hughes that a speech devoted to *Pierce* "might precipitate a dispute which would serve no useful purpose except to enable some fanatics and extremists to ventilate their views."[28] Guthrie never learned whether *Pierce* would provoke controversy among the nation's attorneys. The spa treatment exacerbated his symptoms. Incapacitated by severe headaches and insomnia, he was forced, to his great distress, to cancel his appearance.

Archbishop Christie of Portland, the architect of the Oregon Catholic school system and tireless opponent of the School Bill, did not live to see his life's work preserved. He died on April 6, less than two months before the Court rendered its decision. Early in his tenure, Christie had said, "I shall build schools first or I shall have an empty cathedral twenty years from now."[29] At his funeral, crowds of schoolchildren filled the church, and the hymns they sang rang into the streets of Portland. St. Mary's Academy carries on his legacy today. The only single-gender high school remaining in Oregon, it is one of the most highly regarded schools in the state.

PART III   **Legacy**

EPILOGUE

The nation plunged deeply into a dialogue on education and religion during that summer of 1925. By the time the Supreme Court issued the *Pierce* decision on June 1, the country's attention was already turning to the next "trial of the century," the Scopes "Monkey Trial." As Clarence Darrow prepared to defend John Scopes, a high school teacher charged in May with violating a Tennessee law prohibiting the teaching of evolution in public schools, both the popular and academic presses pondered the impact of the School Bill decision on academic freedom and parental and religious liberty. Most commentators expected the Scopes case to reach the Supreme Court, and they hotly debated whether *Pierce* provided grounds for the Court to find the Tennessee law unconstitutional. The applicability of *Pierce* to the antievolution law was by no means clear, since the Tennessee law regulated only public schools. But many scholars claimed that *Pierce* offered a plausible argument that the law violated parental rights, among other deficiencies.[1]

William Jennings Bryan, leading proponent of antievolution legislation and prosecutor in the Scopes trial, argued that the *Pierce* decision lent support to state enactment of antievolution laws.

> The Oregon case affirms the right of the parent to guard the religious welfare of the child, and this, I think, is decisive in our case. The Oregon case also affirms the right of the state to control the schools to the extent of compelling the teaching of anything that the state deems necessary, and ex-

plicitly declaring the right of the state to prohibit the teaching of anything "manifestly inimical" to the public welfare. The words "manifestly inimical" might be in a large way open for construction, but certainly the state legislature or the state Supreme Court, rather than the United States Supreme Court, would be the power to decide what is "manifestly inimical."[2]

Attorney Thomas O'Mara advised Father Burke that the Scopes case could achieve the constitutional protection of intellectual liberty missing from the *Pierce* decision. He wrote that the "Tennessee Evolution case carries the advantage to us of focusing attention more intensively upon pedagogical liberty." O'Mara predicted that Catholic education would benefit, regardless of the outcome: "Without having anything in jeopardy ourselves, we stand to gain in almost any event." If the courts upheld the power of the state to prohibit the teaching of evolution in public schools, the stature of private schools as bastions of intellectual freedom would be "greatly enhanced." If the law was invalidated, "a magna charta of educational liberty would be written." O'Mara expressed concern that the Supreme Court might "through inadvertence" modify *Pierce* when it ruled on the Tennessee law. But he decided that any change in precedent was "highly improbable" given that the Oregon case was "fresh" in the minds of the justices. More troubling to O'Mara was the "misfortune" that the Scopes case "is going to be handled largely from the standpoint of attempting to demonstrate the validity of evolutionary theory rather than from the standpoint of asserting the integrity of impartial instruction." He hoped that when the case reached the Supreme Court, the justices would "stand for the ideal of intellectual liberty."[3]

July belonged to the "Monkey Trial," and by the time the proceedings opened on July 10, press coverage dominated front pages across the country. The jury granted Darrow's request to convict so that the case could be appealed, but 18 months later, the Tennessee Supreme Court upheld the antievolution law against arguments that it violated the liberty interests protected by *Pierce* and *Meyer*. The state court misread both cases, ignoring the parental rights issue and finding the cases irrelevant because they dealt with statutes affecting "individuals, corporations, and private institutions." The Scopes case never made it to the U.S. Supreme Court, for the Tennessee court overturned the conviction on a technicality.[4]

The momentum for compulsory public education died with the *Pierce* decision. The Oregon district court opinion in 1924 had rattled the movement leaders. Later that same year, voters in Michigan and Washington soundly defeated initiatives compelling public education. The Supreme Court's rejection of state monopoly of education as a primary means of values inculcation dealt a blow to the progressive education agenda. After the decision, advocates of compulsory public schooling proposed a federal constitutional amendment to overrule *Pierce,* but they garnered little support. Despite these losses, the progressive vision of public schools as the guarantors of assimilation did not disappear. Nor did the nativist hostility to private schools, particularly those populated primarily with ethnic and religious minorities. *Pierce* may have prohibited closure of these schools, but it did not preclude regulation. Nativists remained determined to put in place laws regulating foreign-language training and patriotism classes.

Only two years after *Pierce,* the Court took up another case concerning parental rights and education. This time the law arose in Hawaii, under the Hawaiian territorial government, and targeted the Japanese community, which had established a flourishing network of private schools. Like *Meyer,* the law limited foreign-language education in private schools. The Hawaiian law provided for comprehensive regulation of foreign-language schools, including prohibiting attendance until a student had completed the first and second grades in public schools and imposing a per pupil permitting fee on the schools. If implemented, the law would have crippled the Japanese schools. In *Farrington v. Tokushige,* the Court found the law unconstitutional. Once again, Justice McReynolds wrote a very brief opinion that asserted, rather than explained, parental liberty. Content merely to cite *Pierce* and *Meyer* for the doctrine "touching rights" guaranteed to school owners, parents, and children concerning school attendance, the Court summarily concluded that Hawaii had acted "without adequate reason."[5]

The Shift to Incorporation of the Bill of Rights

Pierce augured additional changes in constitutional doctrine. The Court's reliance on Fourteenth Amendment liberty made the holding compatible with, if not identical to, the many precedents protecting economic liberties. But the Court's recognition of "personal," as compared to economic, rights, even if incidental to the antistatist message of the opinion, nevertheless signaled a willingness to extend the reach of the Fourteenth Amendment. *Pierce* hinted at how far this reach might stretch. The conclusion that parents have a constitutional right to make basic choices about how to educate their children, including the type of knowledge and values imparted, implicated fundamental First Amendment principles that were only beginning to be formulated by the Court. *Pierce*'s expansive reading of liberty reveals a Court poised to expand federal judicial review of state laws impacting fundamental rights. The opinion's reliance on substantive due process kept the Court in familiar doctrinal territory, even as it extended the scope of constitutional liberty. *Pierce* thus served as a bridge to the doctrinal transformation that would occur when the Court applied the Bill of Rights to the states. Only one week later, the Court crossed that bridge in *Gitlow,* when it "assumed," for the first time, that freedom of speech is one of the liberties protected against state infringement by the Fourteenth Amendment. Although dicta, the Court substantially expanded its reach over state law when it stated: "for present purposes, we may and do assume that freedom of speech and of the press . . . are among the fundamental personal rights and 'liberties' protected by the due process clause of the Fourteenth Amendment from impairment by the states."[6]

Why the Court took that step in *Gitlow* rather than *Pierce* discloses a good deal about the jurisprudence of the times and the litigation of the cases. The Court in *Meyer* had already acknowledged a constitutional basis for parental rights in the due process clause. Substantive due process, although not uncontroversial, remained supported by decades of precedent. Parental rights in particular bore a strong cultural and historical pedigree. By contrast, the connection between the educational interests at stake in *Pierce* and First Amendment principles derived from a theory of freedom of thought that at that time appeared primarily in the dissents of Justices Holmes and Brandeis. For the Court to strike down the Oregon law on First Amendment grounds would have required a dramatic expansion of constitutional law encompassing both the incorporation of the Bill of Rights and a redefinition of the First Amendment. Instead, the Court risked little by deciding *Pierce* on existing precedent.

The *Pierce* parties did not push the Court on the incorporation issue. Although the Sisters argued that the law interfered with religious liberty, they clearly focused their case on parental rights. The parties in *Gitlow,* however, pressed the Court, devoting a considerable part of their briefs to incorporation. Unlike *Pierce,* the *Gitlow* case offered the Court the opportunity to change constitutional doctrine incrementally. *Gitlow* involved a prosecution for political speech and, apart from the incorporation question, raised archetypical First Amendment issues. The Court could thus resolve the case without disturbing precedents regarding free speech. By upholding the conviction while at the same time opening the door to incorporation of the Bill of Rights, the Court was able to introduce a major interpretive shift without actually implementing it. With *Pierce* and *Gitlow,* the Court managed to expand the constitutional meaning of liberty with minimal doctrinal disruption.

Pierce and *Gitlow* set the stage for the Court to enlarge dramatically its protection of individual rights, but no immediate shift occurred. To the contrary, during the 1920s, the Court showed little inclination to extend individual rights into uncharted waters. *Gitlow,* by affirming yet another conviction of a radical for distribution of socialist literature, highlights the importance of *Pierce* as an antistatist decision. Despite a powerful dissent by Justice Holmes, the *Gitlow* majority displayed scant tolerance for unconventional views. In the 1927 case *Buck v. Bell,* the Court upheld, against constitutional challenge, a Virginia law providing for the involuntary sterilization of certain mentally disabled individuals, concluding its opinion with the now infamous statement by Justice Holmes that "three generations of imbeciles are enough."[7] The Court apparently saw no connection between the private realm of parental prerogatives protected in *Pierce* and the right of an individual not to be involuntarily sterilized. It would take the Court another 15 years to hold, in *Skinner v. Oklahoma,* that decisions relating to marriage and procreation are fundamental to an individual and part of the "basic civil rights of man."[8] *Buck v. Bell* makes it clear that while *Pierce* was a liberty-enhancing case, it would be a mistake to overemphasize this part of the decision. The Court's constitutional protection of parental rights was quite consistent with its conservative judicial philosophy. Parental rights came before the Court bearing a distinguished common-law pedigree and a near unanimous social consensus on their legitimacy. The Court risked little in confirming their constitutional stature.

Gitlow, ironically, by opening the door to incorporation of the First Amendment, threatened the legitimacy of *Pierce* as precedent, as did other dramatic changes in the Court's constitutional jurisprudence during the 1920s and 1930s. *Gitlow*'s assumption that the First Amendment applied to the states carried significant implications for cases involving education and religion.[9] Educational freedom and religious liberty also could be expected to fall under the protection of the First Amendment. Freedom of thought, in fact, had been described by Father Burke and others as the essence of the

Pierce dispute. It was entirely plausible that the Court, in future cases concerning education, would ignore parental rights to focus on First Amendment analysis. If so, *Pierce* would become an anachronistic transition case whose doctrinal foundations were no longer relevant.

Pierce *and the Decline of Substantive Due Process*

Shifts in the Court's interpretation of substantive due process also boded ill for the continued vitality of parental rights. The *Lochner* era ended in the 1930s, when the Court, facing a country battered by economic disaster, abandoned its guardianship of economic liberties as fundamental rights and began to sustain federal and state legislation designed to alleviate the social and economic suffering of the Depression. The Court's rejection of heightened protection for economic liberties cast a shadow on the continued validity of *Pierce*. The justices sudden willingness to uphold regulation of economic liberty under the Fourteenth Amendment as long as it met a minimal standard of rationality placed parental rights on constitutional quicksand, since *Pierce* sprang from the same expansive reading of the due process clause now discarded by the Court. No cases concerning parental rights came to the docket during this era, but the doctrinal transformation left unresolved the fate of parental liberty.

Given the significant changes in constitutional doctrine following *Pierce*, the Court, by the 1930s, seemed poised either to ignore the School Bill decision or to discredit it. Neither scenario occurred. *Pierce*, instead, has endured, and remains part of the established canon of constitutional law. Since the 1920s, more than 144 Supreme Court cases have cited *Pierce* as authority.

That *Pierce* survived as precedent raises provocative questions about its legacy. The case defies easy categorization. In decisions from the 1920s through the 1960s, *Pierce* is variously described as protecting not only parental rights but also economic liberty, free speech, and religious liberty. The Court's efforts during this period to recast the doctrinal basis for the case may well have been driven by an interest in protecting parental rights from the black hole of cases discredited by its rejection of *Lochner*. Until the 1960s, the Court rarely invoked substantive due process, preferring instead to protect individual liberties by application of the Bill of Rights to the states.

Despite this identity crisis, *Pierce* became influential primarily in two areas of constitutional law: as a foundational case supporting the right of privacy and other personal liberty interests under the Fourteenth Amendment and as the standard borne by parents seeking to mold public education. The first legacy relies on *Pierce* predominantly as a theoretical cornerstone, citing it as evidence of the Court's long history of protecting unenumerated personal rights under the due process clause. In this line of cases, parental rights continue to maintain a degree of constitutional vitality. But as a doctrinal matter, the rights specifically recognized in *Pierce* matter less than the Court's willingness to insulate certain fundamental interests from intrusive government regulation, even when those interests are not detailed in the Constitution. By contrast, parental rights do form the core of the second legacy of *Pierce*. The movement for school choice revisits the themes of education, religious liberty, and parental prerogative so central to the School Bill case.

The modern meaning of *Pierce* draws from both legacies, and the antistatist heart of the opinion remains central to most new decisions that cite *Pierce* as precedent. But the most important lesson to be drawn from *Pierce* is both broader than parental rights and more subtle than simple antistatism. The central concern of *Pierce* is the substantial threat to liberty posed by state-compelled identity. This issue once again has become pivotal in a number of highly controversial cases that require the Court to address the meaning of personal identity and self-determination. The significance of *Pierce* to this debate can best be understood by examining the impact of the decision on constitutional canon.

In the decades following *Pierce,* the religious intolerance associated with the passage of the School Bill led the Court, on several occasions, to describe *Pierce* as a case about religious liberty, despite the obvious fact that the Court decided the case on other grounds. The persistent social and legal tensions surrounding parents, religion, and education make the Court's description of *Pierce* understandable, if not doctrinally precise. In 1937, Justice Cardozo's opinion in *Palko v. Connecticut* identified *Pierce* as a case about free exercise. The next year, in footnote 4 of *United States v. Carolene Products,* often described as the most significant footnote in constitutional law, the Court, in explaining why the presumption of constitutionality normally accorded legislation may not apply when government regulation impacts certain minority groups or fundamental rights, described *Pierce* as a case about religious discrimination.[10] Similarly, Justice Frankfurter said *Pierce* is a Bill of Rights case about religious liberty, both in his opinion for the Court in *Minersville School District v. Gobitis,* upholding the state's authority to require children to recite the Pledge of Allegiance, and in his dissent in *West Virginia State Board of Education v. Barnette*, when three years later the Court overruled *Minersville*.[11]

The Court's discussion of *Pierce* in a number of cases concerning religious liberty blends parental rights and religious freedom, seeming to confirm the opinion of justices like Frankfurter that *Pierce* would have been decided under the free exercise clause of the First Amendment if that claim had been available to the plaintiff. But these cases also recognize parental rights as a separate constitutional claim. For example, in *Prince v. Commonwealth of Massachusetts*, a case involving the right of a Jehovah's Witness to have her child sell religious literature, in violation of child labor laws, the Court cited *Pierce* as precedent both when it described the First Amendment right of parents to give their children religious education and when it proclaimed, "It is cardinal with us that the custody, care and nurture of the child reside first in the parents."[12] Similarly, in *Wisconsin v. Yoder*, concerning the right of Amish parents to have their children excused from mandatory school attendance, the Court declared that the parental rights recognized in *Pierce* were "beyond debate," while at the same time explaining, "It is clear that such an intrusion by a State into family decisions in the area of religious training would give rise to grave questions of religious freedom comparable to . . . those presented in *Pierce*." In *Yoder*, the Court, acknowledging its rather enigmatic reading of *Pierce*, concluded, "However read, the Court's holding in *Pierce* stands as a charter of the rights of parents to direct the religious upbringing of their children."[13]

Not surprisingly, the Court occasionally invoked the First Amendment speech clause when citing *Pierce*. The *Pierce* opinion, by describing educational choice as a fundamental parental prerogative, forges a connection to freedom of thought, a core First Amendment principle. State compelled public schooling may threaten the ability of parents to transmit their values and beliefs through the education process. Justice Brandeis, a member of the *Pierce* Court, cited *Pierce* as standing for the First Amendment "right to teach," in his 1927 concurrence in *Whitney v. California*. Justice Brandeis implicitly drew a close parallel between *Pierce* liberty and First Amendment values when he argued that the founders believed that "the freedom to think as you will" is indispensable to truth.[14] *Griswold v. Connecticut*, the case establishing a constitutional right of privacy, made the point explicitly, identifying *Pierce* and *Meyer* as First Amendment speech cases that protect "freedom of inquiry, freedom of thought, and freedom to teach."[15]

In *Tinker v. Des Moines School District,* the Court, upholding the First Amendment rights of students to protest the Vietnam War by wearing black armbands, relied in part on *Pierce* and *Meyer.* The Court referenced both the due process foundations of *Pierce* and *Meyer* and the First Amendment to explain that "it can hardly be argued that either students or teachers shed their constitutional rights to freedom of speech or expression at the schoolhouse gate."[16] *Tinker* also made clear the close connection between educational liberty, the First Amendment, and antistatism. Citing *Meyer's* repudiation of the Spartan system of education through comprehensive indoctrination, the Court concluded that "state-operated schools may not be enclaves of totalitarianism." Students, the Court argued, "may not be regarded as closed-circuit recipients of only that which the state chooses to communicate."[17]

The taint of *Lochner* continued to dog *Pierce.* Justice Felix Frankfurter's initial mixed response to *Pierce* hardened into condemnation; he refused to sign onto Justice Rutledge's opinion in *Prince* because it relied on *Pierce* and *Meyer.* Writing to Rutledge, Frankfurter complained, "On the road to your conclusion in the *Prince* case you are guided by several landmarks to which thus far I do not yield acceptance." Naming *Pierce* and *Meyer,* Frankfurter concluded, "I shall turn out to be a very bad prophet indeed if this Court will not come to rue the implications of *Pierce v. Society of Sisters.*"[18] In *Bolling v. Sharpe,* the federal companion case to the landmark *Brown v. Board of Education,* the parents urged the Court to recognize parental rights under the Fifth Amendment, which governs federal regulation.[19] They argued that segregated schools violated the rights of parents to direct the education of their children. Chief Justice Earl Warren's original draft adopted the parents' argument, concluding that segregation violated the right to knowledge and education protected in *Pierce* and *Meyer.* This passage disappeared from the final opinion, apparently because of the anti-*Lochner* objections of Justices Hugo Black and Felix Frankfurter.[20]

Efforts to recast *Pierce* as a First Amendment case abated with the resurgence of substantive due process in the 1960s. The "liberty" rights that reemerged derived from privacy concerns, not economic ones, and unlike the Court in the *Pierce* era, the Warren Court embraced an expansive definition of constitutional liberty. *Pierce* was lauded as one of the doctrinal lynchpins of personal privacy rights. Justice Harlan, in an influential 1961 dissent in *Poe v. Ullman,* which laid the foundation for the right of privacy the Court would recognize four years later, struggled to articulate the constitutional significance of

Pierce. Like the Court in *Prince* and *Yoder,* he speculated that *Pierce* and *Meyer* "today" would "probably" have been decided under the First Amendment rights of conscience and expression. But he went on to argue that it was not "wrong" to rest those decisions on liberty, because the privacy of the home and family life is so "fundamental" that it draws its protection from more than one constitutional right. *Pierce* and *Meyer,* Harlan concluded, delineate the "private realm of family life which the state cannot enter."[21]

Justice Harlan's argument illustrates how antistatism links *Pierce* and the Court's due process doctrine. Describing the guarantees of due process as "bulwarks" against "arbitrary legislation," Harlan explained that the Court had "again and again" rejected any attempt to limit liberty to the freedoms found in the Bill of Rights. Instead, the Court defined liberty as "a rational continuum which, broadly speaking, includes a freedom from all substantial arbitrary impositions and purposeless restraints." *Pierce* implicates both First Amendment and liberty values, because these values overlap. Due process is "more general and inclusive" than the specific prohibitions in the Bill of Rights, but both reflect fundamental rights that belong "to the citizens of all free governments." Citing *Pierce,* Harlan concluded that "the purposes of those guarantees and not their text, the reasons for their statement by the Framers and not the statement itself," justify their protection as liberty interests under the Fourteenth Amendment.[22]

AFTERWORD *Pierce* Redux

In the landmark case *Griswold v. Connecticut,* the Court recognized a constitutional right of privacy and cited *Pierce* as support for this right. *Griswold* has nothing to do with parental rights—it invalidated a state law prohibiting the use of contraceptives—but it, too, focuses on the relationship between individual and state and on the limits democracy imposes on state power. The appellants challenging the law described *Pierce* in civic terms, as precedent protecting the right of an individual to "sustain his position as citizen rather than subject." The appellants had to convince the Court that striking down the statute would not be resurrecting *Lochner. Pierce* and *Meyer,* they argued, validly recognize fundamental personal liberties and should not be compared to *Lochner*'s unprincipled insulation of economic liberties. They assured the Court that they requested only adherence to *Pierce,* not "reinstatement" of *Lochner.*[1]

Pierce *and Privacy*

After *Griswold* came a line of cases protecting the privacy of an individual to make certain fundamental personal choices intimately connected to the meaning of family, including marriage, contraception, abortion, and cohabitation. In *Roe v. Wade,* the Court described the right protected in *Pierce* as "implicit in the concept of ordered liberty."[2] The Court's treatment of *Pierce* as a cornerstone of privacy doctrine recognizes that the School Bill case made a fundamental statement about the limits of state control over the individual.

The constellation of rights protected as "liberties" under the Fourteenth Amendment is best described as points on a line marking the outer limits of governmental authority over intimate personal and family decisions. The Court has identified a number of these points—including the right to marry, the right to choose whether to have a child, the right to refuse medical treatment, and the right of homosexuals to engage in sexual intimacy. As in *Pierce*, these decisions focus primarily on setting the boundaries of state control over the individual. They offer little insight into the nature or scope of the rights protected.

On occasion, the Court has explained the relationship between defining rights and demarcating state power. In *Moore v. City of East Cleveland*, a grandmother, relying in part on *Pierce*, challenged a housing ordinance that defined "family" in a way that precluded her grandsons from residing in her home. The city sought to distinguish *Pierce*, arguing that the case did not protect grandparents' rights or a family unit other than the nuclear family. A plurality of the Court rejected such a narrow interpretation of *Pierce*, refusing to "close our eyes to the basic reasons why certain rights associated with the family have been accorded shelter." Quoting Justice Harlan's dissent in *Poe*, the Court explained that its due process jurisprudence represents "the balance which our Nation, built upon postulates of respect for the liberty of the individual, has struck between that liberty and the demands of an organized society." Unlike other cases of the *Lochner* era, *Pierce* and *Meyer* survive, the Court concluded, precisely because they strike the appropriate balance between state power and rights valued by society.[3] In *Moore*, the Court recognized that the threat of standardization of the individual by the state extends beyond public education. Quoting *Pierce*, the Court found that the Constitution "prevents East Cleveland from standardizing its children— and its adults—by forcing all to live in certain narrowly defined family patterns."[4] As *Moore* makes clear, the import of the modern cases on substantive due process lies not in how specifically the Court defines the metes and bounds of the particular liberty at stake but in the very act of line drawing. The Court's protection of a sphere of personal choice does not simply articulate liberty; it defines it.

The privacy cases share with *Pierce* a preoccupation with draconian governmental control over significant personal choices. The consistent thread in all these decisions is the Court's distrust of regulation that infringes on choices deemed central to self-identity. The link between liberty and identity was recognized as early as 1937, when, in *Palko v. Connecticut,* the Court described freedom of thought as "the matrix, the indispensable condition, of nearly every other form of freedom." Justice Cardozo's opinion went on to conclude that the "domain of liberty" recognized by the Court includes "liberty of the mind as well as liberty of action."[5]

Nowhere is the connection between *Pierce* and the modern substantive due process cases more obvious than in recent decisions addressing abortion and homosexual sodomy. The essence of *Pierce,* the Court's rejection of state efforts to "standardize" its citizens forms the constitutional core of the Court's discussion of liberty in these opinions. The Court's decision in *Planned Parenthood of Southeastern Pa. v. Casey,* reaffirming the right of a woman to choose abortion prior to viability of the fetus, discusses the liberty interest at stake in language that directly evokes *Pierce*'s disquiet about the standardizing effects of state-monopolized education: "At the heart of liberty is the right to define one's own concept of existence, of meaning, of the universe, and of the mystery of human life. Beliefs about these matters could not define the attributes of personhood were they formed under compulsion of the State."[6] In *Lawrence v. Texas,* which invalidates a Texas statute making it a crime for two persons of the same gender to engage in certain intimate acts, the Court wrote that "freedom extends beyond spatial bounds." It described that freedom as one of identity and personality: "Liberty presumes an autonomy of self that includes freedom of thought, belief, expression, and certain intimate conduct." The Court rejected the state's authority to "control" an individual's "destiny" by criminalizing consensual sexual conduct between adults.[7]

The Shift from Privacy to Liberty

Casey and *Lawrence* mark a shift in the Court's approach to substantive due process. *Casey* and *Lawrence* return the language of substantive due process to the analysis of "liberty" addressed in *Pierce.* Prior to *Casey,* the Court held in a number of cases that the due process clause protects a right of privacy. The Court's recognition of a constitutional right of privacy has been highly controversial, primarily because of the absence of any explicit reference in the Constitution to privacy. Critics charge that the Court's privacy analysis is based on the predilections of the justices and not the constitutional text.

In *Casey* and *Lawrence,* the Court jettisons the language of privacy and speaks once again of constitutional liberty. The opinion in *Casey* begins with the statement "Liberty finds no refuge in a jurisprudence of doubt."[8] The first paragraph in *Lawrence* alludes to the same constitutional interest, describing both the spatial liberty of an individual to be free from unwarranted governmental intrusions into the home and the "more transcendent" liberty that "presumes an autonomy of self."[9] Of course the meaning of liberty is no more apparent than the definition of privacy, but liberty, unlike privacy, is firmly grounded in constitutional text.

The import of this shift may be more than semantic. In *Casey* and *Lawrence,* the Court's reliance on liberty rather than privacy signaled a retreat from the heightened judicial protection given fundamental rights. If this trend continues, Fourteenth Amendment liberty interests will carry significantly less constitutional weight. The Court's revival of liberty analysis admirably focuses interpretation on the constitutional text, but this shift will serve ultimately to impair individual rights if the Court fails to accord liberty interests the same vigorous constitutional protection given other constitutional rights.

Both *Casey* and *Lawrence* owe a great deal to *Pierce.* In all three cases, the Court rejects regulation that compels the individual to conform to the majority's conception of personhood. In doing so, the Court makes clear that liberty includes the right not to be controlled by the state in certain significant personal choices. More important, the shared characteristic of this liberty is the protection of attributes of personal identity from compulsion by the state. *Casey* and *Lawrence* offer a definition of liberty grounded in personal identity that reflects the same antiauthoritarian value so central to *Pierce.* The danger perceived by the Court from the regulations at issue in each of these cases is that of the majority dictating the destiny of those individuals who would choose a different path. In the end, governmental efforts to compel conformity to a democratically defined ideal undermine the very autonomy and individuality essential to the preservation of democracy. Liberty, as articulated in these cases, is the right not to be turned into an object to serve state goals.

Parental Rights and Modern Education

The constitutional future of parental rights per se is less certain. The immediate effect of *Pierce* confirmed Felix Frankfurter's concern that the case offered opportunity for "mischief" by state regulators. In a number of states, *Pierce* spurred legislation increasing the requirements for compulsory school attendance. But *Pierce* and *Meyer* also inspired a movement advocating parental choice, particularly in public education. Touted as the "Magna Charta" of parental rights, *Pierce* galvanized parents seeking greater influence over state education policy. Parental choice has enjoyed considerable success as a social and political movement, achieving education reforms through legislatures and school boards. All 50 states authorize some form of homeschooling in lieu of public school attendance. Advocates for parental rights led the fight for the adoption of school voucher plans. *Pierce* continues to lend authority to parents demanding a voice in the formulation of public education priorities and programs.

Pierce has not been as successful in securing parents a constitutional right to influence public education policy. As early as 1944, with expectations about government regulation already transformed by the New Deal, Justice Frankfurter advised his colleague Justice Wiley Rutledge that the Court might some day "rue the implications of *Pierce*" on the Court's review of education policy.[10] Justice Frankfurter's fears proved unwarranted. To the contrary, *Pierce* has not dramatically realigned the constitutional balance of power between parents and state over education. The Court's statement in *Pierce* that the child is "not the mere creature of the state," although carrying a clear antistatist message, just as clearly affirms significant government authority over the education of children. As a result, *Pierce* has been only marginally successful in securing parental rights in education; modern courts applying *Pierce* to disputes between parents and educators tend to read the case narrowly. Most conclude that *Pierce* goes no further than precluding the state from preempting the education process by requiring all children to attend public schools. The modern expansion of state and federal regulatory authority over education further blurs the line drawn in *Pierce* between state and parental control. Courts have been unwilling to strike down state education policy in the name of parental rights, deferring to the traditional and paramount authority of the state over education.

The deference accorded the state is apparent in two Supreme Court cases concerning school discipline and school curriculum. Like *Tinker,* these cases involve efforts by schools to limit First Amendment expression. Unlike *Tinker,* the Court upheld the authority of the schools to restrict First Amendment activities that interfere with the school environment. In *Bethel School District v. Fraser,* the Court upheld the right of a high school to discipline a student for delivering a lewd speech at a school assembly. The Court explained that the inculcation of democratic values is "truly" the mission of the schools and that the "determination of what manner of speech in the classroom or in school assembly is inappropriate properly rests with the school board."[11] In *Hazelwood School District v. Kuhlmeier,* the Court upheld the school principal's authority to edit a school newspaper that was produced as part of a journalism class. Instead of the strict scrutiny typically applied to state attempts to limit expression, the Court merely evaluated whether the school acted reasonably, stressing the "oft-expressed view" that the "education of the Nation's youth is primarily the responsibility of parents, teachers, and state and local school officials."[12] Even *Tinker* explains that the Court "has repeatedly emphasized the need for affirming the comprehensive authority of the States and of school officials ... to prescribe and control conduct in the schools."[13]

The Court's willingness to defer to school officials, even when faced with First Amendment claims, sends a strong message to lower courts reviewing government decisions concerning education. Courts typically respond to this directive by rejecting efforts by parents to tailor curriculum to parental preferences. The assertion of parental rights may have helped secure the passage of legislation permitting homeschooling, but courts repeatedly deny claims by parents that *Pierce* guarantees them the right to homeschool free from state regulation of curriculum, textbooks, or teacher qualifications. *Pierce* has also not persuaded the courts that the state must acquiesce when parents seek to remove their children from required classes. In a number of cases involving mandatory health or sex education, courts have questioned the applicability of *Pierce* to challenges to curriculum policy. They severely limit the scope of the decision, finding that once parents exercise their right to choose public or private schooling, their fundamental right to control the education of their children is "substantially limited." *Pierce,* these courts conclude, does not give parents the right to restrict the flow of information in public schools and certainly does not give them a fundamental constitutional right to "dictate the curriculum."[14] *Pierce* is a case primarily about state coercion: the case precludes the state from compelling parents to send their children to public school, but it cannot be read either to endow parents with any positive right to prescribe education policy or to impose a constitutional obligation on the state to conform to parental wishes. The authority of *Pierce* ends at the schoolhouse door.

Wisconsin v. Yoder, the 1972 case upholding the rights of Amish parents to be granted an exemption from laws mandating school attendance for their 14- and 15-year-old children, marks the Court's only significant protection of parental rights in education outside *Pierce* and *Meyer*. But the result in *Yoder* is best explained by the conjunction in the case of parental rights and a claim of free exercise under the First Amendment. The Court relied on *Pierce* to reject the state's claim that it is entitled, as *parens patriae* and against the wishes of the parents, to "save" an Amish child by requiring an additional two years of compulsory formal high school education. But the Court also made clear the significance of the free exercise claim to the favorable outcome for the parents, by concluding that "when the interests of parenthood are combined with a free exercise claim of the nature revealed by this record, more than merely a 'reasonable relation to some purpose within the competency of the State' is required to sustain the validity of the State's requirement under the First Amendment."[15] *Yoder* ultimately narrows the reach of *Pierce*. The Court emphasized the relationship between *Pierce* and religious liberty, describing the holding as a "charter of the rights of parents to direct the religious upbringing of their children." More recently, in *Employment Division v. Smith,* the Court said *Pierce* involved the same kind of "hybrid" constitutional claim as *Yoder,* one that joined a claim of parental rights with a claim of free exercise. In *Smith,* the Court suggested that the synergistic union of these two constitutional interests best explains the outcome in *Pierce,* ignoring, once again, the fact that *Pierce* did not involve a free exercise claim.[16]

Some of the reluctance by the courts to expand *Pierce*'s impact on education may stem from the civil rights era. Although parents seeking to dismantle segregation often relied on parental rights, so did the parents seeking to preserve it. After *Brown v. Board of Education,* a number of southern states implemented state-subsidized voucher programs so white parents could send their children to private, segregated schools. Other states adopted "freedom of choice" programs that ostensibly allowed parents to transfer their children out of segregated schools but that were intended to maintain the status quo. The Court finally struck down these programs in a 1968 case, *Green v. County School Board of New Kent County.*[17] The Court also confronted efforts to maintain segregation that relied directly on the parental rights protected by *Pierce*. In *Norwood v. Harrison,* a case invalidating a Mississippi program that provided free textbooks to all schools, including those engaging in racial discrimination, the Court rejected any suggestion that *Pierce* could be used to justify segregation. The Court cautioned that the *Pierce* holding was "not without limits." It chastised the state for failing to recognize the opinion's "limited scope" when the state argued that parents of children attending private, segregated schools have a right to receive textbooks on equal footing with public schools. *Pierce,* the Court made clear, merely protects the right of private schools to exist; the opinion "said nothing of any supposed right of private or parochial schools to share with public schools in state largesse."[18] Similarly, in *Runyon v. McCrary,* private schools engaging in racial discrimination claimed that the prohibition on segregation imposed by the Civil Rights Act interfered with parental rights. The Court once again dismissed the parental rights argument, reading *Pierce* narrowly to hold simply that parents have a constitutional right to send their children to private school. Parents, the Court concluded, "have no constitutional right to provide their children with private school education unfettered by reasonable government regulation."[19]

During the second half of the twentieth century, this "reasonable government regulation" extended to far more than civil rights guarantees. The dramatic expansion of federal and state regulation of education undermines the significance of *Pierce* as a constraint on education policy. The modern Court's validation of extensive government control over education clearly demonstrates none of the hostility to regulation evident during the *Pierce* era. Whether this validation evinces less of a commitment by the Court to antistatist principles is less obvious. The Court's disdain for the School Bill was not due merely to an antipathy to regulation. To the contrary, the Court was quite careful to draw a generous sphere of legitimate government authority in matters pertaining to education. The severe solution imposed by the School Bill, the elimination of private education in the state, forced the Court to consider the outer limit of permissible government regulation. Compelled public education transgressed that boundary because it eliminated parental options. Modern challenges to burdensome education regulation, however onerous, simply do not present the same degree of threat to individual choice that roused the Court in *Pierce. Casey* and *Lawrence,* by contrast, concern the same identity compulsion at the core of *Pierce* and attest to the continued vigor of antistatist jurisprudence.

But apart from its antistatist rationale, *Pierce* ultimately offers little guidance on significant issues concerning parents, children, and education. The marginal impact of the decision on the control of education policy reflects a recognition that these issues are far more complex than the question of state coercion presented in *Pierce.* Modern education theorists still debate the benefits of compulsory public schooling, including whether persuasive justifications that were lacking in *Pierce* now exist. The progressives of the 1920s supported mandatory public education because they perceived that public schools offered the best means to instill values of tolerance, equality, and democracy into all children. The inculcation of these values remains vital to many modern theorists.[20] Other than prohibiting the elimination of private schools, *Pierce* leaves unanswered how far the state may go to control the ideas imparted in public and private schools. A compelled curriculum devoted to democratic values does not limit parental choice as directly as the Oregon School Bill. But any state effort to exert comprehensive control over the transmission of ideas implicates *Pierce*'s rejection of state authority to "standardize" its children.

Pierce does not provide insight into how the educational interests of the child are to be addressed in this polarized struggle between parents and state. Extensive state authority over educational choice and curriculum can be more readily justified if one rejects or qualifies the *Pierce* assumption that children belong to their parents. Parental rights concerning education are necessarily qualified by the modern legal recognition that children are entitled to some degree of self-autonomy and independence. That autonomy assumes that children may have an interest in their education and preparation for citizenship that is distinct from the dictates of their parents. *Pierce* frames the constitutional parameters of the debate between parents and state over education, but it does so in the context of a direct and draconian effort by the state to control parental choice. *Pierce*'s endorsement of parental rights in education has been enervated by the complex realities of modern education. Cases like *Tinker* and *West Virginia v. Barnette,* protecting the First Amendment interests of students, complicate the analysis of rights in an educational environment, although neither of these cases involve discord between parents and children.

Despite these doctrinal erosions, the right of parents to direct the education of their children carries particular resonance in matters of religious education. The perception persists that the parental liberty protected in *Pierce* is particularly tied to religious freedom. Recent changes in First Amendment doctrine may enhance that connection, as the Court appears poised to allow increasing public financial assistance to parochial schools. With that increased support may come renewed efforts to shape education policy through parental rights.

The relationship between the state and parochial schools has changed dramatically since the *Pierce* era. In 1947, the Supreme Court first held that the establishment clause of the First Amendment applies to the states through the Fourteenth Amendment. In a series of cases dealing with public finance and parochial schools, the Court's interpretation of the establishment clause as designating a "wall of separation" led it to validate the no-aid policies of the states. The Court's commitment to separationism led it to ignore the often-nefarious anti-Catholic history behind these policies. As recently as 2004, in *Locke v. Davey,* the Court upheld, against a free exercise challenge, a provision of the Washington state constitution that denied public scholarship funds to students preparing for the ministry.[21] The Court rejected arguments that the state constitutional provision amounted to a "baby-Blaine Amendment," grounded in anti-Catholic hostility, attributing it instead to historic antiestablishment interests of the state in prohibiting the use of taxpayer dollars to support the clergy.

Today, state regulation affecting religious schools is more likely to involve efforts to publicly underwrite parochial education than to restrict it. The separationists are now a minority on the Court, and recent decisions have greatly expanded the ability of the state to assist parochial schools without running afoul of the establishment clause. Justice Thomas's plurality opinion for the Court in *Mitchell v. Helms,* upholding the state's provision of educational materials to Catholic schools, denounces the Court's historically restrictive view of permissible government aid to religious schools, criticizing it as "hostility" to sectarian schools that has "a shameful pedigree that we do not hesitate to disavow." In concluding that the Court should no longer invalidate all aid allocated directly to parochial schools, Thomas declared, "This doctrine, born of bigotry, should be buried now."[22]

The most significant victory for the movement for school choice and the most telling example of the political and legal changes since the days of the School Bill came in the 2002 landmark opinion *Zelman v. Simmons-Harris.* After almost two centuries of public hostility toward Catholic education, the Court upheld, against an establishment clause challenge, the use of publicly funded vouchers in religious schools. The briefs and the opinions in the case read, for the most part, like a paean to parochial schools for the academic excellence and values-based education too often missing in public schools. Although the advocates of parental rights played a substantial role in the push for school vouchers, the holding in *Zelman* is based on the establishment clause, not parental rights. Only Justice Thomas, in his concurring opinion, mentioned *Pierce,* when he described the voucher program as a permissible aspect of parental choice protected by *Pierce*.[23] But *Zelman* is perhaps the ultimate vindication for the opponents of the Oregon School Bill. *Pierce* protects the right of parents to choose private education for their children; *Zelman* authorizes the state to subsidize that choice with public funds.

Parental Rights outside of Education

The fate of parental rights outside the education context offers further proof of the ambiguity generated by *Pierce*. The case has proved effective precedent for securing basic procedural fairness for parents facing state efforts to limit or terminate their parental rights. But it has been wielded more successfully as a shield than a sword; courts are disinclined to find that *Pierce* requires the state to accommodate parental choices. As early as 1944, in *Prince v. Commonwealth of Massachusetts,* the Court upheld the conviction of a guardian aunt who allowed her nine-year-old niece to solicit on behalf of Jehovah's Witnesses, in violation of child labor laws. The Court rejected the aunt's argument that *Pierce* required deference to her decision. It acknowledged that *Pierce* recognizes the "private realm of family life that the state cannot enter," but it upheld the application of the child labor laws, concluding that "the family itself is not beyond regulation in the public interest," even as against a claim of religious liberty.[24] *Prince* stands for a widely recognized limitation on parental rights: parental decisions will not be upheld if they jeopardize the health or safety of the child or impose significant social burdens. More recently, courts consistently reject challenges to curfew ordinances based solely on parental rights. In a characteristic opinion, one court concludes that the "intimate family matters" protected in *Pierce* do not extend to "a parent's right to unilaterally determine when and if children will be on the streets."[25] Like the education cases, these decisions reveal that courts typically refuse to read *Pierce* as granting parents a right to veto the application of laws with which they disagree.

Protection of parental rights has engendered conflict as other rights within the family have evolved. The patriarchal family model of the common law has waned as the rights of women and children have increased. The *Pierce* Court's depiction of children as "belonging" to their parents invokes a property relationship that largely has been discredited by subsequent doctrinal developments. In particular, enhanced judicial protection for the rights of minors creates tensions with the parental prerogatives recognized in *Pierce*.

Parental rights have been asserted as justification for limiting the rights of minors in matters of health care, religion, and privacy. Typically, parental prerogatives prevail when the interests of parents and minor children conflict. In *Parham v. J.R.*, the Court accorded substantial deference to parents when it refused to find that minor children who have been committed to a mental institution enjoy the same due process protections as adults. The Court recognized the child's liberty interest in not being confined unnecessarily but found in favor of the "plenary authority" of parents, subject only to an independent medical judgment. This prerogative, the Court argued, derives from the "Western civilization concepts of the family as a unit with broad parental authority over minor children." The Court rejected the children's claim that commitment could occur only after a formal adversarial hearing, concluding that a full adversarial proceeding would undermine parental control. Even the risk that some parents would abuse their authority does not justify placing the state between parent and child. The Court, citing *Pierce* for the proposition that the child is not the "mere creature of the state," confirmed the antistatist heart of the opinion when it concluded, "The statist notion that governmental power should supersede parental authority in *all* cases because *some* parents abuse and neglect children is repugnant to American tradition."[26]

Parental prerogative does not always prevail when it is pitted against the privacy interest of a minor. In numerous cases involving challenges to laws limiting minors' access to contraception and abortion, the state has argued that the restrictions permissibly advance the constitutional right of parents to control the upbringing of their children. The Supreme Court has invalidated a number of these restrictions, upholding the limited privacy interests of minors, even against an assertion of parental authority. Parental authority also does not preclude criminal prosecution for a child's death when faith healing fails, even when combined with a free exercise claim. Although courts continue to give great weight to parental interests when they conflict with those of their minor children, the state has become increasingly involved in family matters through laws specifically designed to protect the rights of minors. These conflicts of rights within the family are likely to dilute the judicial weight given to parental rights as courts seek greater legal nuance to accommodate competing interests.

The most recent significant Supreme Court case on parental rights outside education is *Troxel v. Granville*, a 2000 case involving a Washington visitation statute. The law in *Troxel* impacted multiple family relationships, pitting a mother against paternal grandparents and the state. The Court was forced to consider whether the mother's decision limiting grandparent visitation prevailed over the contrary decision of the state. The six-to-three decision upholding parental rights generated six separate opinions. The badly splintered opinions cast doubt on the constitutional vitality of parental rights. Although eight of the justices recognized some constitutional protection for parental rights, none was willing to give significant weight to them; all eight recognized the authority of the state to intrude on parental rights in appropriate situations. The various opinions acknowledge parental rights but, admitting that these rights are ill defined, decline to articulate their "metes and bounds."[27]

The analytical disarray concerning *Pierce* can be explained in large part because *Pierce* provides little guidance for a case like *Troxel,* which requires the Court not simply to designate the outer limits of state authority but to weigh the valid and competing interests of multiple parties, including the state. Justice Stevens, dissenting, found *Pierce* inapplicable, because *Troxel* did "not present a bipolar struggle between the parents and the State over who has final authority to determine what is in a child's best interest." Justice Stevens questioned the relevance of *Pierce* to disputes not involving education, noting that while *Pierce* is a "source of broad language" concerning parental rights, "the constitutional principles and interest involved in the schooling context do not necessarily have parallel implications in this family visitation context, in which multiple overlapping and competing prerogatives of various plausibly interested parties are at stake."[28] Justice Kennedy, in dissent, opined that had *Pierce* been decided today, it probably would have been "grounded upon First Amendment principles protecting freedom of speech, belief, and religion." He cautioned against reading parental rights too broadly, arguing that courts "must use considerable restraint, including careful adherence to the incremental instruction given by the precise facts of particular cases, as they seek to give further and more precise definition to the right."[29]

The Court's ambivalence about the constitutional weight to be given to parental rights continues to surface in cases since *Troxel.* In a case concluding that a federal statute grants parents independent, enforceable rights concerning the education of their disabled children, the Court cited *Pierce* for the proposition that parents have a "recognized legal interest in the education and upbringing of their child, " but it made no mention of the constitutional stature of this interest.[30] In a recent First Amendment case involving student speech, Justice Thomas, in a concurring opinion, specifically disassociated *Pierce* from First Amendment claims. Criticizing the Court's description of *Pierce* as a First Amendment case in the 1969 *Tinker* case, Justice Thomas insists that *Pierce* "has nothing to say" on the speech rights of students, because the case "simply upheld the right of parents to send their children to private school."[31]

Both the disinclination by the Court to expand parental rights and the continuing debates among the justices about the constitutional weight these rights carry are not surprising. If the Court truly was preoccupied in *Pierce* with defining the limits to state power, the vulnerability of parental rights per se should not be surprising. The Court's equivocation on parental rights also is due, in part, to the more far-reaching question of the fate of unenumerated constitutional rights and whether they will continue to receive special protection from the Court.

Past, Present, and Future

Pierce is more controversial today than the day it was decided. The Court's defense of substantive due process remains the focus of intense and enduring criticism. For some courts and commentators, parental rights are anachronistic remnants of patriarchal history that must be tempered with a modern appreciation for the liberty interests of children and the more complex social goals of the contemporary state. To advocates of parental rights, *Pierce* too often fails to advance parental prerogatives in controversies over major issues, such as homeschooling and curriculum control.

But *Pierce* remains significant precisely because its constitutional meaning extends beyond parental rights. *Pierce* and its modern progeny, including *Casey* and *Lawrence,* address fundamental questions about the meaning of personhood in a democratic society. These cases share a concern with protecting significant, personal choices integral to individual identity from unjustified government intrusion. *Pierce* protects a liberty basic to our constitutional order, no matter how it is named. Justice Harlan made precisely this point in his dissent in *Poe,* when he argued that *Pierce* could legitimately be considered a decision based either on substantive due process or on the First Amendment because "the purposes of those guarantees and not their text, the reasons for their statement by the Framers and not the statement itself," justify their protection as liberty interests under the Fourteenth Amendment.[32]

Justice Harlan's dissent and the *Pierce* opinion suggest a constitutional connection between Fourteenth Amendment liberty and the First Amendment. The intellectual liberty protected in *Pierce,* the right not to be standardized by compulsory public education, is inextricably linked to fundamental First Amendment values. Numerous opinions describe freedom of thought as the essence of the First Amendment and, ultimately, of liberty itself. Justice Harlan explained the importance of education to liberty in 1908, in his dissent in the *Berea College* case: "The right to impart instruction . . . is, beyond question, part of one's liberty as guaranteed against hostile state action by the Constitution of the United States."[33] In *West Virginia v. Barnette,* the Court, in striking down a state resolution requiring all public school children to salute the flag, addressed explicitly the relationship between education, nationalism, and the First Amendment and concluded, "If there is any fixed star in our constitutional constellation, it is that no official, high or petty, can prescribe what shall be orthodox in politics, nationalism, religion, or other matters of opinion."[34]

Justice Brandeis eloquently elucidated the relationship between liberty, identity, and the First Amendment in his renowned concurrence in *Whitney v. California:* "Those who won our independence believed that the final end of the state was to make men free to develop their faculties. . . . They valued liberty both as an end, and as a means. . . . They believed that freedom to think as you will and to speak as you think are means indispensable to the discovery and spread of political truth."[35] In *Griswold,* Justice Douglas, writing for the majority, linked educational choice to core First Amendment values, reaffirming the "principle" of *Pierce* and *Meyer:* that "the State may not, consistently with the spirit of the First Amendment, contract the spectrum of available knowledge."[36] Justice Douglas's statement, like much of the debate on the Court over the constitutional values protected by *Pierce,* suggests that the *Pierce* Court's protection of parental rights served also to safeguard a basic liberty of the individual, one closely aligned to First Amendment axioms. *Pierce, Casey,* and *Lawrence* join liberty to First Amendment principles by soundly rejecting state authority to compel conformity to a state determined identity.

Pierce may repudiate state authority to standardize its citizens but it offers little guidance for determining when the state crosses that line. The essential question posed by *Pierce,* the appropriate constitutional balance between individual liberty and nationalist interests, remains in flux and impacts a far broader range of liberties than privacy rights. The Court's rejection of compelled public schooling in the service of nationalism leaves unresolved the evidence that the state must present to prevail on future claims invoking national security. It took the turmoil of the civil rights movement for the Court to agree that political dissent should be protected by the First Amendment unless it presents a true threat of imminent harm. But the Court never overruled the World War I dissent cases, such as *Schenck v. United States,* and their fate may still be tested if the combined trauma of war and social unrest visit us again. National security interests shift inevitably with the exigencies of the times. The profound issue advanced by democracy-enforcing cases like *Pierce* is whether the line of protected liberty must retreat in response.

The Oregon initiative presented in stark relief the question of whether the state's interest in fostering citizenship justified state monopoly of education. The Court's answer, that the Constitution precludes actions by the state to "standardize" children, affirms a principle basic to our constitutional order. Standardization—of education and ultimately of identity—is at odds with our understanding of liberty. The story of the School Bill is the story of the struggle to protect the individual from a state imposed identity. *Pierce,* and its legacy, remind us that this struggle continues.

NOTES

INTRODUCTION

1. See, e.g., "See Reign of Terror as Aim of Plotters," *New York Times,* June 4, 1919; "Palmer Warns Red They Can Not Succeed," *New York Times,* June 18, 1919; "Charges I.W.W. Plot," *New York Times,* October 1, 1920.

2. Robert K. Murray, *Red Scare: A Study in National Hysteria, 1919–1921* (Minneapolis: University of Minnesota Press, 1955), 17.

3. John Daniels, *America via the Neighborhood* (New York: Harper, 1920), 249–50.

4. David A. Horowitz, Peter N. Carroll, and David D. Lee, *On the Edge: A New History of Twentieth-Century America* (Eagan, Minn.: West, 1990), 160–61.

5. Kenneth T. Jackson, *The Ku Klux Klan in the City, 1915–1930* (Oxford: Oxford University Press, 1967), 19.

CHAPTER 1

1. *New Age* 28 (1920): 322.

2. *New York Times,* May 19, 1922.

3. Eckard V. Toy, "Ku Klux Klan in Oregon," in *Experiences in a Promised Land,* ed. G. Thomas Edwards and Carlos A. Schwantes (Seattle: University of Washington Press, 1986), 278.

4. David B. Tyack, "The Perils of Pluralism: The Background of the Pierce Case," *American Historical Review* 74 (October 1968): 79.

5. *Clarion* on the Klan, quoted in Jackson, *Ku Klux Klan in the City,* 197; Ben Olcott to *New York World,* September 22, 1921, as quoted in the *Oregonian,* May 15, 1922.

6. Toy, "Ku Klux Klan in Oregon," 271.

7. Ben Olcott, "Proceedings of Governors' Conference," in Lawrence J. Saalfeld, *Forces of Prejudice in Oregon, 1920–1925* (Washington, D.C.: Catholic University of America, 1950), 50.

8. Ku Klux Klan Membership Form, Lutheran Schools Committee, Compulsory Education Bill in Oregon, 1922–1925, MSS 646, Oregon Historical Society Research Library.

9. *Oregonian,* February 28, 1922, 5; *Oregonian,* April 18, 1922, 4; Waldo Roberts,

"The Ku-Kluxing of Oregon," *Outlook,* March 14, 1923, 491; Jackson, *Ku Klux Klan in the City,* 198.

10. Ku Klux Klan, Ben Titus, November 2, 1922, Lutheran Schools Committee, Compulsory Education Bill in Oregon, 1922–1925, MSS 646, Oregon Historical Society Research Library.

11. *Oregon Voter,* March 25, 1922, 5.

12. E. Kimbark MacColl, *The Growth of a City: Power and Politics in Portland, Oregon, 1915 to 1950* (Portland, Ore.: Georgian Press 1979), 164.

13. Olcott, "Proceedings of Governors' Conference," 138.

14. *Capital Journal,* August 18, 1922, reprinted in *Mt. Scott Herald,* August 25, 1922, 1.

15. *Portland Telegram,* May 1, 1923.

16. "Ku Klux Klan Is Busy," *Oregon Voter,* January 21, 1922, 14.

17. Oregon State Archives, Official Documents, Proclamation of Governor Olcott, document no. 5458.

18. *Oregon Journal,* May 14, 1922.

19. *Oregon Voter,* December 30, 1922.

20. Saalfeld, *Forces of Prejudice in Oregon,* 32–33.

21. Burt C. Jones to Jas. R. Ryan, Associate Director, Legal Department, August 11, 1922, box 14, folder 7 (Church: Church and State: Oregon School Case, 1922–1923), National Catholic Welfare Conference Collection, American Catholic History Research Center and University Archives (hereafter NCWC Collection, ACUA), Catholic University of America, Washington, D.C.

22. *Oregon Voter,* May 27, 1922, 356.

23. Olcott quoted in Toy, "Ku Klux Klan in Oregon," 279.

24. Olcott quoted in Steve Neal, *McNary of Oregon: A Political Biography* (Portland: Oregon Historical Society, 1985), 1.

CHAPTER 2

1. *Catholic Sentinel,* July 13, 1922.

2. *Oregon Voter,* July 15, 1922.

3. *Oregonian,* August 2, 1922.

4. *Coos Bay Times,* October 28, 1922.

5. *Catholic Sentinel,* June 22, 1922.

6. The editor made no reference to the measure for several weeks. See Fr. Wilfred Schoenberg, S.J., *Defender of the Faith* (Portland: Oregon Catholic Press, 1993), 180.

7. *Oregonian,* September 17, 1922, 6.

8. *Coos Bay Times,* October 30, 1922.

9. *Coos Bay Times,* October 31, 1922.

10. Burton J. Hendrick, "The Initiative and Referendum and How Oregon

Got Them," *McClure's Magazine* 37, no. 3 (July 1911): 240. Allen H. Eaton, *The Oregon System: The Story of Direct Legislation in Oregon* (Chicago: A. C. McClurg, 1912), 3; David Schuman, "The Origin of State Constitutional Direct Democracy: William Simon U'Ren and 'The Oregon System,'" *Temple University Law Review* 67 (1994): 949; Robert T. Johnston, *The Radical Middle Class, Populist Democracy, and the Question of Capitalism in Progressive Era Portland, Oregon* (Princeton: Princeton University Press, 2003), 122.

11. Joint Committee on Direct Legislation, "The Initiative and Referendum," 4th ed. (n.p., n.d. [1893/94], pamphlet at Oregon State Library, Salem), quoted in Johnston, *Radical Middle Class,* 122.

12. *Oregonian,* May 9, 1894, 4; *Oregonian,* March 17, 1894, 4.

13. *Oregonian,* May 9, 1894, 4.

14. *Oregonian,* May 14, 1902, 8.

15. Eaton, *Oregon System,* v–vi.

16. *Oregonian,* December 12, 1904, 8.

17. *Kadderly v. City of Portland,* 74 P. 710, 720 (Or. 1903).

18. *Pacific States Telephone & Telegraph Co. v. State of Oregon,* 223 U.S. 118 (1912).

19. Eaton, *Oregon System,* 50–52.

20. Johnston, *Radical Middle Class,* 124; Eaton, *Oregon System,* v.

21. Dudley G. Wooten, *Remember Oregon* (Denver: American Publishing Society, 1923), 4.

22. Eaton, *Oregon System,* 6.

23. *Portland Telegram,* October 26, 1922.

CHAPTER 3

1. Archbishop Christie to Father John Burke, July 13, 1922, box 14, folder 7 (Church: Church and State: Oregon School Case, 1922–1923), NCWC Collection, ACUA, Catholic University of America, Washington, D.C.

2. Lutheran Schools Committee to Rev. Titus Lang, October 12, 1922, Lutheran Schools Committee, Compulsory Education Bill in Oregon, 1922–1925, MSS 646, Oregon Historical Society Research Library.

3. Christie to Burke, July 13, 1922.

4. William G. Ross, *Forging New Freedoms: Nativism, Education, and the Constitution, 1917–1927* (Lincoln: University of Nebraska Press, 1994), 139.

5. *Hamilton v. Vaughan,* 179 N.W. 553, 558 (Mich. 1920).

6. Edward Kelly to Cardinal Gibbons, in Thomas J. Shelley, "Oregon School Case and the National Catholic Welfare Conference," *Catholic Historical Review* 75, no. 3 (July 1989): 440.

7. Campaign flyer, August 28, 1920, Lutheran Schools Committee, Compulsory Education Bill in Oregon, 1922–1925, MSS 646, Oregon Historical Society Research Library.

8. *The School?* (Denver: American Publishing Society, 1923), Lutheran Schools Committee, Compulsory Education Bill in Oregon, 1922–1925, MSS 646, Oregon Historical Society Research Library.

9. Lutheran Campaign Committee to Lutheran Pastors and Teachers, Michigan District of the Evangelical Lutheran Synod, September 26, 1921, Lutheran Schools Committee, Compulsory Education Bill in Oregon, 1922–1925, MSS 646, Oregon Historical Society Research Library.

10. Rudolph Messerli to Rev. Titus Lang, October 12, 1922, Lutheran Schools Committee, Compulsory Education Bill in Oregon, 1922–1925, MSS 646, Oregon Historical Society Research Library. Proponents also failed to gather sufficient signatures to place the measure on the ballot in Michigan in 1923. After another court challenge, sponsors prevailed in placing the measure on the ballot in 1924, when it again was defeated, by a margin close to the 1920 loss. Voters in Washington State defeated a similar measure on the same day.

11. *Oregon Journal,* June 16, 1922.

12. Christie to Burke, July 13, 1922.

13. James R. Ryan to Francis E. McMahon, June 26, 1922, box 14, folder 7 (Church: Church and State: Oregon School Case, 1922–1923), NCWC Collection, ACUA, Catholic University of America, Washington, D.C.

14. John J. Burke to Archbishop Christie, July 30, 1922, box 14, folder 7 (Church: Church and State: Oregon School Case, 1922–1923), NCWC Collection, ACUA, Catholic University of America, Washington, D.C.

15. John J. Burke to Archbishop Christie, September 11, 1922, box 14, folder 7 (Church: Church and State: Oregon School Case, 1922–1923), NCWC Collection, ACUA, Catholic University of America, Washington, D.C.

16. Wooten, *Remember Oregon,* 14.

17. Ibid., 12.

18. Ibid.

19. Ibid., 12–13.

20. Ibid., 10–12.

21. Ibid., 13–14.

22. Messerli to Lang, October 12, 1922.

23. Ibid.

24. Letter from Lutheran Schools Committee, August 1922, Lutheran Schools Committee, Compulsory Education Bill in Oregon, 1922–1925, MSS 646, Oregon Historical Society Research Library; letter from Lutheran Schools Committee, August 31, 1922, Lutheran Schools Committee, Compulsory Education Bill in Oregon, 1922–1925, MSS 646, Oregon Historical Society Research Library.

25. Stephen Arthur Lowell to Lutheran Schools Committee, October 10,

1922, Lutheran Schools Committee, Compulsory Education Bill in Oregon, 1922–1925, MSS 646, Oregon Historical Society Research Library.

26. David. E. Lofgren to Lutheran Schools Committee, September 23, 1922, Lutheran Schools Committee, Compulsory Education Bill in Oregon, 1922–1925, MSS 646, Oregon Historical Society Research Library.

27. *Oregonian,* November 5, 1922, 10.

28. *Oregon Voter,* January 4, 1919, 25.

29. Walter M. Pierce, *Oregon Cattleman-Governor-Congressman: Memoirs and Times of Walter M. Pierce,* ed. Arthur H. Bone (Portland: Oregon Historical Society, 1981), 135.

30. Ibid., 134.

31. Ben Titus, "I Was a Klansman," *Portland Telegram,* November 6, 1922, 1.

32. Walter Pierce to Grace Wick-Merritt, December 2, 1922, Lutheran Schools Committee, Compulsory Education Bill in Oregon, 1922–1925, MSS 646, Oregon Historical Society Research Library.

33. Statement by Walter Pierce, La Grande, Oregon, September 3, 1922, Lutheran Schools Committee, Compulsory Education Bill in Oregon, 1922–1925, MSS 646, Oregon Historical Society Research Library.

CHAPTER 4

1. *Spectator,* October 14, 1922

2. Quotations from campaign ads throughout this chapter are from Lutheran Schools Committee, Compulsory Education Bill in Oregon, 1922–1925, MSS 646, Oregon Historical Society Research Library.

3. Wooten, *Remember Oregon,* 7.

4. *Portland Telegram,* March 12, 1923.

5. State of Oregon, "Proposed Constitutional Amendments and Measures (with Arguments)," (Salem, 1922) (hereafter *Voters' Pamphlet*), *Voters' Pamphlet,* Lutheran Schools Committee, Compulsory Education Bill in Oregon, 1922–1925, MSS 646, Oregon Historical Society Research Library.

6. Lutheran Schools Committee, Compulsory Education Bill in Oregon, 1922–1925, MSS 646, Oregon Historical Society Research Library; Masons, *Reasons Why,* ibid.

7. *Voters' Pamphlet.*

8. *Oregon Voter,* March 25, 1922, 5.

9. Masons, *Reasons Why,* Lutheran Schools Committee, Compulsory Education Bill in Oregon, 1922–1925, MSS 646, Oregon Historical Society Research Library.

10. Edward Alsworth Ross, *Social Control: A Survey of the Foundations of Order* (New York: Macmillan 1901), quoted in Paul C. Violas, "Progressive Social Phi-

losophy: Charles Horton Cooley and Edward Alsworth Ross," in Clarence J. Karier, Paul C. Violas, and Joel H. Spring, *Roots of Crisis: American Education in the 20th Century* (Chicago: Rand McNally, 1973), 40–65.

11. *Oregon Voter,* October 7, 1922, 14.

12. "The Public School Bill," *Oregon Teacher's Monthly,* October 1922, 12.

13. *Cottage Grove Sentinel,* November 3, 1922.

CHAPTER 5

1. *The Oregon School Fight: A True History* (Portland, Ore.: A. B. Cain, 1924), 9.

2. Campaign literature quoted in this chapter is from Lutheran Schools Committee, Compulsory Education Bill in Oregon, 1922–1925, MSS 646, Oregon Historical Society Research Library.

3. Dudley Wooten, *24 Reasons against Laws to Abolish Private Schools and to Create a State Monopoly of Schools* (Denver: American Publishing Society, 1923), 10.

4. Tyack, "The Perils of Pluralism," 88–89.

5. William D. Wheelwright, Debate on School Bill, in *Oregon Voter,* October 7, 1922, 20.

6. Wooten, *24 Reasons,* 11.

7. "Educators Oppose Oregon School Bill," *Hood River Glacier,* October 19, 1922.

8. Sister Christine Mary, "The Case of the Sisters of the Holy Names vs. The State of Oregon," (1958), Holy Names Heritage Center.

9. Ibid.

10. "The Cost to Oregon," *Capital Journal,* October 21, 1922.

11. *Oregon Voter,* October 7, 1922, 19.

CHAPTER 6

1. *State v. Hosmer,* 72 Or. 57 (1914).

2. Sister Christine Mary, "The Case of the Sisters of the Holy Names vs. The State of Oregon," (1958), 1, Holy Names Heritage Center.

3. *Oregonian,* June 21, 1921, 22.

4. Sister Christine Mary, "Case of the Sisters," 6; *Glendale (Oregon) News,* October 12, 1922.

5. Quotation from Edward C. Day, "Right of Child to an Education in the Public School," *New Age* 31 (1923): 325; see also "More Concerning the Public Schools," *New Age* 28 (1920): 355. Campaign flyer, Lutheran Schools Committee, Compulsory Education Bill in Oregon, 1922–1925, MSS 646, Oregon Historical Society Research Library.

6. *Oregon Voter,* March 25, 1922, 5.

7. Tyack, "The Perils of Pluralism," 79; Ben Titus, "I Was a Klansman," *Portland Telegram,* November 6, 1922, 3.

8. Jackson, *Ku Klux Klan in the City,* 205.

9. Campaign ads, Lutheran Schools Committee, Compulsory Education Bill in Oregon, 1922–1925, MSS 646, Oregon Historical Society Research Library.

10. Saalfeld, *Forces of Prejudice in Oregon,* 24–25.

11. George Estes, *The Old Cedar School* (Portland, Ore.: Luther I. Powell, 1922).

12. Ibid.

13. Ibid.

14. *Oregon School Fight,* 19.

15. "Plans of Oregon Bigots Denounced by Father O'Hara," press release, July 24, 1922, box 14, folder 7 (Church: Church and State: Oregon School Case, 1922–1923), NCWC Collection, ACUA, Catholic University of America, Washington, D.C.

16. Ibid.

17. "Suggestions to Speakers," Non-Sectarian and Protestant Schools Committee, Lutheran Schools Committee, Compulsory Education Bill in Oregon, 1922–1925, MSS 646, Oregon Historical Society Research Library.

18. Philip Hamburger, *Separation of Church and State* (Cambridge, Mass.: Harvard University Press, 2002), 405 n. 36.

19. Ibid., 391–478.

20. Wooten, *24 Reasons,* 8.

21. *Oregon School Fight,* 9.

22. Ibid., 16.

23. "School Bill Is Held Boon for Catholics; Measure Attacked," *Pendleton (Oregon) Tribune,* November 1, 1922.

24. *Bend Bulletin,* October 20, 1922.

25. Sister Christine Mary, "Case of the Sisters," 9.

CHAPTER 7

1. *Oregonian,* November 5, 1922, 5, 19.

2. Johnston, *Radical Middle Class,* 109.

3. MacColl, *Growth of a City,* 144.

4. Oregon State Archives, *Oregon at War!* http://arcweb.sos.state.or.us/exhibits/war/intro/postwar.html.

5. Pierce, *Oregon Cattleman-Governor-Congressman,* 130.

6. Ibid., 131.

7. William J. Preston, Jr., *Aliens and Dissenters* (Cambridge, Mass.: Harvard University Press, 1963), 152–80; Murray, *Red Scare,* 58–66.

8. Murray, *Red Scare*, 61–63; Johnston, *Radical Middle Class*, 225.

9. *Oregonian*, December 21, 1918; MacColl, *Growth of a City*, 157.

10. *Oregon Journal*, January 16, 1919, 1; *Oregonian*, January 17, 1919, 10; Pierce, *Oregon Cattleman-Governor-Congressman*, 131.

11. *Oregon Journal*, January 15, 1919; *Oregon Journal*, January 16, 1919.

12. *Oregon Journal*, January 16, 1919.

13. *Oregon Voter*, January 18, 1919, 7.

14. MacColl, *Growth of a City*, 157.

15. Pierce, *Oregon Cattleman-Governor-Congressman*, 133.

16. Ibid.

17. *Oregonian*, January 4, 1920, 20.

18. *Oregonian*, January 20, 1919, 10.

19. Report of the Civil Liberties Committee, National Lawyers Guild, Oregon Chapter, May 24, 1938, 7–10, Oregon Historical Society Research Library.

20. Oregon Laws 1919, Chapter 19, sec. 1.

21. *Oregon Journal*, January 4, 1920, 1.

22. *Oregon Statesman* (Salem), November 3, 1922.

23. From *Public Opinion*, as quoted in John Higham, *Strangers in the Land: Patterns of American Nativism, 1860–1925*, (Piscataway, N.J.: Rutgers University Press, 1955), 55.

24. Higham, *Strangers in the Land*, 198.

25. David H. Bennett, *The Party of Fear: From Nativist Movements to the New Right in American History* (Chapel Hill: University of North Carolina Press, 1988), 185.

26. Murray, *Red Scare*, 9.

27. Bennet, *Party of Fear*, 189.

28. "Reds Rely on Cash of 'Pink' Bolsheviki," *New York Times*, September 15, 1923.

29. *Schenck v. United States*, 249 U.S. 47 (1919).

30. *Frohwerk v. United States*, 249 U.S. 204, 209 (1919).

31. *Debs v. United States*, 249 U.S. 211 (1919).

32. *Abrams v. United States*, 250 U.S. 616 (1919).

33. *Abrams v. United States*, 250 U.S. at 628.

34. David Tyack, Thomas James, and Aaron Benarot, *Law and the Shaping of Public Education* (Madison: University of Wisconsin Press, 1987), 173.

35. Murray, *Red Scare*, 171.

36. "Reds Are Ruining Children of Russia," *New York Times*, June 13, 1919.

37. *Oregonian*, October 1, 1919, 10.

38. *Oregon School Fight*, 7.

39. A. & A.S.R. School Committee, *Reasons Why* (International News Service, 1922); campaign ad titled "The Roman Monopoly" appeared in the *Silverton Tri-*

bune, October 13, 1922. Both are found in Lutheran Schools Committee, Compulsory Education Bill in Oregon, 1922–1925, MSS 646, Oregon Historical Society Research Library.

40. "Free Public Schools America's Noblest Monument," *Oregonian,* November 5, 1922.

41. "Radicalism Held Issue for Oregon," *Portland Telegram,* October 26, 1922; Johnston, *Radical Middle Class,* 242.

42. *Oregon School Fight,* 9.

43. Ibid., 11.

44. Ibid., 15.

45. Ibid., 17.

46. Ibid., 18.

47. Lutheran Schools Committee, *"The Truth" about the So-Called Compulsory Education Bill,* (Portland, Ore.: Lutheran Schools Committee, 1922), 10.

48. *Oregonian,* November 5, 1922.

49. *Oregonian,* October 29, 1922; *Astorian,* November 2, 1922.

50. Wooten, *24 Reasons,* 8.

51. "The Cost to Oregon," *Capital Journal,* October 21, 1922.

52. "School Bill Out-Prussias Prussia, Is Avowal of *San Francisco Argonaut,*" *Portland Telegram,* October 28, 1922.

53. Both cartoons appeared, respectively, in the *Portland Telegram,* November 1 and November 6, 1922.

CHAPTER 8

1. MacColl, *Growth of a City,* 170.

2. *Oregonian,* October 21, 1922, 16.

3. *Oregonian,* October 19, 1922, 14.

4. *Oregonian,* October 20, 1922, 8.

5. *Oregonian,* October 25, 1922, 6.

6. MacColl, *Growth of a City,* 170–71.

7. *Capital Journal,* August 18, 1922. The *Mt. Scott Herald* reprinted the editorial on its front page, August 25, 1922, 1.

8. Jackson, *Ku Klux Klan in the City,* 209.

9. *Corvallis Gazette-Times,* October 28, 1922.

10. "Eyes of Nation Watching Forces of Intolerance in Struggle to Seize Oregon," *Portland Telegram,* October 20, 1922.

11. "Education and the State," *Oregonian,* November 6, 1922.

12. "The School Bill," *Oregon Journal,* October 26, 1922.

13. "Portland Press 'Pussyfooting' on Ku Kluxism Says Salem Editor," *Mt. Scott Herald,* August 25, 1922, 1.

14. *Portland Telegram,* November 4, 1922, 3.

15. *Capital Journal,* October 26, 1922.

16. *Portland Telegram,* October 26, 1922.

17. *Hood River Glacier,* November 3, 1922.

18. Campaign ads, Lutheran Schools Committee, Compulsory Education Bill in Oregon, 1922–1925, MSS 646, Oregon Historical Society Research Library.

19. *Portland Telegram,* October 13, 1922.

20. Dean Collins, "School Bills, School Bills," *Oregon Voter,* September 30, 1922.

21. "Masonry the Goat," *Capital Journal,* November 4, 1922.

22. *Oregonian,* November 5, 1922, 1.

23. "There Is No Joy in Pierce Camp," *Oregonian,* November 1, 1922.

24. "Campaign Seems Like Horse Race," *Oregonian,* November 5, 1922.

25. *Oregonian,* November 7, 1922; *Oregonian,* November 8, 1922, 1, 8.

26. Sam A. Kozer, *Biennial Report of the Secretary of State* (Salem, Ore., 1923), 112, in Johnston, *Radical Middle Class,* 368 n. 11; *Oregon Blue Book and Official Directory, 1923–24* (Salem: Oregon State Printing Department, 1923), 170.

27. Wooten, *Remember Oregon,* 7.

28. *Oregonian,* November 8, 1922, 1; Johnston, *Radical Middle Class,* 232.

29. Saalfeld, *Forces of Prejudice in Oregon,* 37.

30. "Klan Candidate Carries Oregon," *New York Times,* November 8, 1922, 3; "What the Klan Did in Oregon Elections," *New York Times,* December 3, 1922, 1.

31. *Baltimore Sun,* November 11, 1922, in *Public Opinion and the Oregon School Law* (Washington, D.C.: National Catholic Welfare Council, 1923), 3–12.

32. *Oregonian,* November 9, 1922.

33. Press release, NCWC News Service, November 14, 1922, box 14, folder 7 (Church: Church and State: Oregon School Case, 1922–1923), NCWC Collection, ACUA, Catholic University of America, Washington, D.C.

CHAPTER 9

1. "School Measure to Be Attacked," *Oregonian,* November 9, 1922.

2. Letter to Prof. A. C. Stellhorn, November 10, 1922, Lutheran Schools Committee, Compulsory Education Bill in Oregon, 1922–1925, MSS 646, Oregon Historical Society Research Library.

3. "Fears School Repression," *New York Times,* December 11, 1922, 7.

4. Archbishop A. Christie to Most Reverend Edward J. Hanna, D.D., November 1922, box 14, folder 7 (Church: Church and State: Oregon School Case, 1922–1923), NCWC Collection, ACUA, Catholic University of America, Washington, D.C.

5. Sister Christine Mary, "The Case of the Sisters of the Holy Names vs. The State of Oregon," (1958), 12, Holy Names Heritage Center.

6. Dr. Slattery to Father Burke, November 9, 1922, box 14, folder 7 (Church:

Church and State: Oregon School Case, 1922–1923), NCWC Collection, ACUA, Catholic University of America, Washington, D.C.

7. Justin McGrath to Father Burke, November 11, 1922, box 14, folder 7 (Church: Church and State: Oregon School Case, 1922–1923), NCWC Collection, ACUA, Catholic University of America, Washington, D.C.

8. Ibid.

9. "To Fight Oregon Law," *Seattle Times,* January 21, 1923.

10. Note to Father Burke on letter from J. A. Walsh to Rev. John P. Carroll, December 7, 1922, box 14, folder 7 (Church: Church and State: Oregon School Case, 1922–1923), NCWC Collection, ACUA, Catholic University of America, Washington, D.C.

11. William D. Guthrie to Father Burke, December 20, 1922, box 14, folder 7 (Church: Church and State: Oregon School Case, 1922–1923), NCWC Collection, ACUA, Catholic University of America, Washington, D.C.

12. William D. Guthrie to Father Burke, January 5, 1923, box 14, folder 7 (Church: Church and State: Oregon School Case, 1922–1923), NCWC Collection, ACUA, Catholic University of America, Washington, D.C.

13. Gordon Lee, *Crusade against Ignorance: Thomas Jefferson on Education* (New York: Bureau of Publications, Teachers College, Columbia University, 1961), 17; Forrest Church, *So Help Me God* (New York: Harcourt Trade, 2007), 105; John Adams, *The Works of John Adams, Second President of the United States* (New York: Little, Brown, 1851), 6:198.

14. Report of the House Committee on Public Lands, in *Barnard's American Journal of Education* 28 (1878): 939, 942, 944.

15. Tyack, *Law and the Shaping of Public Education,* 154.

16. *State v. Bailey,* 61 N.E. 730 (Ind. 1901).

17. *People v. Ekerold,* 105 N.E. 670 (N.Y. 1914); *State v. Counort,* 124 P. 910 (Wash. 1912).

18. Ken I. Kersch, *Constructing Civil Liberties* (New York: Cambridge University Press, 2004), 247.

19. Ibid., 260.

20. Ellwood Cubberly, *Changing Conceptions of Education* (Boston: Houghton Mifflin, 1909), 63, cited in Kersch, *Constructing Civil Liberties,* 251.

21. Winthrop D. Lane, "The National Crisis in Education," *Survey* 44 (1920): 299, cited in Kersch, *Constructing Civil Liberties,* 258.

22. "Dr. Butler Opposes Education Bureau," *New York Times,* January 16, 1922, 12.

23. "Opposes Federal Rule over Schools," *New York Times,* December 28, 1923, 4.

24. "Fears Federal Rule in Education Bill," *New York Times,* December 12, 1924, 20.

25. Guthrie to Burke, January 5, 1923.

26. "Fears Federal Rule in Education Bill," 20.

CHAPTER 10

1. NCWC Administrative Committee, Minutes, January 11, 1923, 51–54, box 10, folder 18 (Church: Church and State: Catholic-Public Schools, 1923–1948), NCWC Collection, ACUA, Catholic University of America, Washington, D.C.

2. Ibid.

3. Ibid.

4. Ibid.

5. Thomas J. Shelley, "Oregon School Case and the National Catholic Welfare Conference," *Catholic Historical Review* 75, no. 3 (July 1989): 449.

6. Edward J. Larson, *Summer for the Gods: The Scopes Trial and America's Continuing Debate Over Science and Religion* (New York: Basic Books, 1997), 36.

7. Ibid., 45.

8. Horace Mann, Mary Tyler Peabody Mann, George Combes Mann, Felix Pecant, *Life and Works of Horace Mann,* vol. 2 (Boston: Lee and Shepard, 1891), 424; John C. Jeffries, Jr., and James E. Ryan, "A Political History of the Establishment Clause," *Michigan Law Review* 100 (2001): 298.

9. "The Bible in Our Common School," *Common School Journal* 14 (1852): 9, quoted in Thomas James, "Rights of Conscience and State School Systems in Nineteenth-Century America," in *Toward a Usable Past: Liberty under State Constitutions,* ed. Paul Finkelman and Stephen E. Gottlieb (Athens: University of Georgia Press, 1991), 126–27.

10. *Commonwealth v. Cooke,* 7 Am. L. Reg. 417 (Mass. Police Ct. 1859).

11. Otto T. Hamilton, *The Courts and the Curriculum* (New York: Teacher's College, Columbia University, 1927) 113, cited in Tyack, *Law and the Shaping of Public Education,* 163.

12. *Donahoe v. Richards,* 38 Me. 379 (1854).

13. Ibid.

14. Jeffries and Ryan, "Political History of the Establishment Clause," 301.

15. Hamburger, *Separation of Church and State,* 324–25.

16. Ibid., 229–40.

17. Jeffries and Ryan, "Political History of the Establishment Clause," 301.

18. Mann, Mann, Mann, and Pecant, *Life and Works of Horace Mann,* 250.

19. Walter Lippmann, *Drift and Mastery,* ed. William Leuchtenburg (Madison: University of Wisconsin Press, 1985), 115.

20. Most Rev. Austin Dowling to Rev. John J. Burke, January 18, 1923, box 14, folder 7 (Church: Church and State: Oregon School Case, 1922–1923), NCWC Collection, ACUA, Catholic University of America, Washington, D.C.

21. Christie to Dowling, January 22, 1923, and Kavanaugh to Burke, February

3, 1923, box 14, folder 7 (Church: Church and State: Oregon School Case, 1922–1923), NCWC Collection, ACUA, Catholic University of America, Washington, D.C.

22. Kavanaugh to Christie, June 21, 1923, box 14, folder 7 (Church: Church and State: Oregon School Case, 1922–1923), NCWC Collection, ACUA, Catholic University of America, Washington, D.C.

23. Dowling to Muldoon, July 20, 1923, box 14, folder 7 (Church: Church and State: Oregon School Case, 1922–1923), NCWC Collection, ACUA, Catholic University of America, Washington, D.C.

24. Dowling to Muldoon, July 21, 1923, box 14, folder 7 (Church: Church and State: Oregon School Case, 1922–1923), NCWC Collection, ACUA, Catholic University of America, Washington, D.C.

25. Hanna to Dowling, July 1923, box 14, folder 7 (Church: Church and State: Oregon School Case, 1922–1923), NCWC Collection, ACUA, Catholic University of America, Washington, D.C.

26. Carroll to Dowling, July 21, 1923, box 14, folder 7 (Church: Church and State: Oregon School Case, 1922–1923), NCWC Collection, ACUA, Catholic University of America, Washington, D.C.

27. Dowling to Hanna, August 5, 1923, box 14, folder 7 (Church: Church and State: Oregon School Case, 1922–1923), NCWC Collection, ACUA, Catholic University of America, Washington, D.C.

28. Hanna to Kavanaugh, July 1923, box 14, folder 7 (Church: Church and State: Oregon School Case, 1922–1923), NCWC Collection, ACUA, Catholic University of America, Washington, D.C.

CHAPTER II

1. "Keynote Strikes Colonel," *New York Times,* September 26, 1912, 2.

2. George Martin, *Causes and Conflicts: The Centennial History of the Association of the Bar of the City of New York, 1870–1970* (New York: Fordham University Press, 1970), 218.

3. Upton Sinclair, *The Goose Step: A Study of American Education* (Whitefish, Mont.: Kessinger, 1922), 53.

4. *A History of the School of Law Columbia University,* ed. Julius Goebel, Jr. (New York: Columbia University Press, 1955), 211.

5. Ibid.

6. Martin, *Causes and Conflicts,* 218.

7. *Pollock v. Farmers' Loan & Trust Company,* 157 U.S. 429 (1895).

8. Edward R. A. Seligman, "Progressive Taxation in Theory and Practice," *American Economic Association Quarterly* 9, no. 4 (1908): 298.

9. "Must Have Economy Republicans Cry," *New York Times,* March 25, 1910, 11.

10. William D. Guthrie, "Constitutionality of the Sherman Anti-Trust Act of 1890," *Harvard Law Review* 11 (1897–98): 80, 81–83.

11. Benjamin Rollins Twiss, *Lawyers and the Constitution: How Laissez Faire Came to the Supreme Court* (New York: Russell and Russell, 1962), 215.

12. Stephen B. Wood, *Constitutional Politics in the Progressive Era: Child Labor and the Law* (Chicago: University of Chicago Press, 1968), 280.

13. William D. Guthrie, *Magna Carta, and Other Addresses* (Freeport, N.Y.: Books for Libraries Press, 1969), 85.

14. Guthrie, "Constitutionality of the Sherman Anti-Trust Act ," 93–94.

15. "Our Constitution Is Rooted in Magna Carta," *New York Times,* February 3, 1929, 133.

16. In 1925, the Court began to apply the protections of the Bill of Rights to limit state power over individuals through selective incorporation under the due process clause of the Fourteenth Amendment.

17. William D. Guthrie, *Lectures on the Fourteenth Article of Amendment to the Constitution of the United States* (Boston: Little, Brown, 1898), 108.

18. Guthrie, "Constitutional Morality," in *Magna Carta, and Other Addresses,* 42–86.

19. Twiss, *Lawyers and the Constitution,* 217.

20. John W. Davis, "William D. Guthrie," *United States Law Review* 70 (April 1936): 197.

21. Guthrie, "Catholic Parochial Schools," in *Magna Carta, and Other Addresses,* 249–50.

22. "Education Bill Opposed," *New York Times,* April 6, 1921, 34.

23. 262 U.S. 390 (1923). The statute did allow foreign languages to be taught as a language course after eighth grade. While most of these English-only laws mandated English instruction, some specifically prohibited the teaching of German. Five challenges to these laws reached the Supreme Court, which rendered the opinion in *Meyer* and the companion cases *Bartels v. Iowa, Bohning v. Ohio, Pohl v. Ohio,* and *Nebraska District of Evangelical Lutheran Synod v. McKelvie* (262 U.S. 404 (1923)).

24. Brief and Argument of State of Nebraska, Defendant in Error, *Meyer v. Nebraska,* 12–15.

25. Ibid., 13. The state's brief also quoted extensively from the opinion of the Nebraska Supreme Court in a case upholding the language law, where the court emphasized the responsibility of the state to "teach [the alien child] love for his country, and hatred of dictatorship, whether by autocrats, by the proletariat, or by any man or class of men" (ibid., 16). Iowa and Ohio made similar arguments in the companion cases.

26. Brief and Argument of Robert T. Meyer, Plaintiff in Error, *Meyer v. Nebraska,* 16–17.

27. Brief of Amici Curiae, William D. Guthrie, *Meyer v. Nebraska*, 3–6.

28. Ernst Freund, *The Police Power, Public Policy, and Constitutional Rights* (Chicago: Callaghan, 1904), sec. 266.

29. Brief of Amici Curiae, William D. Guthie, *Meyer v. Nebraska*, 4–8.

30. Cf. Brief of Plaintiff in Error at 14 with Oral Argument of Arthur F. Mullen, on Behalf of Plaintiffs-in-Error, *Meyer v. Nebraska*, 7–8. Transcript of Oral Argument in *Landmark Briefs and Arguments of the Supreme Court of the United States: Constitutional Law*, Phillip B. Kurland and Gerhard Caspar, eds. v. 21 (Arlington, VA: University Publications of America, 1975), 769.

31. Transcript of Oral Argument of Arthur F. Mullen, *Meyer v. Nebraska*, 9–10.

32. Ibid., 13. The Court had not yet incorporated any provisions of the Bill of Rights through the Fourteenth Amendment. There was some discussion at oral argument of whether the Fourteenth Amendment's due process clause incorporated religious liberty and free speech. Mullen also claimed that religious liberty was protected as a privilege and immunity under the Fourteenth Amendment.

33. Father Burke to J. P. Kavanaugh, March 1, 1923, box 14, folder 7 (Church: Church and State: Oregon School Case, 1922–1923), NCWC Collection, ACUA, Catholic University of America, Washington, D.C.

34. *Meyer v. Nebraska*, 262 U.S. 390, 399 (1923).

35. Ibid., 400.

36. Ibid., 401–2.

37. Ibid., 390, 402.

38. *Bartels v. Iowa*, 262 U.S. 404, 412 (1923) (Holmes, J., dissenting). Justices Holmes and Sutherland did join the Court in striking down the Ohio law prohibiting only the teaching of German: see *Bohning v. Ohio*, 262 U.S. 404 (1923).

39. William Howard Taft to George L. Fox, July 31, 1923, Taft Papers, reel 255, Library of Congress.

40. Hanna to Dowling, July 1923, box 14, folder 7 (Church: Church and State: Oregon School Case, 1922–1923), NCWC Collection, ACUA, Catholic University of America, Washington, D.C.

41. Hanna to Kavanaugh, July 1923, box 14, folder 7 (Church: Church and State: Oregon School Case, 1922–1923), NCWC Collection, ACUA, Catholic University of America, Washington, D.C.

CHAPTER 12

1. Alfred Powers and Howard McKinley Corning, eds., *History of Education in Portland* (Portland, Ore.: Adult Education Project, 1937), 102.

2. St. Mary's Academy Chronicles, January 30, 1924, Holy Names Heritage Center.

3. Kavanaugh to Christie, June 21, 1923, box 14, folder 7 (Church: Church

and State: Oregon School Case, 1922–1923), NCWC Collection, ACUA, Catholic University of America, Washington, D.C.

4. Ibid.

5. Dowling to Muldoon, July 20, 1923, box 14, folder 7 (Church: Church and State: Oregon School Case, 1922–1923), NCWC Collection, ACUA, Catholic University of America, Washington, D.C.

6. Ross, *Forging New Freedoms,* 161.

7. Christopher Kauffman traces this tension to turf and policy battles during World War I between the Knights and the National Catholic War Council: see *Faith and Fraternalism: The History of the Knights of Columbus, 1882–1982* (New York: Harper, 1982), 283.

8. McCamant to Van Winkle, August 24, 1923, Oregon State Archives, Department of Justice Records, Case Files, *Pierce v. Society of Sisters.*

9. Guthrie to Kavanaugh, October 5, 1923, box 14, folder 7 (Church: Church and State: Oregon School Case, 1922–1923), NCWC Collection, ACUA, Catholic University of America, Washington, D.C.

10. Ibid.

11. Guthrie to Kavanaugh, January 3, 1924, box 14, folder 8 (Church: Church and State: Oregon School Case, January–June 1924), NCWC Collection, ACUA, Catholic University of America, Washington, D.C.

12. Burke to Guthrie, January 3, 1924, box 14, folder 8 (Church: Church and State: Oregon School Case, January–June 1924), NCWC Collection, ACUA, Catholic University of America, Washington, D.C.

13. *Berea College v. Kentucky,* 211 U.S. 45 (1908).

14. Kavanaugh to Guthrie, January 5, 1924, box 14, folder 8 (Church: Church and State: Oregon School Case, January–June 1924), NCWC Collection, ACUA, Catholic University of America, Washington, D.C.

15. Guthrie to Burke, January 4, 1924, box 14, folder 8 (Church: Church and State: Oregon School Case, January–June 1924), NCWC Collection, ACUA, Catholic University of America, Washington, D.C.

16. Ross, *Forging New Freedoms,* 162.

17. *Berea College,* 211 U.S. 45 (1908), Transcript of Record.

18. *Berea College,* 211 U.S. 45, 68 (1908) (Harlan, J., dissenting).

19. John Locke, *Two Treatises of Government* (Cambridge: Cambridge University Press, 1988), chap. VI, sec. 58, p. 306, and sec. 69, p. 313; John Stuart Mill, *On Liberty* (1869), chap. V, par. 12–13, http://www.bartleby.com/130/5.html.

20. William C. Sprague, *Blackstone's Commentaries,* abridged, 9th ed. (Chicago: Callaghan and Company, 1915), 86.

21. *People ex rel. O'Connell v. Turner,* 55 Ill. 280 (1870).

22. *Ex parte Crouse,* 4 Wharton 9 (Pa. 1839).

23. *Risting v. Sparboe,* 162 N.W. 592, 594 (Iowa 1917).

24. Lutheran School Defense Committee to the Pastors and Teachers of the Michigan District, Lutheran Schools Committee, Compulsory Education Bill in Oregon, 1922–1925, MSS 646, Oregon Historical Society Research Library.

25. See, e.g., Pope Pius XI, *Rappresentanti in Terra* ("Encyclical Letter on Christian Education," December 31, 1929), par. 32–33, cited in Anne Fremantle, *The Papal Encyclicals in Their Historical Context* (New York: Mentor-Omega Books, 1963), 224.

26. Burke to Guthrie, December 12, 1923, box 14, folder 7 (Church: Church and State: Oregon School Case, 1922–1923), NCWC Collection ACUA, Catholic University of America, Washington, D.C.

CHAPTER 13

1. Guthrie to Kavanaugh, January 2, 1924, box 14, folder 8 (Church: Church and State: Oregon School Case, January–June 1924), NCWC Collection, ACUA, Catholic University of America, Washington, D.C.

2. Ibid.

3. Guthrie to Burke, October 22, 1923, box 14, folder 7 (Church: Church and State: Oregon School Case, 1922–1923), NCWC Collection, ACUA, Catholic University of America, Washington, D.C.

4. *Terrace v. Thompson,* 263 U.S. 197 (1923).

5. *Pennsylvania v. West Virginia,* 262 U.S. 553, 593 (1923).

6. Guthrie to Kavanaugh, January 3, 1924, box 14, folder 8 (Church: Church and State: Oregon School Case, January–June 1924), NCWC Collection, ACUA, Catholic University of America, Washington, D.C.

7. Kavanaugh to Burke, December 15, 1923, box 14, folder 7 (Church: Church and State: Oregon School Case, 1922–1923), NCWC Collection, ACUA, Catholic University of America, Washington, D.C.

8. Brief on Behalf of Plaintiff, Society of the Sisters of the Holy Names of Jesus and Mary, *Pierce v. Society of Sisters;* District of Oregon, Portland; U.S. District Courts (Rg 21); National Archives, Pacific AK Region (Seattle), 10–17.

9. Ibid.

10. Ibid., 24–29.

11. Ibid., 48–91.

12. Ibid., 101–2.

13. Brief on Behalf of Plaintiff, Hill Military Academy, *Pierce v. Society of Sisters;* District of Oregon, Portland; U.S. District Courts (Rg 21); National Archives, Pacific AK Region (Seattle), 35–40.

14. Brief on Behalf of Defendants, Walter M. Pierce, Gov. of Oregon, *Pierce v. Society of Sisters;* District of Oregon, Portland; U.S. District Courts (Rg 21), National Archives, Pacific AK Region (Seattle).

15. Brief on Behalf of Defendants' Motion to Dismiss, *Pierce v. Society of Sisters;* District of Oregon, Portland; U.S. District Courts (Rg 21), National Archives, Pacific AK Region (Seattle), 26, 46–53.

16. Brief on Behalf of Defendants, Walter M. Pierce, Gov. of Oregon, *Pierce v. Society of Sisters;* District of Oregon, Portland; U.S. District Courts (Rg 21), National Archives, Pacific AK Region (Seattle), 32.

CHAPTER 14

1. Section 266 of the Federal Judicial Code, 28 U.S.C. 380, required that a three-judge court hear all requests for injunctions seeking to restrain enforcement of state statutes claimed to be unconstitutional. Its successor statute, 28 U.S.C. 2281, was invoked in *Brown v. Board of Education,* among other landmark cases. Section 2281 was repealed in 1976. In district court today, three-judge panels are required only when required in an act of Congress or to challenge the constitutionality of the apportionment of federal or state voting districts (28 U.S.C. 2284).

2. Transcript of Discussions, Motions, *Oregon School Fight,* 55.

3. Ibid., 54.

4. Ibid., 61.

5. Ibid., 64.

6. Ibid., 68.

7. Ibid., 69–78.

8. Ibid., 81–82.

9. Ibid., 82–83.

10. Ibid., 87–88.

11. Ibid., 95.

12. Ibid., 94.

13. Ibid., 97–98.

14. Ibid., 100–102.

15. Ibid., 104.

16. Ibid., 104–11.

17. Ibid., 115.

18. Ibid., 124.

19. Ibid., 123–31.

20. Guthrie to Kavanaugh, January 28, 1924, box 14, folder 8 (Church: Church and State: Oregon School Case, January–June 1924), NCWC Collection, ACUA, Catholic University of America, Washington, D.C.

21. Burke to Guthrie, February 11, 1924, box 14, folder 8 (Church: Church and State: Oregon School Case, January–June 1924), NCWC Collection, ACUA, Catholic University of America, Washington, D.C.

22. Burke to Guthrie, April 1, 1924, box 14, folder 8 (Church: Church and

State: Oregon School Case, January–June 1924), NCWC Collection, ACUA, Catholic University of America, Washington, D.C.

23. *Society of Sisters v. Pierce*, 296 F. 928, 933 (D.C. Ore. 1924).

24. Ibid., 937.

25. Ibid., 938.

26. McCamant to Moore, Oregon State Archives, Department of Justice Records, Case Files, *Pierce v. Society of Sisters.*

27. *Oregon School Fight*, 144–45.

28. *Grants Pass Spokesman*, April 26, 1924.

29. "Court Invalidates Oregon School Law," *New York Times*, April 1, 1924, 1; "The Oregon School Law," *New York Times*, April 2, 1924, 18.

30. Kavanaugh to Guthrie, April 1, 1924, box 14, folder 8 (Church: Church and State: Oregon School Case, January–June 1924), NCWC Collection, ACUA, Catholic University of America, Washington, D.C.

31. William D. Guthrie, "The Oregon Compulsory Public School Law," *Columbia Magazine*, June 1924.

32. Willis to McCamant, Oregon State Archives, Department of Justice Records, Case Files, *Pierce v. Society of Sisters.*

CHAPTER 15

1. Hanna to DeLai, February 28, 1925, box 14, folder 10 (Church: Church and State: Oregon School Case, January 1925), NCWC Collection, ACUA, Catholic University of America, Washington, D.C.

2. McGrath to Burke, April 18, 1925, box 14, folder 10 (Church: Church and State: Oregon School Case, January 1925), NCWC Collection, ACUA, Catholic University of America, Washington, D.C.

3. Guthrie to Burke, April 7, 1924, box 14, folder 8 (Church: Church and State: Oregon School Case, January 1925), NCWC Collection, ACUA, Catholic University of America, Washington, D.C.

4. Guthrie to Burke, February 24, 1925, box 14, folder 10 (Church: Church and State: Oregon School Case, January 1925), NCWC Collection, ACUA, Catholic University of America, Washington, D.C.

5. *New York Times*, October 15, 1923, 2; *Oregonian*, January 30, 1925.

6. McCamant to Van Winkle, June 4, 1924, Oregon State Archives, Department of Justice Records, Case Files, *Pierce v. Society of Sisters.*

7. Brief on Behalf of Appellee, Society of the Sisters of the Holy Names of Jesus and Mary, *Oregon School Cases, Complete Record* (Baltimore: Belvedere Press, 1925), 276.

8. Burke to Guthrie, March 10, 1925, box 14, folder 10 (Church: Church and State: Oregon School Case, January 1925), NCWC Collection, ACUA, Catholic University of America, Washington, D.C.

9. Memo to Board of Directors and General School Board, March 19, 1924, and letter to Rev. J. C. Baur, August 4, 1924, Lutheran Schools Committee, Compulsory Education Bill in Oregon, 1922–1925, MSS 646, Oregon Historical Society Research Library.

10. Chamberlain to Van Winkle, December 11, 1924, Oregon State Archives, Department of Justice Records, Case Files, *Pierce v. Society of Sisters.*

11. Van Winkle to Chamberlain, January 3, 1925, Oregon State Archives, Department of Justice Records, Case Files, *Pierce v. Society of Sisters.*

12. Chamberlain to Van Winkle, January 10, 1925, Oregon State Archives, Department of Justice Records, Case Files, *Pierce v. Society of Sisters.*

13. E. W. Cornell to William R. Stansbury, Clerk, August 28, 1924, RG 267, entry 21, case file 30548, Appellate Case Files, 1792–2004, *Pierce v. Society of Sisters,* National Archives, Washington, D.C.

14. William Guthrie to William R. Stansbury, January 13, 1925, RG 267, entry 21, case file 30548, Appellate Case Files, 1792–2004, *Pierce v. Society of Sisters,* National Archives, Washington, D.C.

15. Willam R. Stansbury to William D. Guthrie, January 16, 1925, RG 267, entry 21, case file 30548, Appellate Case Files, 1792–2004, *Pierce v. Society of Sisters,* National Archives, Washington, D.C.

16. Guthrie to Ryan, February 20, 1925, box 14, folder 10 (Church: Church and State: Oregon School Case, January 1925), NCWC Collection, ACUA, Catholic University of America, Washington, D.C.

17. Ibid.

18. Nicholas Murray Butler, *Across the Busy Years: Recollections and Reflections* (New York: Scribner, 1939–40), 1:357–58.

19. Felix Frankfurter, "Chief Justices I Have Known," *Supreme Court Historical Society Yearbook 1980,* (1980), 3.

20. W. H. Taft, "Mr. Wilson and the Campaign," *Yale Review,* October 1920, 19–20.

21. Felix Frankfurter, "The United States Supreme Court Molding the Constitution," *Current History* 32, no. 2 (May 1930): 239.

22. Ibid.

23. Quoted in Alpheus Thomas Mason, *The Supreme Court from Taft to Burger* (Baton Rouge: Louisiana State University Press, 1979), 50.

24. Roscoe Pound, "Liberty of Contract," *Yale Law Journal* 18 (1909): 454, 457.

25. Quoted in Frankfurter, "United States Supreme Court Molding the Constitution," 238.

26. Quoted in Mason, *Supreme Court from Taft to Burger,* 57.

27. *Adkins v. Children's Hospital,* 261 U.S. 525, 561 (1923).

28. *Truax v. Corrigan,* 257 U.S. 312, 376 (1921) (Brandeis, J., dissenting).

29. Mason, *Supreme Court from Taft to Burger,* 67.

30. *United States v. Cruikshank,* 92 U.S. 542, 554 (1875).

31. *Slaughterhouse Cases,* 83 U.S. 36 (1873).

32. *Allgeyer v. Louisiana,* 165 U.S. 578, 588 (1897).

33. *Meyer v. Nebraska,* 262 U.S. 390, 399 (1923).

34. Guthrie to Ryan, July 10, 1924, box 14, folder 9 (Church: Church and State: Oregon School Case, July 1924), NCWC Collection, ACUA, Catholic University of America, Washington, D.C.

35. *Meyer v. Nebraska,* 262 U.S. 390, 399 (1923).

36. Pound, "Liberty of Contract," 466.

CHAPTER 16

1. Brief of Appellant, Attorney General of the State of Oregon, *Pierce v. Society of Sisters, Oregon School Cases, Complete Record,* 148.

2. Brief of Appellant, Governor of the State of Oregon, *Oregon School Cases, Complete Record,* 100.

3. McCamant to Moore, January 30, 1925, Oregon State Archives, Department of Justice Records, Case Files, *Pierce v. Society of Sisters.*

4. Brief of Appellant, Governor, *Oregon School Cases,* 102–3.

5. Ibid., 115–16.

6. Brief of Appellee, Society of Sisters, *Oregon School Cases,* 238–84.

7. Supplement to Brief of Appellant, Governor of the State of Oregon, *Oregon School Cases,* 129.

8. Brief of Appellee, Society of Sisters, *Oregon School Cases,* 275.

9. Ibid., 279–80.

10. *Permoli v. Municipality No. 1 of the City of New Orleans,* 44 U.S. 589, 609 (1845).

11. Brief of Appellee, Society of Sisters, *Oregon School Cases,* 275–76.

12. Ibid., 276–77.

13. Brief of Appellant, Governor, *Oregon School Cases,* 98.

14. Brief of Appellee, Society of Sisters, *Oregon School Cases,* 239–40.

15. Supplement to Brief of Appellant, Governor, *Oregon School Cases,* 130.

16. Brief of Wm. A. Williams, Amicus Curiae, on Behalf of the North Pacific Union Conference of Seventh-Day Adventists, *Oregon School Cases,* 605.

17. Brief of Louis Marshall, Amicus Curiae, on Behalf of the American Jewish Committee, *Oregon School Cases,* 615.

18. William D. Guthrie to William R. Stansbury, February 19, 1925, RG 267, entry 21, case file 30548, Appellate Case Files, 1792–2004, *Pierce v. Society of Sisters,* National Archives, Washington, D.C.

19. William R. Stansbury to William D. Guthrie, February 23, 1925, RG 267,

entry 21, case file 30548, Appellate Case Files, 1792–2004, *Pierce v. Society of Sisters,* National Archives, Washington, D.C.

20. Inaugural Address of Calvin Coolidge, March 4, 1925, available at www.bartleby.com/124/pres47.html.

21. Ryan to O'Mara, March 18, 1925, and Burke to Guthrie, April 20, 1925, box 14, folder 10 (Church: Church and State: Oregon School Case, January 1925), NCWC Collection, ACUA, Catholic University of America, Washington, D.C.

CHAPTER 17

1. Burke to O'Mara, March 23, 1925, box 14, folder 10 (Church: Church and State: Oregon School Case, January 1925), National Catholic Welfare Conference Collection, ACUA, Catholic University of America, Washington, D.C.

2. Oral Argument, *Oregon School Cases,* 626–28.

3. Oral Argument of Willis S. Moore on Behalf of Appellant, Attorney General, *Oregon School Cases,* 634–39.

4. Ibid., 642.

5. Ibid., 643.

6. Ibid., 644, 646.

7. Ibid., 642–50.

8. Oral Argument of William D. Guthrie, on Behalf of Appellee, Society of Sisters, *Oregon School Cases,* 653.

9. Ibid., 651–55.

10. Ibid., 660.

11. Ibid., 656–62.

12. Ibid., 664–66.

13. Ibid., 666–67.

14. Ibid., 669.

15. Ibid., 670.

16. Ibid., 671.

17. Ibid., 672.

18. Oral Argument of Kavanaugh, on Behalf of Appellee, Society of Sisters, *Oregon School Cases,* 674.

19. Ibid., 673–80.

20. Oral Argument of George E. Chamberlain, on Behalf of Appellant, Governor, *Oregon School Cases,* 681–82.

21. Ibid., 683.

22. Ibid.

23. Ibid., 688.

24. Ibid., 687–88.

25. Ibid.

26. Ibid., 690–91.

27. Ibid., 690–92.

28. The transcript of the oral argument in the *Hill Military* case is not available because no stenographic record was made.

29. Burke to Dougherty, March 18, 1925, box 14, folder 10 (Church: Church and State: Oregon School Case, January 1925), NCWC Collection, ACUA, Catholic University of America, Washington, D.C.

30. Burke to O'Mara, March 23, 1925.

31. Ibid.

32. Ryan to O'Mara, March 18, 1925, box 144, folder 64 (Office of the General Secretary), NCWC Collection, ACUA, Catholic University of America, Washington, D.C.

33. Ibid.

34. Objection to Petition of Public School Defense League, April 24, 1925, RG 267, entry 21, case file 30548, Appellate Case Files, 1792–2004, *Pierce v. Society of Sisters,* National Archives, Washington, D.C.

35. *New York Times,* May 11, 1925.

CHAPTER 18

1. "Hughes Fears Laws Endanger Liberty," *New York Times,* September 3, 1925, 27.

2. *Gitlow v. New York,* 268 U.S. 652 (1925).

3. Ibid., 672 (Holmes, J., dissenting).

4. Philippa Strum, ed., *Brandeis on Democracy* (Lawrence: University Press of Kansas, 1995), 93.

5. William Howard Taft, *Liberty under Law* (New Haven: Yale University Press, 1922), 24.

6. Ibid., 50.

7. Ibid., 29.

8. *Pierce v. Society of Sisters,* 268 U.S. 510, 534 (1925).

9. Ibid.

10. Ibid.

11. Ibid., 536.

12. George Sutherland to William H. Church, June 8, 1925, Sutherland Papers, Library of Congress.

13. Taft to Charles P. Hillis, June 9, 1925, Taft Papers, reel 274, Library of Congress.

14. Editorial, *New Republic,* June 17, 1925, reprinted in Philip B. Kurland, *Felix Frankfurter on the Supreme Court: Extrajudicial Essays on the Court and the Constitution* (Cambridge, Mass.: Harvard University Press, Belknap Press, 1970), 177–78.

15. Interview with Sister M. Benildis, June 30, 1958, and congratulatory messages in "The Case of the Sisters of the Holy Names vs. State of Oregon," Holy Names Heritage Center, 16–17.

16. *New York Times,* June 2, 1925.

17. Marshall to Burke, June 6, 1925, box 14, folder 11 (Church: Church and State: Oregon School Case, January 1925), NCWC Collection, ACUA, Catholic University of America, Washington, D.C.

18. William Clerkin to Clerk of the Supreme Court, June 5, 1925, RG 267, entry 21, case file 30548, Appellate Case Files, 1792–2004, *Pierce v. Society of Sisters,* National Archives, Washington, D.C.

19. James Hamilton to Isaac H. Van Winkle, June 3, 1925, Oregon State Archives, Department of Justice Records, Case Files, *Pierce v. Society of Sisters.*

20. Editorial, *New Republic,* June 17, 1925.

21. *Oregonian,* June 2, 1925.

22. *Corvallis Gazette-Times,* June 2, 1925. Democrat Eldon Watkins defeated Republican Congressman Clifton N. McArthur, an outspoken critic of the Klan and the School Bill, in the 1922 election. McArthur died a year later.

23. *Oregonian,* June 3, 1925.

24. Chapter 317, Laws of 1925, State of Oregon, *Constitutional Amendments Adopted and Laws Enacted by the People at the General Election Together with the General Laws and Joint Resolutions, Concurrent Resolutions, and Memorials Adopted by the Thirty-third Regular Session of the Legislative Assembly* (Salem: Oregon State Printer, 1925), 637.

25. Kurland, *Felix Frankfurter on the Supreme Court,* 177–78.

26. Burke to Kavanaugh, June 10, 1925, box 14, folder 11 (Church: Church and State: Oregon School Case, January 1925), NCWC Collection, ACUA, Catholic University of America, Washington, D.C.

27. O'Mara to Burke, July 1, 1925, box 14, folder 11 (Church: Church and State: Oregon School Case, May 1925), NCWC Collection, ACUA, Catholic University of America, Washington, D.C.

28. Guthrie to Burke, July 2, 1925, box 14, folder 11 (Church: Church and State: Oregon School Case, May 1925), NCWC Collection, ACUA, Catholic University of America, Washington, D.C.

29. St. Mary's Academy, Chronicles, April 6, 1925, Holy Names Heritage Center.

EPILOGUE

1. See, e.g., William Waller, "The Constitutionality of the Tennessee Anti-Evolution Act," *Yale Law Review* 35 (1925–26): 192; Blewett Lee, "Anti-Evolution Laws Unconstitutional," *American Bar Association Journal* 11 (1925): 417, 421. See also Larson, *Summer for the Gods,* 220. The Supreme Court did not consider the

constitutionality of antievolution statutes until 1968, in *Epperson v. Arkansas,* where it held that the laws violated the establishment clause.

2. Bryan to Austin Peay, June 27, 1925, and Bryan to Samuel Untermeyer, June 11, 1925, Bryan Papers, Library of Congress.

3. O'Mara to Burke, July 1, 1925, box 14, folder 11 (Church: Church and State: Oregon School Case, May 1925), NCWC Collection, ACUA, Catholic University of America, Washington, D.C.

4. *Scopes v. State,* 154 Tenn. 105 (1927). The Tennessee Supreme Court, finding that the jury, not the judge, should have determined the fine imposed, dismissed the case.

5. *Farrington v. Tokushige,* 273 U.S. 284, 298–99 (1927).

6. *Gitlow v. New York,* 268 U.S. 652 (1925).

7. *Buck v. Bell,* 274 U.S. 200, 207 (1927).

8. *Skinner v. Oklahoma,* 316 U.S. 535 (1942) (invalidating an Oklahoma law providing for the involuntary sterilization of certain habitual criminals).

9. *Gitlow,* 268 U.S. 652, 666.

10. *United States v. Carolene Products,* 304 U.S. 144, 152 (1938). The footnote is considered important because it lays the groundwork for modern analysis of equal protection and fundamental rights, by suggesting that the Court should engage in stricter scrutiny of legislation that discriminates against minorities or fundamental rights.

11. *Minersville School District v. Gobitis,* 310 U.S. 586, 599 (1940); *West Virginia State Board of Education v. Barnette,* 319 U.S. 624, 656 (1943).

12. *Prince v. Commonwealth of Massachusetts,* 321 U.S. 158, 165–66 (1944). Justice Stewart, dissenting in *School District of Abington Township v. Schempp,* a case challenging Bible reading in public school, claimed, "It has become accepted that the decision in *Pierce* . . . was ultimately based upon the recognition of the validity of the free exercise claim involved in that situation" (374 U.S. 203, 312 (1963)).

13. *Wisconsin v. Yoder,* 406 U.S. 205, 231–33 (1972).

14. *Whitney v. California,* 274 U.S. 357, 373 (1927) (Brandeis, J, concurring).

15. *Griswold v. Connecticut,* 381 U.S. 479, 482–83 (1965).

16. *Tinker v. Des Moines School District,* 393 U.S. 503, 506 (1969).

17. *Tinker,* 393 U.S. 511.

18. J. Frankfurter to J. Rutledge, January 22, 1944, file 2040, box 99, Felix Frankfurter Papers, Library of Congress, Manuscript Div.

19. Brief of Petitioners, Spottswood Thomas Bolling, et al., *Bolling v. Sharpe,* 347 U.S. 497 (1954), 1953 WL 48693.

20. See Dennis J. Hutchinson, "Unanimity and Desegregation: Decision-making in the Supreme Court, 1948–1958," *Georgetown Law Journal* 68 (1979–80), 1, 45–48.

21. *Poe v. Ullman,* 367 U.S. 497, 541–44 (1961) (Harlan, J., dissenting).

22. Ibid.

AFTERWORD

1. *Griswold v. Connecticut,* 381 U.S. 479 (1965), Appellant's Brief, p. 23, file date 2/11/1965, U.S. Supreme Court Records and Briefs, 1832–1978, Thomson Gale, doc. DW3900564675.

2. *Roe v. Wade,* 410 U.S. 113, 153 (1973).

3. *Moore v. City of East Cleveland, Ohio,* 431 U.S. 494, 500–501 (1977).

4. *Moore,* 431 U.S. 506.

5. *Palko v. Connecticut,* 302 U.S., 319, 326–27.

6. *Planned Parenthood v. Casey,* 505 U.S. 833, 851 (1992).

7. *Lawrence v. Texas,* 539 U.S. 558, 562, 578 (2003).

8. *Planned Parenthood,* 505 U.S. 844.

9. *Lawrence,* 539 U.S. 562.

10. Frankfurter to Rutledge, January 22, 1944, cited in Gerald T. Dunne, *Hugo Black and the Judicial Revolution* (New York: Simon and Schuster, 1977), 266.

11. *Bethel School District v. Fraser,* 478 U.S. 675, 683 (1986).

12. *Hazelwood School District v. Kuhlmeier,* 484 U.S. 260, 273 (1988).

13. *Tinker v. Des Moines School District,* 393 U.S. 507.

14. *Brown v. Hot, Sexy and Safer Productions,* 68 F.3d 525, 533 (1995); *Fields v. Palmdale School District,* 427 F.3d 1197 (2005).

15. *Wisconsin v. Yoder,* 406 U.S. 205, 233 (1972).

16. *Employment Division v. Smith,* 494 U.S. 872, 881 (1990).

17. *Green v. County School Board of New Kent County,* 391 U.S. 430 (1968).

18. *Norwood v. Harrison,* 413 U.S. 455, 461–62 (1973).

19. *Runyon v. McCrary,* 427 U.S. 160, 161–62 (1976).

20. See Amy Gutmann, *Democratic Education* (Princeton: Princeton University Press, 1987), 1–70; Stephen Macedo, *Diversity and Distrust* (Cambridge, Mass.: Harvard University Press, 2000), 229–79.

21. *Locke v. Davey,* 540 U.S. 712 (2004).

22. *Mitchell v. Helms,* 530 U.S. 793, 828 (2000).

23. *Zelman v. Simmons-Harris,* 536 U.S. 639, 680 (2002) (Thomas, J., concurring).

24. *Prince v. Commonwealth of Massachusetts,* 321 U.S. 158, 166 (1944).

25. *Hutchins v. District of Columbia,* 188 F.3d 531, 541 (D.C. Cir. 1999). Courts that invalidate juvenile curfew laws generally do so on First Amendment vagueness or overbreadth challenges.

26. *Parham v. J.R.,* 442 U.S. 584, 602–3 (1979).

27. *Troxel v. Granville,* 530 U.S. 57, 78 (2000) (Souter, J., concurring).

28. *Troxel,* 530 U.S. 86 (Stevens, J., dissenting).

29. *Troxel,* 530 U.S. 95–96 (Kennedy, J., dissenting).

30. *Winkelman ex rel. Winkelman v. Parma City School District,* 550 U.S. 516, 529 (2007).

31. *Morse v. Frederick,* 127 S. Ct. 2618, 2636 (2007) (Thomas, J., concurring).

32. *Poe v. Ullman,* 367 U.S. 497, 544 (1961) (Harlan, J., dissenting).

33. *Berea College v. Kentucky,* 211 U.S. 68 (Harlan, J., dissenting).

34. *West Virginia State Board of Education v. Barnette,* 319 U.S. 624, 642 (1943).

35. *Whitney v. California,* 274 U.S. 357, 375 (1927) (Brandeis, J., concurring).

36. *Griswold,* 381 U.S. 482.

Index

abortion. *See* procreation decisions
Abrams v. United States (1919), 71, 196
acculturation. *See* Americanization of immigrants; assimilation
Adams, John, 94
Adkins v. Children's Hospital (1923), 165
Adventists. *See* Seventh Day Adventists
African Americans, 45, 67
Akron Beacon Journal, 202
Alien Act (1798), 68
Allgeyer v. Louisiana (1897), 134, 167
Alphonse, Mother Superior, 126
American Bar Association, 72. *See also* Hughes, Charles Evans
American Communist Labor Party, 70
American Communist Party, 70
American Federation of Patriotic Voters, 58
Americanization of immigrants: Committee on Public Schools and, 38; Guthrie on Oregon School Bill and, 187; *Meyer* on state monopoly over education and, 122, 248n. 25; Oregon legislature's promotion of, 203; progressives on public schools and, 95–96, 211; Protestantism and goal of, 105; public schools and, 95, 211; School Bill advocates on, 39; Sisters' suit on School Bill and claims of, 140–41; Supreme Court and national interests in, 196–97; as virtue of public education, 2–3; Wooten on private schools and, 46. *See also* immigrants; nativists and nativism
American Jewish Committee, 178
American Know-Nothing Party, 102–3
American Legionnaires, 65–66
American Patriotic Association, 67
American Protective Association, 38, 107
amicus curiae brief(s): Guthrie's, on *Meyer,* 118–24, 162–63; Lutheran Schools Committee considers, 159; Public School Defense League, 194; for School Bill appellate case, 177–78; Stansbury on submission of, 161

Amish parents, mandatory school attendance for children of, 216, 224–25
anarchists, immigration denied for, 69
anti-Catholicism: establishment clause and, 228; of fundamentalists, 101; history in Oregon of, 50–52; Oregon School Bill and, 52–56, 81; in small Oregon towns, 9
antielitism, 39–40, 41, 46. *See also* elites
antimask law, Oregon, 13
antistatism: Harlan on *Pierce* link of due process to, 218; personal identity, *Pierce* and, 215; *Tinker* on educational liberty, First Amendment and, 217. *See also* state power
antitrust laws, federal, Guthrie on, 115
Arkansas, compulsory public education considered in, 26
Ash, Robert, 160
assimilation. *See* Americanization of immigrants
Associated Press, 132
Astoria Budget, 79
attorney general, Oregon. *See* Van Winkle, Isaac H.

"Baby Blaines," 106, 228. *See also* Blaine Amendment
Bailey v. Drexel Furniture Company (1922), 116
Baker, George L.: on compulsory public education, 52; on criminal syndicalism bill, 65; on evils of Bolshevism, 64; with Klan in newspaper photo, 11; on October labor strikes, 77–78; on the "Reds" vs. German immigrants, 63; Sisters of St. Vincent and, 54
Baldwin, Roger, 108
ballot initiatives. *See* initiatives
Baltimore Sun, 84
Bartels v. Iowa (1923), 248n. 23, 249n. 38
Barzee, C. W., 74
Baur, Rev. John C., 31–32
Bean, Robert S., 144, 145
Beard, Charles A., 114
Beecher, Lyman, 103

National Catholic Welfare Council; Roman Catholic Church

Catholic School Defense League, 100–101

Catholic schools: allegations of substandard education in, 53; Christie and growth in Oregon of, 27; educational progressives concerns about, 107–8; Guthrie omits data on growth of, 162; history of, 105–6; opposition to School Bill by, 3–4; Oregon School Bill and, 22. *See also* parochial schools

Catholic Sentinel, 12, 17

Catholic Truth Society, 89–90

"Catholic Welfare League," 81

Cayuse tribe, Whitman Mission attack by, 50–51

Chamberlain, George, 160–61, 176–77, 188–92

Chicago, Haymarket Square bombing in (1886), 69

child labor laws, 96, 116, 216, 229

children: disabled, parental rights concerning education of, 231; educational interests of, parents vs. state on, 227; playing on the streets, *Pierce* and, 229; in private schools, as unpatriotic, hostility and prejudice toward, 132; in private schools, Chamberlain on rights of, 189; in private schools, Guthrie on rights of, 185; in private schools, Kavanaugh on rights of, 147–48; right to attend private schools of, 130. *See also* minors; procreation decisions

Chinese, denied property ownership in Oregon, 67

Christian Science Monitor, 92

Christie, Archbishop Alexander: asks for NCWC legal assistance, 23, 24, 90; Burke on turf battles of, 193; campaign plans of, 27–28; canvassing strategy of, 30–31; on court challenge to School Bill, 85; forms Catholic Truth Society, 89–90; on Kavanaugh as legal counsel, 108; Knights of Columbus commitment for litigation costs and, 92–93, 110; NCWC grants request for assistance by, 98; on Oregon and national legal counsel, 109; organizes Catholic Civic Rights Association, 29; on *Pierce* opinion, 205; on reasons for opposition to School Bill, 43; on Society of Sisters as plaintiff for School Bill suit, 125; turf battle with national Catholic leadership and, 99–100

citizens, educated. *See* democracy, American

Claxton, Philander, 47

"clear and present danger" test, 71

Cleland John B., 15

Clerkin, William, 202

Cleveland, Grover, 69

Colorado, compulsory public education considered in, 156

Columbia University, Guthrie and, 113, 114–15

commerce clause, federal, 116. *See also* contracts clause and contractual obligations; police powers

Committee on Americanization of Public Schools, 38

common law, 134–35, 168, 185–86. *See also* natural law

Common School Journal, 103

common schools, 95, 102

communism and communist governments: compulsory public education as monopoly under, 62; Guthrie on, 117; Odale on threat of, 67; Taft Court's fear of government expansion and, 165–66. *See also* Bolsheviks/Bolshevism; Soviet Union

Communist Party members, campaign to deport immigrant members of, 2

"Compulsory Education Bill," 36–37, 76. *See also* Oregon School Bill

compulsory public education. *See* Oregon School Bill

Constitution, Oregon, Supreme Court queries of Moore on questions of, 181

Constitution, U.S.: concerns on Oregon System and, 20; contracts clause (Article I, Sec. 10), 126–27, 130, 139–40, 177, 188; lack of references to parental rights in, 45; religious liberty and, 57–61; on republican government in states (Article IV, Sec. 4), 20, 190

constitutional law, Guthrie as expert in, 113

constitutions, state, on importance of education and public schools, 95

contraception, minors' access to, parental rights and, 230

contracts clause and contractual obligations: due process under Fourteenth Amendment and, 134; Kavanaugh's oral argument before Supreme Court on, 188; School Bill appellate briefs on, 177; Sisters' suit on School Bill in violation of, 130, 139–40; Society of Sisters' relationship with Oregon under, 126–27; Taft Court on, 165. *See also* economic liberty interests

Coolidge, Calvin, 136, 163, 179

Cornell, E. W., 161

corporations: Kentucky Constitution on power to alter charters of, 133; as plaintiff in *Meyer,* Guthrie on, 170; protections under liberty clause of Fourteenth Amendment, 199. *See also* contracts clause and contractual obligations

required for teaching in public or private schools, 67

English-only education laws, 118–24, 248n. 23

Episcopalians/Episcopal Church, 43, 55, 177–78

equality, Guthrie on, 116–17

Escaped Nun from Mount Angel Convent, The (Hosmer), 51

Espionage Act (1917), 2, 63, 69, 70–71, 196

establishment clause: Fourteenth Amendment and, 228. *See also* free exercise of religion; religious freedom

Etherlind, Sister Mary, 51

Evans, Walter, 11

Everest, Wesley, 66

evolution, public schools teaching, 101, 209–10

Exalted Cyclops of Portland Klan No. 1, 10

Ex parte cases. *See* name of party

faith healing, child's death from, criminal prosecution of parents for, 230

Farrington v. Tokushige (1927), 211

federal district courts, three-judge panel requirements for, 144, 252n. 1

federalism, in state response to injunction against School Bill, 142

federal land grants, 95, 96

Federation of Patriotic Societies (FOPS), 37–38

Fenlon, Father John B., 99

First Amendment: Espionage and Sedition Acts and, 70–71; establishment clause, 228; as federal not state application, 57–58; *Gitlow* on, 212–13; Harlan on *Pierce* and *Meyer* under, 217–18; juvenile curfew laws and, 260n. 25; *Pierce* cited as precedent on, 216; *Pierce* opinion and incorporation of, 211–14; protections of student interests by, 227

First Families of Portland, 18

flag salutes, 233

Flegel, A. F., 59

founders of the United States, private schools and, 46, 185

Four Horsemen of the Apocalypse, 164

Fourteenth Amendment: Court's shift from privacy to liberty under, 221–22; governor's brief on parental rights and, 171; Groesbeck on compulsory public education and, 24; Guthrie lectures on, 113; Guthrie on *Meyer* and First Amendment protections under, 184; Kavanaugh on parental rights and, 147–48; liberty clause protections for corporation under, 199; McCamant on parental rights and, 150; *Meyer* on parental rights un-

der, 121; parental rights, economic liberty and, 166–68; *Pierce* opinion and incorporation of Bill of Rights under, 211–14; rights protected as "liberties" under, 220; School Bill opponents on parental rights and, 45; Sisters' brief on religious liberty, parental rights and, 174; Sisters' complaint on personal liberties protected by, 130; state brief on liberty only for natural persons, 170; Taft on parental rights under, 124. *See also* due process; economic due process; parental rights; privileges and immunities clause; substantive due process

Frankfurter, Felix: condemnation of *Pierce* by, 217; on opportunity for "mischief" by state regulators, 204, 222–23; patriotic societies on liberalism of, 73; on *Pierce* opinion, 202, 215–16; on Supreme Court and public opinion, 200; on Supreme Court from 1913 to 1926, 164; on Taft's leadership on Supreme Court, 163

Freedom of Education (O'Hara speech), 16

free exercise of religion: Cardozo's description of *Pierce* as, 215; child's death after faith healing, criminal prosecution of parents and, 230; as element of education, Guthrie on, 176; parental rights in *Yoder* and, 225; *Pierce* decision on, 4; as protection under Fourteenth Amendment, 130; School Bill opponents on interference with, 58; Stewart in *Abington Township* on *Pierce* and, 259n. 12. *See also* establishment clause; religious freedom

"Free Public Schools, America's Noblest Monument" (ad), 39

"Free Public Schools, Open to All, Good Enough for All, and Attended by All" (ad), 39

"Free Public Schools for Red-blooded Children" (ad), 40

free speech. *See* speech, freedom of

Freund, Ernst, 119

Frohwerk, Jacob, 71

Frohwerk v. United States (1919), 71

fundamentalist/fundamentalism: post–World War I use of term, 101. *See also* Protestants

Gallagher, Michael J., 25–26

Gasparri, Pietro Cardinal, 156

German(s): anarchists, Haymarket Square bombing and, 69; as immigrants, nativist furor over, 24; vigilante squads in search of, 63

Gibbons, Bishop Edmund F., 99–100

Gibbons, James Cardinal, 25

Gifford, Fred L.: anti-Catholic School Bill ads by, 52–53; FOPS break over public utilities with, 38; on Klan as legitimate patriotic organization, 10–11; on Klan backing for Gov. Pierce, 34–35; Nov. 1922 election and candidates endorsed by, 84; offers Klan assistance to Portland with labor strikes, 77; Oregon School Bill endorsement by Masons and, 16, 17; parochial and private schools for children of, 60; Pierce confrontation with, 158

Gilbert, William B., 144–45, 146–47, 148

Gitlow v. New York (1925), 196, 212–13

governance, link in U.S. between education and, 94–95, 197, 200–201

governor, Oregon. *See* Pierce, Walter M.

Grand Lodge of Oregon, 15. *See also* Scottish Rite Masons

grandparents' rights, housing ordnances on nuclear families and, 220

Grant, Ulysses S., 106

Grants Pass Spokesman, 154

Green, B. A., 78

Green v. County School Board of New Kent County (1968), 225

Gregory XVI, Pope, 106

Griswold v. Connecticut (1965), 216, 219, 233

Groesbeck, Alex J., 24, 26

guarantee clause, on republican governments in states, 190–91

Guthrie, William D.: as advocate in School Bill challenge, 112; amicus brief on *Meyer* by, 118–24; as an attorney of stature, Dowling on, 110; on *Berea College* case, 133; brief for School Bill appeal, 173–75; briefs international Catholic leadership, 156; Burke on School Bill as violation of intellectual and religious liberty and, 179; as Catholic legal counsel, Burke on, 108; on Chamberlain's brief for the appeal, 161; on common-law heritage supporting parental rights, 168; conservative Court's respect for traditional family and, 167; criticism of, 114–15; on district court decision on injunction, 155; early life and education, 112–13; on extra time for oral argument, 178, 180–81; general opinion on Oregon School Bill by, 93–94; on Kavanaugh's preparation for Jan. 1924 hearing, 137; as legal counsel, 109, 110–11; legal views and significant cases of, 114–17; on mandatory attendance laws and Oregon case, 98; on *Meyer* case and School Bill case filing, 124; oral argument before Supreme Court, 183–87; on parental rights, 136, 166–67; *Pierce* opinion and, 204–5; on pleadings by Sisters

vs. Hill Military Academy, 131; on prematurity issue and jurisdiction, 170; preparations for Supreme Court, 161–62; on the presentations at the hearing on the injunction, 151–52; public relations strategy of, 157; Public School Defense League amicus brief and, 194; state brief on Fourteenth Amendment liberty and, 170; studies Oregon politics, 158; supplies transcript copies as part of the record, 194; use of Leopold/Loeb murder case by, 158–59

Hadley, Arthur, 47

Hall, Charles, 8, 13, 23, 33, 80

Hally, Patrick J. M., 93

Hamilton, James, 25, 194, 202

Hamilton v. Vaughan (Mich. 1920), 24, 45

Hammer v. Dagenhart (1918), 116

Hanley, P. J., 93

Hanna, Archbishop Edward J.: on control of legal counsel, 110–11; formal agreement between NCWC and Christie and, 99–100; on Guthrie and McEnerney as legal counsel, 109; letter to Vatican on School Bill before Supreme Court, 156; on McEnerney as legal counsel, 108; *Meyer* opinion and negotiations with Kavanaugh, 123–24; NCWC administrative meeting Jan. 1923 and, 93

Hanson, Ole, 64

Hanzen, Henry M., 79

Harding, Warren G., 3, 71, 72, 163

Harlan, John Marshall (1877–1911), 134

Harlan, John Marshall (1955–1971), dissent in *Poe* on right of privacy, 217–18, 220, 232–33

Harvard, 47. *See also* private colleges and universities

Hawaii, foreign-language education in private schools in, 211

Hayes, Rutherford B., 106

Haymarket Square bombing, Chicago (1886), 69

Hazelwood School District v. Kuhlmeier (1988), 224

Hershkopf, Bernard, 204

Hill, Joseph A., 89, 129

Hill, Joseph Wood, 129

Hill Military Academy: allotted one hour for oral argument, 181; Gifford's son attends, 60; Guthrie on pleadings by, 131; hearing on injunction by, 144; injunction against School Bill and, 141–42; McCamant's case for dismissing injunction by, 145–46; opposition to School Bill by, 3–4; *Pierce* opinion and, 199; as plaintiff, Guthrie on religious liberty and,

175; suit challenging School Bill by, 129. *See also* Veatch, John C.

Hold-Up Legislature (1897), 19

Holmes, Oliver Wendell, Jr.: absences during oral argument, 180, 184; dissent in *Abrams* on antiwar pamphlets, 70–72; dissent in *Gitlow,* 196, 213; dissents on freedom of thought, 212; on experimentation and democracy, 166; Guthrie's transcript copies for, 194; on language laws and assimilation, 122, 249n. 38; McCamant's expectation of, 172; *Pierce* opinion and, 200; as Taft Court member, 164; on Taft Court's fear of government expansion, 165

homeschooling, 96, 223, 224

homosexual sodomy, 220, 221

Hoover, J. Edgar, 2

Hosmer, J. E., 51

House of Representatives, educational land policy (1826) and land grants by, 94–95

housing ordinances on nuclear families, grandparents' rights and, 220

Hughes, Bishop John, 105

Hughes, Charles Evans, 195–96, 204–5

human rights, Sisters' suit on School Bill and questions of, 141

Hume, Hugh, 60

Humphrey, Lester, 11

Hurlburt, Tom, 11

ideological conformity, of early twentieth century, 2

Illinois: compulsory public education considered in, 156; English language instruction mandated in schools, 107; Supreme Court on parental rights, 135

immigrants: association with radicalism in America, 68; Catholic, during the 19th century, 103; Catholic, to Oregon during World War I, 51; decried in School Bill promotion pieces, 73–74; federal financial incentives to "Americanize," 97; nativist furor over, 1–2; newspapers on radicals as, 68; perceived as enemy during World War I, 69; perceived as threats to small towns in Oregon, 9; as percentage of Oregon population, 67; *Pierce* decision on bigotry against, 4; as threat to American democracy, 61; as voters, Michigan education initiative and, 26. *See also* Americanization of immigrants; assimilation

Immigration Act (1903), 69

Immigration Acts (1921–24), 72

income tax, federal, 115

Indiana: compulsory public education consid-

ered in, 156; mandatory school attendance law in, 95–96

Industrial Workers of the World (IWW, "Wobblies"): American Legionnaires storm headquarters of, 65–66; as easy political target, 65; newspapers on alien status of, 68; October strikes seen as radicalism by, 77–78; in Oregon, 63–64; perceived as radical aliens, 69; Seattle General Strike of 1919 and, 64

inheritance tax, federal, 115

initiatives (ballot): Chamberlain on Supreme Court approval of, 190; development in Oregon of, 18–21; on public education in Michigan, 24–27. *See also* Oregon School Bill

injunction against School Bill: arguments for plaintiff in, 139–42; district court ruling on, 152–54; Guthrie on *Berea College v. Kentucky* and, 132; Guthrie on cases supporting, 138; Guthrie on presentations during hearing on, 151–52; Guthrie on strategy for, 137–38; hearing set for Jan. 1924, 137; Kavanaugh amends, 130–32; Kavanaugh files, 130; Kavanaugh's concerns about, 138–39; Kavanaugh's rebuttal to state's motion to dismiss, 146–47; McCamant on justifications for the law, 149–50; McCamant on state's motion to dismiss, 145–46; McCamant's role as government counsel, 144–45; Myers closing government argument at hearing, 150–51; omission of parents from, 132–33; plaintiffs against state monopoly of education in, 147–49; prematurity issue addressed in hearing, 144–45; state response to, 142–43; three-judge panel open hearing on, 144, 252n. 1; Veatch's rebuttal to prematurity claim, 146

injunctions against state law when injury is pending, *Pennsylvania v. West Virginia* on, 138

"In Justice to American Principles" (ad), 44, 58, 75

intellectual liberty: Burke on School Bill as violation of religious liberty and, 179, 192; under First Amendment, Brandeis on, 216; fundamental First Amendment values and, 233; O'Mara on Scopes case and, 210; parental rights to, Guthrie's brief on, 176; personal identity and, 221; Ryan on School Bill as violation of religious liberty and, 193

interest group litigation, Catholic School Defense League as model for, 100–101

International Longshoremen (union), 77

Invisible Empire. *See* Ku Klux Klan

Iowa, compulsory public education considered in, 156

Italy, rise of fascism in, 195

Japanese in Hawaii, education and parental rights issues for, 211
Jefferson, Thomas, 57, 94
Jehovah's Witnesses, child labor laws and, 216, 229
Jenkins, Leon, 11
Jewish League for Preservation of American Ideals, 45
Jews and Jewish interests, 1–2, 45, 105, 138
Johnson, James A., 53
Joint Committee on Direct Legislation, 18–19
judicial review, Guthrie on, 117

Kadderly v. City of Portland (Or. 1903), 20
Kalmer, Rev. Leo, 159
Kavanaugh, John P.: amended bill of complaint by, 131–32; applies to Supreme Court Bar, 157–58; argument against state monopoly of education, 147–49; on *Berea College* case, 133; Burke on School Bill as violation of intellectual and religious liberty and, 179; Catholic Civic Rights Association and, 29; on challenges of plaintiff and need for local counsel, 128–29; concerns for Jan. 1924 hearing, 138–39; on court scheduling hearing, 137; on district court decision on injunction, 155; files the Society of Sisters suit, 130; Guthrie's compliments on presentation at hearing by, 151–52; Knights of Columbus commitment for litigation costs and, 92–93; legal counsel selection controversy and, 108, 109, 110; *Meyer* opinion and Hanna's negotiations with, 123–24; offers legal assistance to Burke, 108–9; oral argument before Supreme Court, 187–88; on prematurity issue and jurisdiction, 145, 170; prior to oral arguments at Supreme Court, 180; on publicity for the case, 132; rebuttal to McCamant on state's motion to dismiss, 146–47; on Society of Sisters as plaintiff for School Bill suit, 126–27; turf battle with national Catholic leadership and, 99, 100
Keating-Owen child labor law, 116
Kelly, Edward D., 25
Kennedy, Anthony M., 231
Kent, Chancellor James, 174
Kentucky Constitution, state power to alter corporation charters under, 133
King James Bible, 102, 104–5. *See also* Bible reading in schools
KKK. *See* Ku Klux Klan
"K.K.K. Plot to Control the State" (Hanzen), 79
Klamath Falls Herald, 79

Knights of Columbus: Burke on turf battles of, 193; Christie, Kavanaugh, and financial gift by, 99; Christie on monitoring Klan-dominated legislature by, 89; commitment for litigation costs, 92–93; Hill Military Academy suit and, 130; NCWC refuses assistance of, 99
Knights of the Ku Klux Klan: growth in Oregon, 8–12. *See also* Ku Klux Klan
Know-Nothing Party, 102–3
Ku Klux Klan: anti-Catholic messages on School Bill to, 53; attacks on reputations of individuals by, 60; boycotts of opposition newspapers by, 12; campaigns against Catholic candidates in other states by, 91–92; on Catholic Church as secretive cult, 54; Christie's opposition strategy and, 27; compulsory public education and, 3; deterioration of Pierce's relationship with, 158; editorial cartoon of, 76; Gov. Pierce deal for support by, 34–35; legislative dominance as embarrassment to Oregon, 128; in Michigan, public education initiative and, 25; negative impact of School Bill support by, 41; Nov. 1922 election and candidates endorsed by, 84; in Oregon, district court decision and, 155; Oregon primary election of 1922 and, 13–14; as Oregon School Bill sponsors, 16–18; as political machine in Oregon, 12–14; political parties in Oregon and, 33; publication of identities of, 47–49; on public education and contempt for minorities, 60; Public School Defense League amicus brief and, 194; on religious separation to protect Protestant dominance, 58; Salem, on Hall's loss in 1922 primary, 13; waning influence in Oregon by, 203, 258n. 22. *See also* Gifford, Fred L.; Knights of the Ku Klux Klan

labor unions, 63, 70, 77, 165. *See also* Industrial Workers of the World
La Grande Provisional Klan, 34. *See also* Ku Klux Klan
laissez-faire jurisprudence, Guthrie as proponent of, 115
Lasenan, Mary, 51
Last Stand of Desperate Despotism, The (Hosmer), 51
Law, Curtis Lee, 101
law-and-order platform, of KKK, 9
Lawrence v. Texas (2003), 221, 226, 232, 233
Leopold, Nathan, 158, 159
liberty: Court's shift from privacy to, 221–22; Harlan on First Amendment and *Pierce* and

ments of, 198–201; enduring controversy of, 232–34; Guthrie and ABA on, 204–5; incorporation of Bill of Rights and, 211–14; as landmark constitutional case, 3–4; national debate on democracy and, 195–97; NCWC reaction to, 203–4; Oregon legislature's reaction to, 203; parental rights, modern education and, 222–29; parental rights outside of education and, 229–32; privacy and, 219–21; public reaction to, 201–3; Tennessee Supreme Court on Scopes case and, 210; unanimity of Court on, 197–98, 200

Pius XI, Pope, 28

Planned Parenthood of Southeastern Pa. v. Casey (1992), 221, 222, 226, 232, 233

Plato, on state as parental authority, 119–20, 121–22, 167, 190

Pledge of Allegiance recitation in schools, 215–16

Poe v. Ullman (1961), 217–18, 220, 232–33

police powers: Chamberlain on School Bill as property rights deprivation due to, 192; federalism issues and, 194; Kavanaugh on Fourteenth Amendment protections from, 148; Lutheran Campaign Committee on parental rights and, 26; McCamant on public education mandate and, 150; Moore on Oregon School Bill as exercise of, 181–82; Mullen in *Meyer* on, 120; O'Hara on parental rights and, 16; reserved to states, Moore on education policy as, 183

political questions, Supreme Court on, 190–91

Pollack v. Farmers' Loan & Trust Company (1895), 115

populism: Gov. Pierce on School Bill and, 35; in Oregon, 18; strength in Oregon of, School Bill proponents and, 40

"Portals of the Nation's Future, Free Public Schools" (ad), 39

Portland, Eldon Watkins, 258n. 22

Portland: elites in, opposition to School Bill by, 47; First Families of, 18; news of *Pierce* effect in, 201; Red Squad to investigate radicalism in, 66–67; School Board elections (1921), anti-Catholic sentiment of, 51–52; shipbuilding industry collapse after World War I, 63–64; turnout for passage of School Bill, 84. *See also* Baker, George L.

Portland Daily Herald, 126

Portland Klan No. 1, 10–11. *See also* Ku Klux Klan

Portland Ministerial Association, 46

Portland Spectator, 36–37

Portland Telegram, 11, 38, 78–79, 81–82

Pound, Roscoe, 165, 168

Powell, King Kleagle Luther, 9, 11, 55, 56, 91

precedents, legal: for economic liberty, 134, 214; for parental rights, 45, 136, 185–86; *Pierce* legacy for, 214–15, 216, 217–18, 219–20

prematurity issue: district court ruling on, 152–53; Guthrie on, 98, 124, 131, 183; Kavanaugh on, 128, 131–32; Kavanaugh rebuts state on, 146–47; McCamant for state case on, 145; Moore on Oregon attorney general's waiver of, 181; *Pierce* on School Bill and, 199; state's appellate case and, 169–70; *Terrace* and *Pennsylvania* on, 138

Presbyterians, on School Bill as human welfare, 74–75

Prince v. Commonwealth of Massachusetts (1944), 216, 217, 229, 259n. 12

privacy, right to: controversy on Court's shift to liberty from, 221–22; minors' access to contraception or abortion and, 230; *Pierce* and *Meyer* as precedents for, 216; *Pierce* as precedent for, 214–15, 217–18, 219–20; *Pierce* decision on, 4

private colleges and universities: antielitist arguments on, 47; elite, Guthrie on School Bill and, 138; Guthrie on Oregon School Bill as threat to, 185; Kavanaugh on School Bill as threat to, 148; *Pierce* opinion on, 199

private schools: allegations of substandard education in, 53; banned in Soviet Union, 73; district court on economic interests of, 154; district court on parental rights and, 153; enrollment in, 46; financial burden of incorporating children into public schools from, 26–27; Guthrie on historical importance of, 186; Guthrie on Oregon School Bill as threat to, 185; national campaign on regulation of, 98; in Nebraska, oral arguments in *Meyer* on, 120; parental rights and racial discrimination by, 226; *Pierce* on School Bill and, 198; *Pierce* opinion on, 199; School Bill advocates' connections to, 60–61; secular, opposition to School Bill by, 45–46; Sisters' suit on School Bill depriving right to teach in, 130; standing to assert parental right, state's appellate case and, 169–70, 181; warning in state's appellate brief on types of, 172–73. *See also* Catholic schools; parochial schools

privileges and immunities clause: evolution of Supreme Court opinion on protections under, 167; Guthrie on, 116; Mullen's claim in *Meyer* of, 249n. 32; parental rights and, 45. *See also* Fourteenth Amendment procreation decisions: Court on individual liberty and, 213; for minors, parental rights and, 230; *Pierce* as precedent for right to, 220; substantive due process and, 221

progressivism/progressive movement: education and, 96–98; Guthrie on, 113–14, 117; Oregon System and, 21; on public schools and assimilation, 211; strength in Oregon of, School Bill proponents and, 40

Prohibitionist Party, 19

property ownership: by aliens, legislation on, 128; by Chinese, 67

property rights: Sisters' suit on School Bill in violation of, 130; Sutherland's question to Chamberlain on, 191–92; Taft Court on, 165

Protestants: on assimilation, 105; on Catholic teachers in public schools, 92; fears of Catholic political ascendance among, 106–7; Gov. Pierce on family history and, 35; KKK on values of, 9–10, 58; Non-Sectarian and Protestant Schools Committee and, 43; pastors, opposition to School Bill by, 46; private schools of, Guthrie on School Bill and, 138; school prayer and, 102, 104. *See also* Bible reading in schools; Non-Sectarian and Protestant Schools Committee

Prudential Ins. Co. v. Cheek (1922), 176

"Prussianism in Education," 75–76

public education: compulsory, financial impact of, 47; compulsory, Kavanaugh on, 147–48; compulsory, Mason's resolution on, 7; compulsory, Michigan initiative on, 24–27; compulsory, modern theorists' debates on, 226–27; compulsory, momentum for, 210–11; compulsory, Moore's oral argument on, 183; Daniels on virtues of, 2–3; fundamentalist influences on, 101; Harlan on right to, 134; modern, parental rights and, 222–29; Moore on Oregon's right to set policy on, 182; open to all, KKK on reviled religious minorities and, 60; parental rights, segregated schools and, 217; progressive agenda for, Taft Court and, 166; Progressive Era and, 96–98; teaching evolution in, 209–10; without class or religious bias, Chamberlain on, 176–77. *See also* education; Oregon School Bill

public opinion: Frankfurter and Supreme Court and, 200; insights for Supreme Court on constitutional guarantees and, 201

public relations campaigns for School Bill challenge, 98, 132, 157, 159

Public School Defense League, 194

public school teachers. *See* teachers

Puffendorf, Samuel, 185

Putnam, George, 11, 79, 80. *See also Capital Journal*

Putney, Albert, 191

radicalism: decried in School Bill promotion pieces, 73–74; of early twentieth century, 2; editorial cartoonists on hysteria over, 76; Holmes and Brandeis on state suppression of, 196; immigrants and Catholics associated with, 68; purging, and protecting patriotism in the schools, 72–73; School Bill as debate on combating influences of, 62; Taft Court's fear of government expansion and, 165–66. *See also* Bolsheviks/Bolshevism; communism and communist governments

radicals: Catholic or Jewish immigrants suspected as, 67–68; vigilante squads in search of, 63

Ramp, Floyd, 63

Reames, Charles L., 64

Reasons Why (Masons' pamphlet), 38–39, 73, 242–43n. 39

Red Scare (1919–20): national debate on democracy and, 195; nativists and, 67–70; in Oregon, 63–67; protecting patriotism in the schools and, 72–73; Supreme Court on, 70–72; U.S. preoccupation with nativism, patriotism, ideological conformity and, 2. *See also* Bolsheviks/Bolshevism; communism and communist governments; national security; socialism

referendums, development in Oregon of, 18–21

religion: molding of American education and, 102–8; Moore on Oregon School Bill and, 182

religious bigotry/intolerance: Chamberlain on Oregon School Bill and, 188–89; Guthrie on Oregon School Bill and, 186–87; *Pierce* decision on, 4; unease of Oregon voters about, 61; Wheelwright on School Bill supporters and, 49. *See also* anti-Catholicism

religious freedom (liberty): Bible reading in schools and, 104–5; Chamberlain on Oregon School Bill and, 191; district court ignoring of, 153; federal Constitution and, 57–61; under Fourteenth Amendment, *Meyer* on, 121, 249n. 32; Freund on freedom of private instruction and, 119; *Gitlow* and, 213–14; Oregon Catholic leadership on opposition based on, 44; *Pierce* as precedent on, 214; *Pierce* on School Bill and, 198; *Pierce* opinion omits, 199; School Bill opponents on, 56–57; Sisters' brief on Oregon School Bill's denial of, 175–76, 184; in state response to injunction against School Bill, 143; state's appellate case on, 177; Supreme Court's description of *Pierce* as, 215–16. *See also* establishment clause; free exercise of religion

religious garb in public schools, 54–55, 91, 92, 128

religious instruction: Moore on Oregon School Bill and, 183; Moore on tolerance in Oregon for, 182; Oregon law to excuse children from public school for, 178–79. *See also* parochial schools

Remember Oregon (Wooten pamphlet), 37

Republican Party, KKK and Masons and, 33

Riddle Enterprise, 154

Rimbach, Rev. J. A., 32

Roberts, Waldo, 10

Roe v. Wade (1973), 219

Roman Catholic Church: in America, political infighting in, 28; Chamberlain on parental rights under, 189; distortions on scripture of, 60; Guthrie and, 117; *Mirari Vos* encyclical (1832), 106–7; portrayal as secretive cult, 54; School Bill passage and, 1; as strengthened by religious hatred against it, 59. *See also* anti-Catholicism; Catholic leadership; Catholics; Catholic schools

Roosevelt, Theodore, 39, 54, 69, 113–14

Roseburg Review, 79

Ross, Edward Alsworth, 40

Ruhl, Robert W., 11

Runyon v. McCrary (1976), 226

Russia. *See* Soviet Union

Russian Revolution (1917), 62

Russians, perceived as enemy during World War I, 69

Rutledge, Wiley B., 216

Ryan, Father James H., 28, 97, 161, 192, 193–94

Sanford, Edward T., 164, 181

San Francisco Argonaut, 75–76

Sawyer, Reuben, 53

Schenck, Charles T., 70–71

Schenck v. United States (1919), 70–71, 234

Schoffen, Elizabeth, 54

school attendance, mandatory: Amish families and, 216; district court on Oregon School Bill and, 153–54; Know-Nothings and laws on, 103; laws on, 95–96; Moore on Oregon School Bill and, 183; Sisters' suit on, 140

School Bill. *See* Oregon School Bill

"School Bill Monopoly or the Government Ownership of Children, The" (Wooten speech), 75

"School Bills, School Bills" protest song, 81–82

school choice: *Pierce* as precedent on, 215. *See also* school voucher plans

school curriculum, state power over education and, 223–24

school discipline, state power over education and, 223–24

School District of Abington Township v. Schempp (1963), 259n. 12

school prayer, Protestant, 102, 104. *See also* Bible reading in schools

school voucher plans, 223, 225, 228–29. *See also* school choice

Scopes, John, 209–10

Scopes "Monkey Trial" (1925), 101, 209–10

Scott, Joseph, 128

Scottish Rite Masons: anti-Catholic messages in School Bill ads by, 52; on district court decision on injunction, 152; funding of School Bill appeal and, 158; Klan and, 14; McCamant's representation of complaint and, 133–34; members with Klan in newspaper photo, 11; national campaign on private school regulation and, 98; Oregon School Bill endorsement by, 16–18; parental rights vs. all-powerful state advocated by, 44; political parties in Oregon and, 33; public rift among, 41; *Reasons Why* (pamphlet), 38–39, 73, 242–43n. 39; resolution on compulsory public education, 7; retain Chamberlain to represent Pierce, 160; Sisters' suit filing and, 130–31. *See also* Grand Lodge of Oregon

Seattle, Wash., General Strike of 1919 in, 64

Sedition Act (1798), 68

Sedition Act (1918), 2, 69, 70–71

self-determination. *See* liberty

separation of church and state: anti-Catholic hostility and, 228; as fundamental American principle, 58; *Mirari Vos* encyclical on, 106–7; Moore on "practical effect" of School Bill and, 183; religious schools as threat to, state's appellate brief on, 177. *See also* establishment clause; religious freedom

Seventeenth Amendment, Oregon System and, 21

Seventh Day Adventists: amicus brief for School Bill appeal, 177–78; Non-Sectarian and Protestant Schools Committee and, 43; *Old Cedar School* ridicule of, 55; on religious liberty, 59; on right and duty of parents, 45; on School Bill as un-American, 74

sex education, Pierce decision and, 224

signature collection: for Oregon School Bill, 15, 23–24; for second Michigan public school bill, 26

Bill, 183; Guthrie and, 113, 159; on language laws and assimilation, 122, 249n. 38; McCamant's expectation of, 172; *Pierce* opinion and, 200; on State constitutional questions, 181; as Taft Court member, 164

Taft, Henry W., 113
Taft, William H.: on extra time for oral argument, 180–81, 186; fears of radicalism, 166; Harding appointment to Supreme Court of, 163; on Oregon System, 21–22; on *Pacific States Telephone & Telegraph,* 190–91; on parental rights for private language instruction, 123; *Pierce* opinion and, 200; projecting School Bill opinion by, 197; Public School Defense League amicus brief and, 194; on state laws violating U.S. constitutional rights, 183
"Take It to Yourselves" (*Corvallis Gazette-Times* editorial), 79
takings. *See* property rights
taxing authority, federal, 116
tax relief, Gov. Pierce on, 35
teach, as First Amendment right, Brandeis on, 216
teachers: Catholic, hired over Protestant minority protests, 92; Catholic, in public schools, discrimination against, 52; English-only education law in Nebraska and, 118, 122; Kavanaugh on economic rights of, 147–48; loyalty oaths for, 73; perceived as radicals, 72–73; as plaintiffs, NCWC dispute over, 132–33; public school, support for School Bill by, 41; Sisters' suit on School Bill depriving right to teach by, 130. *See also* economic liberty interest; religious garb in public schools
Terrace v. Thompson (1923), 138, 145
Texas, compulsory public education considered in, 26, 156
textbooks, 73, 224, 225–26
Thirteenth Amendment, 71
Thomas, Clarence, 228–29, 232
"Three Souls with the Same Thought" (editorial cartoon), 76
Tinker v. Des Moines School District (1969), 217, 223, 224, 227
Titus, Benjamin E., 10
Towner-Sterling Bill, 97
Troxel v. Granville (2000), 230–31
Truth about the So-Called Compulsory Education Bill, The (Bauer tract), 31–32
24 Reasons (Wooten pamphlet), 31, 37, 38–39, 44–45, 75
Twiss, Benjamin, 115

unions, 63, 70, 77, 165. *See also* Industrial Workers of the World
Unitarians, on Bible reading in public schools, 102
United Mine Workers, 70
United States v. See name of party
U'Ren, William S., 19, 21

vaccinations, parental refusal of, 96
Van Devanter, Willis, 164
Van Winkle, Isaac H.: on Chamberlain's brief for the appeal, 161; Chamberlain's role in appeal and, 160; Hamilton and, 202; Hill Military Academy suit against, 129; on McCamant and state appeal, 158; supplemental brief to state's appellate brief by, 171–72
Veatch, John C., 129, 146, 149, 152, 180
vigilante squads, in Oregon, 63, 64
Virginia, involuntary sterilization law in, 213
"Vote No" stickers, 32
voters: in Michigan, immigrants as, 26; in Oregon, Nov. 1922 election discontent among, 41–42; in Oregon, Pierce and pool for, 36. *See also* initiatives
Voters' Pamphlet: in favor of School Bill, 17, 38; on opposition to School Bill, 32, 44, 56–57, 59

Walsh, J. A., 93
war. *See* Alien Act; Espionage Act; Sedition Act; World War I
Warren, Earl, 217
Warren Court, constitutional liberty under, 217–18
Washington (state): compulsory public education considered in, 26, 156, 211, 238n. 10; constitutional provision for public scholarship funds for theology students, 228; multiple family relationships and visitation law in, 230–31
Washington, George, 94
West, Oswald, 127
Western American (KKK publication), 41, 79
West Virginia State Board of Education v. Barnette (1943), 216, 227, 233
Wheelwright, William, 17, 49
White, Edward D., 164
Whitman Massacre (1847), 50
Whitney v. California (1927), 216, 233
Williams, George, 19
Wilson, Woodrow, 69, 164
Wisconsin v. Yoder (1972), 216, 224–25
Withycombe, James, 34, 64
Wobblies. *See* Industrial Workers of the World

Wolverton, Charles E., 144, 146–47, 152–54
women: increased rights for, *Pierce*'s family model and, 229; turnout for passage of School Bill by, 84. *See also* abortion; procreation decisions
Woodward, William F., 40–41, 49
Wooten, Dudley G.: canvassing strategy of, 30–31; on divisions among Catholics, 29–30; on private schools and Americanization of immigrants, 46; on reasons for opposition to School Bill, 43–44; on religious tolerance as true "Americanism," 58–59; on School Bill as Russian Sovietism, 75; Slattery on competence of, 91; on voters abstaining from School Bill vote, 83

World War I: anti-Catholic attitudes in Oregon during, 51; economic collapse after, 70; national debate on democracy and, 195–96; nationalism after, regulating education and, 96–97; nativism during, 69; political dissent cases, 2, 70–72, 234; Portland shipbuilding industry collapse after, 63–64
Wyoming, compulsory public education considered in, 26

Yale, 47, 113. *See also* private colleges and universities
Yoder. See Wisconsin v. Yoder

Zelman v. Simmons-Harris (2002), 228